The Education of a Traitor

A Memoir of Growing Up in Cold War Russia

Svetlana Grobman

Musings Publishing

COLUMBIA, MISSOURI

Musings Publishing
3212 S Old Ridge Rd.
Columbia, Missouri 65203

Photographs property of Svetlana Grobman
Editor: Jenny McDonald
Manufactured in the United States of America

Publisher's Note: This work is a literary memoir. The experiences and conversations recounted here are the result of the author's recollections. Therefore, they are a subjective account of events that occurred in her life. Her perceptions and opinions are entirely her own.

The Education of a Traitor/Svetlana Grobman. -- 1st ed.
ISBN: 978-0692312285 (pbk.)
Grobman, Svetlana, 1951—Childhood. Coming-of-age-stories. Jews—Soviet Union—Biography. Soviet Union—Anti-Semitism. Ukraine—World War, 1939-1945—German atrocities. Soviet Union—Cold War. Soviet Union—Social conditions—20th century. Immigrants.

For Alex and Amelia

The distinction between the past, present, and future is only a stubbornly persistent illusion.

—ALBERT EINSTEIN

ABOUT THE AUTHOR

Svetlana Grobman is a Jewish immigrant from Russia who was born in Moscow in 1951. She moved to the United States in 1990. While living in Russia, Grobman was an engineer and an editor for the Soviet Encyclopedia. Now she is a librarian and freelance writer living in Columbia, Missouri. *The Education of a Traitor* is Grobman's first book, and she is currently working on her second.

CONTENTS

PROLOGUE

I am running along the twisted streets of a strange town. It is late and the streets are dark and silent except for the sound of my shoes tapping desperate Morse code signals into the black world. A winding street climbs to a tower on top of a hill whose windows are as dark as everything else in this town. Where are the people? Are they all asleep? Or … dead? No, no! I won't think about death! I carry a message for these people. An important message! I'll think of something nice instead, like flowers or, better yet, mountains—the way they appear in the night, dim silent giants propping up a sky encrusted with glimmering stars.

I reach the tower door and try to open it. The door is locked. I ring a bell. No answer. I ring again—twice, three times. I keep my finger pressed on the bell button and listen to the piercing sounds sinking into the depth of the house. I shout, "Is anybody there?"

Muffled footsteps sound behind me. I turn sharply. Nobody. I continue ringing. More footsteps. I turn again. Not a soul. My heart is about to jump out of my chest, and my voice is breaking, "Open, open, please!"

Suddenly, the door flies open and a tall silhouette appears in the dark hallway, "I've been waiting for you." I recoil. "Yes, we've been waiting for you," echoes behind me, too.

I spin around—two more silhouettes loom in the street. I freeze. How did they know I'd come at this hour? Nobody was supposed to know! Did they spy on me? Is this a trap?

I jerk and try to shrink away from the door, but several invisible hands grab my shoulders, pull my clothes, and push me back into the dark doorway. I fight them silently and vigorously—until I feel the barrel of a gun against my spine.

"Let me go!" I scream, but no sound comes out of my throat, not even a squeak. Something slippery and cold tightens its grip around my neck, blinds my eyes, and squeezes my chest. "Leave me alone!" I try again. "I know nothing! Let me go-o-o-o!"

With all my strength, I try to break away, only to wake up to the sounds of my own moaning.

Ever since I can remember, I have had nightmares. A week rarely goes by without me waking up at night screaming. Nightmares are as much a part of my life as the pop-up spring thunderstorms in my home country, Russia, or the vibrant fall colors of the American Midwest, where I live now.

For a long time, my nightmares were about wars. This is no surprise, since I was born in Moscow six years after the Great Patriotic War (the Second World War) ended, and I grew up in the shadow of its grim memories. War stories were as common in my childhood as lullabies are for the American child. These stories were everywhere, in books, in movies, and on TV—about Russian soldiers and partisans, about the suffering of our civilians, about ill-fated lovers caught in the ravages of war, and whatever else war stories can be about.

The stories were heroic, moralizing, and sad, because the main characters always died. Some of them died in battle, struck by bullets or shrapnel. Others were crushed by tanks or torn apart by bombs, and others were betrayed by traitors and died under torture. Even those who almost survived the war died on the last day—or the day after—while they were preparing to go back home. There was no escape for them. Heroes died because that was what made them heroes, and traitors died because that was what our justice demanded.

As for the millions of people displaced by chance and misfortune—POWs or civilians—they remained under a cloud of suspicion. How could they surrender alive? Why didn't they die the way heroes did? If they came back, they were sent to Siberian gulags. If they disappeared in the maze of the world, they were quickly forgotten, as if they had never been born. Everything was black and white, with no nuances and no half tones. History—in our judgment—had mercy for no one, since, clearly, there was no higher honor or a better destiny than to die for our country.

Time and again, I would turn over the last page of a book and ask myself, could I run forward into heavy fire? Could I endure torture, knowing that in the end I'd be hanged by the Germans, like the eighteen-year-old partisan, Zoya Kosmodemyanskaya, died on a freezing November day in 1941, with her head held high, shouting, "I am happy to die for my people!"? Would I have the courage to intercept machine-gun fire with my own body, like another young hero, Alexander Matrosov, who threw himself onto a German pill-box in February 1943 to allow his unit to advance?

That was what true patriots did, and I longed to be a true patriot. I just did not want to be a *dead* patriot. There must be a way of proving my worth to my country while staying alive, I thought to myself, like being a good student, following the precepts of Grandfather Lenin, which we studied in school, and of course, loving my homeland and never, ever, under any circumstances, leaving it.

Yet leave it I eventually did. By the time of my departure, I no longer felt patriotic toward the country of my birth, and I did not care about being called a traitor for abandoning it. I learned that the land I loved so much never cared for me. In fact, it did not care for anybody, only for its pompous marches in Red Square, its false pretenses, and its power to imprison us.

It didn't take me too long to acquire this knowledge—most of my education would be complete by the age of fifteen. After that, all I could do was wait and hope—wait to grow up, and hope that the Soviet regime would release its grip on me, and others like me, to finally let us go.

CHAPTER ONE

BIRCH TREES

To celebrate my birth in 1951, my parents planted two birch trees beside our apartment house in Moscow. I cannot actually remember this, but my parents have told me about it so often that, eventually, I began to feel as though I were there with them, watching my father dig two holes in the thawed ground and lower two spindly saplings into their depths. I do remember growing up with these trees and being proud of the fact that my arrival in this world was marked by something alive and symbolic, for birches are symbols of my mother country Russia, as bald eagles are symbols of the United States. This is why, to this day, birch trees remain an anchor for my early memories.

My entire body quivers from coughing. Coughs fill my lungs, my throat, my head, and our whole apartment. There is so much coughing that my grandmother opens our second floor kitchen window to dilute the cough-filled atmosphere with fall air. She holds me by the window on her large warm bosom. Her arms are strong and soft.

"Inhale deeply. Now exhale. Inhale again. Good girl. Everything is going to be all right. Just breathe."

Wet needles cool my face. I am still coughing, but my breathing eases, and I can look around. Dark-gray clouds move slowly above me. Below me, the same color is repeated in the wet pavement of the street and the wooden rectangle of a fence in front of our house, inside of which two slim birches stretch their bare branches toward me in a gesture of sympathy. I am getting cold and Grandma closes the window, muttering under her breath, "I'm too old for this ..."

I spend a lot of time with Grandma. Mom is mostly "at work" and Dad is "on a business trip," although I do not know what that means. All I know is that Mom comes home every night and Dad does not. Mom often arrives tired—it must be because she carries a heavy bag. I have peeked into her bag a couple of times, so I know its contents: several shiny metal containers, bundles of tiny pointed bottles filled with transparent liquid, boxes of pills, cupping-glasses, and a long rubber tube with a large black disk at one end and a forking metal part with small ear pieces on the other.

The rubber tube thing looks like fun, and I would love to use it on my blue-eyed doll, Masha—to push the ear pieces into my ears, place the cool disk onto Masha's cloth body, and command, the way Mom does, "Breathe, don't breathe…"

Dad, when he comes home, does not bring anything interesting except heavy thick books. His books are boring, though—no colors or pictures, just a tangled mass of letters, lines, and numbers. I do not like them—they distract Dad from reading to me. Grandma does not like them either. "A family man," she sneers when Dad is not around, "should be thinking about making *parnose* (a living, Yiddish), not reading books."

I miss having other kids around. Once, I overheard Mom telling somebody that when they tried to put me in day care, I got sick and they almost "lost" me, so now they have to keep me at home. I do not remember being lost. I am not sure that is even possible in our small apartment, where the grandparents occupy one room and my parents and I occupy half the kitchen.

The apartment is crammed with bulky furniture and there is so little open space that even I have a hard time hiding here when my older cousins—Mom's niece and nephew—condescend to play hide-and-seek with me during their visits.

A big chunk of the room is taken up by a round wooden table covered with a dark-maroon tablecloth and encircled with straight-back heavy chairs. Behind the table sits an aluminum-frame bed with a headboard that is decorated with dull metal balls. A large wardrobe is propped up against the wall on the right—its key sticks tantalizingly from a keyhole well above my head; and a sideboard on the left displays plates and glasses that Grandma uses for special occasions.

In the kitchen are a little sofa for me, a couch for my parents, a counter with two *kerosinki* (one-burner oil-stoves), and an iron wash-stand with a wash basin—the house has no running water.

When I am bored, I wander to the landing, but I never stay there long. The light on the landing is low, and a steep staircase to the first floor seems to teem with shadowy dangers. Also, as soon as I step outside our door, a smell of cats envelops me like a dense cloud. The odor comes from the next-door apartment occupied by a sick old woman. Her husband died a long time ago, and her only son was killed in the Second World War ten years ago.

I rarely see that woman. Like many invalids and cripples living in the victorious city, she is almost invisible. No facilities exist to accommodate people like her or help them get around, so they just rot in their smelly little rooms, unnoticed by the rest of us.

When Grandma goes grocery shopping, she leaves me outside. Together, we negotiate the dark staircase—Grandma walks and I half-slide my way down sitting on my rear and pushing with my hands against the cool surface of the steep stone stairs. Grandma opens a squeaky front door and we find ourselves next to a weathered wooden gate that leads to a small garden with my birch trees. Grandma lets me in and closes the gate. "Stay put and don't cry," she says. "Be brave, *bubala* (Yiddish term of endearment)." Then she adjusts the dark triangle of her headscarf, firmly places a small purse under her armpit, and leaves.

I watch her softly rounded figure blend into the dim air of the street and swallow my rising tears. "Grandma will come back soon," I console the birches, and they nod agreeably in the wind.

I am used to talking to these trees. They are my age, although they grow much faster than I do, and I have to look up to see their fuzzy crowns against the cold-blue sky. Often, I hug their flaky trunks in hopes that this closeness will spark a magical power of growth, and I will shoot up as fast as they do.

I will return to these trees numerous times throughout my life in Moscow. The last time I come, I will be thirty-nine years old and about to leave Russia for good. I will desperately wander around my grandparents' old neighborhood, trying to find the patch of earth where the little girl I used to be talked to the trees, but I will not find it. The house will be demolished by then, and clusters of gray concrete-block clones will have mushroomed in its place. The little garden of my childhood with its trees and flowers will be gone, leaving me forever uprooted.

Yet that is still in the future. For now, I pick a daisy and start tormenting it, tearing off its bright petals, one by one, while monotonously lamenting—the way I have heard Mom do, "He loves me, he loves me not …"

I'm three years old

By the time Grandma comes back—two large string-bags in her arms and her headscarf crooked—I am in tears. I've been alone forever, and I'm scared that she might not come back for me. What am I going to do then? Grandma looks at me and sighs. We both know that taking me along does not make things better. We are shoved by ageless-looking women whose whole lives are spent waiting and who, even as they talk, eye each other suspiciously. Together but utterly separate, they are united only by righteous indignation against anyone who tries to jump ahead in line.

Grandma rarely talks to strangers. When she does, people near us exchange glances—her Russian is tainted with a distinct Yiddish accent, although I am too young to understand that. Grandma does not talk much to me either, just holds my hand in hers.

"Stand still," she says—her face a mask of tired resignation. But I have a sensation of something running up and down my legs, and my hand—the one that she holds in hers—grows heavy and numb. I pull it from Grandma's grip and shake it, while Grandma mutters to herself, "I'm too old for this ..."

CHAPTER TWO

GRANDPARENTS

I play alone a lot. There are no children in our small apartment house, and Grandma is too busy to play with me. For one thing, the wooden floor of the apartment needs to be meticulously scrubbed. Grandma brings buckets of water from the outside water pump and crawls around the floors with her bottom sticking up and her head lowered down—both hands slapping a wet cloth like a pendulum: right, left, right, left ...

Grandma also does a lot of cooking. This takes a long time, for our *kerosinki* are slow and everything has to be made from scratch. Dough needs to be mixed, green cabbage needs to be chopped and pickled, and chickens need to be plucked and singed.

Washing is another major undertaking. Grandma warms up water on the *kerosinki* and pours it into a zinc washtub. She fetches an aluminum washboard and a piece of strong smelling brown soap and rubs clothes and linen against the washboard. I am eager to help her, but she never lets me. "This is not a game," she says as she orders me to stay away from the sparkling soapy splashes.

Mom uses the same washtub to bathe me; the adults go to a bath-house. Every Saturday, they head there with a sack of clean clothes, towels, and soap. Grandpa also takes leafy birch twigs to lash himself in a *parilka* (steam room)—a favorite activity for bath-house aficionados. He carries vodka in his sack, too, and when he comes home, his cheeks are flushed, and he laughs and tells jokes that he has heard in the bath-house.

These jokes are mostly the kind not told in polite company, but I do not know this. Nor do I understand what is funny about them, or why Grandma gets upset with her husband. Puzzled, I watch my grandfather—middle height, slightly overweight, with soft facial features and a balding head—facing his much shorter and more rounded spouse.

"Shhh! *Zug gornisht*, Raphail, say nothing! The *kind* (child) is listening!"

"Okay, okay, my *gelibte* (sweetheart). I'll be quiet like a mouse. Isn't it funny, though?" And, infuriating my grandmother, he repeats the joke again, bursting into laughter long before the punch line.

In comparison to Grandma, who expects something bad to happen at any moment, my grandfather is an optimist and fun to be around. Despite his family's modest circumstances, he brings home smiles and laughter. He puts me on his lap and asks me how my day has been, and, sometimes, as I am tucked into bed, sounds of his guitar follow me into my dreams.

Grandfather always comes home hungry. As soon as Grandma hears his key turning in the keyhole, she starts serving dinner. Grandpa's dinner is usually the same: a small piece of roasted meat with a hearty portion of potatoes drowned in gravy and a shot of his favorite pepper-flavored vodka "*Pertsovka,*" accompanied by a pickle—a must-have addition to vodka for every self-respecting Muscovite male.

I am envious that Grandma never tries to push soup on him, although she always asks if he wants some. This is a nightly ritual between them.

"Raphail, do you want some soup?" Grandma's hands are rooted on her hips.

"Nope, my sweetheart. Liquid should come only from a bottle!" Grandpa responds energetically and, as if letting me know that turning soup down is a privilege of adult life, flashes a broad, crescent-moon smile accompanied by a wink.

When Grandpa smiles, deep wrinkles dance around his pale green eyes, and sparkles of hidden laughter jump out of his pupils. He has a nice baritone voice, too. When he is in a good mood—which corresponds with trips to the bath-house, paychecks, visits of relatives, or holidays—all accompanied by consumption of fair amount of "*Pertsovka*"—he plays his guitar and sings. Both of my grandparents came from the Ukraine, so many of Grandpa's favorite songs are Ukrainian. They are often sad and melancholy, which may account for the sorrow in his voice and the tears in his eyes:

"Don't be afraid of the cold night, my sweetheart. I'll warm your little feet in my fur hat and I'll carry you in my arms …"

I sit next to Grandpa—my hand resting on his knee, my eyes fixed on his lips—and diligently sing along in a thin little voice, thoughtlessly repeating the words that mean nothing to me, yet I am still overtaken by the song's heart-rending sounds and the despair in the singer's voice. After a while, Grandpa stops singing and just plays the guitar with his eyes closed, and I watch his thick fingers, with the flat yellowish fingernails of an old smoker, run up and down the fretboard, as if trying to find a solution to the injustices of life.

There are times when the sadness of his song overcomes Grandpa, and he puts his guitar aside, reaches for a bottle of *Pertsovka*, and continues drinking—silently and gloomily.

"*Genug* (enough already, Yiddish), Raphail!" Grandma appears in front of him, attempting to take the bottle away.

At this point, Mom puts her medicine-smelling hands on my shoulders, "Let me take you to bed," and pulls me away, while behind us Grandpa thunders curses toward "this damn woman who never understood me!" And if I look back, "Mama, why is Grandpa upset?," I see my grandmother—a disapproving expression written on her face—slowly and quietly retreat from the table, like a general who has lost a battle but still believes in the sanctity of her mission.

These storms never last long, nor does Grandpa ever strike his wife. In fact, the next morning is likely to start with another familiar "song":

"*Fanusechka* (diminutive from Fannie), my *gelibte*, forgive me, an old fool. I don't know what came over me. Please, don't turn away. Just look at me, would ya?"

Grandma, seemingly disgusted, appears deaf to the steady stream of her husband's regrets. Everybody else exchanges glances. We all know that soon she will forgive him, and he will be nice and attentive to her—the way he normally is—until the next explosion.

Despite occasional flashes of Grandfather's alcohol-induced temper, my grandparents get along very well—that is, as well as anybody I know. His part in their union is making a living—as modest as it is—her part is everything else. She is a homemaker—a common designation for women of her generation, especially before the war. It is less common in the 1950s, for the war left millions of women widowed and many returning soldiers invalids or hopeless alcoholics, forcing women to take over men's places.

Grandma is very lucky. She has not lost anyone from her immediate family. Her husband, stationed on the Finnish border in 1939, survived two wars with Finland—the short Winter War and the longer Continuation War—and, in 1946, came back to his family with his limbs intact, suffering only from a post-traumatic stress disorder. Their older daughter, my aunt, who turned 18 in 1942, was also drafted into the army and sent to the front as a telegrapher. Yet she, too, survived and even married a sergeant from her battalion. In 1945, she returned home pregnant with my cousin Sima, her war-time husband killed.

My aunt in uniform, 1944

Grandma, with her younger children—my mother then 15 and her brother 12—evacuated to Siberia, as many panic-stricken Muscovites did during the war. They lived in a barracks with twenty other families and almost no heat during the frigid Siberian winters.

All of them worked fourteen hours a day: Mother on the assembly line at a factory manufacturing parts for tanks and cannons, her younger brother as an electrician, and Grandma as a seamstress repairing damaged military uniforms. Their pay—a meager *paek* (ration) of bread, lard, and rotten potatoes—was small enough to starve them to death slowly. So Grandma sold their last possessions for food at a local market, and my mother and her brother roamed the local fields looking for rotting vegetables and cow pies for heating fuel.

Mother (before she married) with her brother and their parents, 1948

Still, they lived, although my uncle came very close to dying, once from pneumonia and another time from an electric shock he suffered while fixing a high-voltage power line. When the war was over, they returned to Moscow, where my pregnant aunt and, later, my grandfather joined them.

Except for heavy lifting, Grandpa does not do much at home, which is typical for the average Muscovite male. Less typical is that Grandma—and not her husband—makes the major decisions in the family: what to buy, how to help the children, or what to fix. She does not seem to like my father very much and rarely talks to him. When she does, it sounds like a monologue that is addressed to nobody in particular.

"Some people don't worry about getting a job that provides for their families. They need a *college education*!" (My father has been taking night classes off and on). "They are too busy studying and don't have enough time when their families need them." A pause. "Of course, what do I know? I've never been to college. I'm not that smart. All I've done all my life is take care of everybody around me."

Dad cringes in his corner and the textbook in his hand begins shaking, as if a mild earthquake is hitting him. His face takes on the martyr-like expression of somebody who's about to lament: "One day you'll be sorry!" but Mom flashes him a "don't-you-say-anything!" glance, and he remains silent.

There is not much Father can say anyway. He does not make enough money to buy an apartment for his family, and he has no *svyazi* (connections) to get one from the government. When I wake up during the night, I sometimes hear Mom whispering to her husband not to pay attention to Grandma's complaints.

CHAPTER THREE

GREAT EXPECTATIONS

Like any young child, I do not evaluate my world. I take it the way it is and adjust my needs accordingly. The good thing is, I do not need much. I have clothes for the cold Moscow winters, a dozen children's books, a blue-eyed doll, Masha, and a second-hand toy dog, Shavka.

Also, I do not care about food. I am a "terrible eater," and the only food I like is sweets. Grandma claims that I have a "sweet tooth." That, I know, is not true. If I *really* had a sweet tooth, I would have a sweet taste in my mouth all the time. As it is, I enjoy sweets only when Mom or Grandma gives me an open-faced sugar sandwich. That is a feast, and to prolong it, I chew the sandwich very, very slowly, savoring every snow-white crystal of sugar as it melts in my mouth.

The only thing better than a sugar sandwich is chocolate. Alas, chocolate is very expensive, and I can have it only on big holidays or the birthdays of my older cousins Sima and Roma, children of Mom's sister Raya. Aunt Raya is now married to a Polish Jew who was cast ashore on the Moscow River by the receding waves of the Great Patriotic War.

Abraham has no family left back in Poland. His parents, siblings, his first wife and their four children—all were lost to the callous hatred of the Nazis and the Polish anti-Semites. Abraham is fifteen years older than my aunt and shorter than her by at least four inches. That said, he is still good-looking, with bright dark eyes, bushy eyebrows, slightly sharp features, and a head of Einstein-like white hair.

Abraham is not an easy man—stern, short-tempered, and demanding. This could be the result of his painful past, although it is entirely possible that he was like that all along. Yet, with the post-war shortage of men, my aunt could not afford to be choosy—Abraham is a decent man, and he adopted Aunt Raya's daughter from her short-lived war-time marriage. He is also a good tailor and a good provider—better than my father at any rate—which allows his wife to stay at home in their own doll-sized house, one street away from us.

The best thing about Abraham, in my view, is that his grateful customers sometimes bring him a box of chocolates—a great addition to our families' gatherings, especially for me and my cousin Roma. Roma is the only child Uncle Abraham and Aunt Raya have together. He is three years older than me and already in second grade. His sister Sima is in fifth grade and, to me, she looks like a consummate grown-up. She no longer wears bows in her blond hair, her skirts fall down to cover her bony knees, and when I ask her a question, her usual answer is: "You won't understand. Why don't you go play with your toys?"

Roma does not pay much attention to me either. He is at his happiest when galloping around the neighborhood with a band of other boys, tornado style—raising dust, shouting, breaking things, and scaring scraggy street cats.

Still, I like visiting their house, especially for my cousins' birthdays. Birthdays in our country are almost as festive as Christmas is in the West. The only holiday that is higher in our hierarchy is New Year's. But unlike New Year's, families celebrate birthdays several times a year, which means more fun and happiness to go around. Children are happy because they get sweets and other presents, and adults because they can "*utopit gore v vine*," drown their sorrows in wine, or, more likely, in vodka.

I rarely get sweets for my birthday. My usual presents are a couple of oranges, a cluster of bananas, or other foods that are hard to come by in Moscow in the 1950s—all of them from that tedious category of things my parents call "good for you." My cousins, on the other hand, get *real* presents *and* chocolate. I never envy them, though. Their toys will be, one day, passed down to me. As for the chocolate, I can share it with them, too. In fact, I am hoping to have some tonight, at the celebration of Roma's eighth birthday.

When my parents, my grandparents, and I enter Aunt Raya's house, food is already on the table. Sauerkraut shows off its cranberry-freckled face in a deep glass bowl. In a dish next to it, two large herrings swim in sunflower oil. A mound of pickles nestles near bottles of vodka, and a splash of grated boiled beets, liberally dressed with mayonnaise, appears in the middle of the table like a spot of blood left by feasting vampires.

I peer into the kitchen—do they have any chocolate?—but Mom orders me to take my place at the table. The dinner is long and abundantly peppered with toasts for Roma's health, success and good luck, his parents' health, success and good luck, the guests' health, success and good luck, and, most importantly, peace in the whole world.

The main course is finished, the dirty plates are taken away, and I hope dessert will follow soon. Too early. The adults keep talking, but now their conversation takes a bitter turn.

"Does anybody even know how many people Stalin *sgubil* (wasted) before and during the war? Millions for sure! And after the war? Millions again!" my father thunders. "Okay, Khrushchev denounced Stalin's cult of personality. Still, tell me, where are the people who carried out his commands all those years, who shot innocent people or squealed on their neighbors?" Father looks around at his silent audience, and his fist hits the table: "They're still among us!"

I stare at the adults, alarmed. What's the matter? Actually, nothing special. It is a typical conversation many families have behind closed doors. Political freedom does not exist in our country, and it will not exist for many more years—if ever. The only places where people can express their unhappiness and let off steam are in their homes, and family gatherings are good outlets for that, since everybody knows that talking politics outside the family circle could be dangerous.

Tonight, though, Mom tries to stop her husband. "Enough, Natán," she says quietly, pulling his sleeve. "It's a birthday party."

"Don't 'enough' me!" Father cuts her off.

Uncle Abraham raises his voice, too. "Fira's right. *Chto proshloe voroshit."* (Don't dig up the past).

Father, exalted by the spirits and the sound of his own voice, turns away from Mom and faces his brother-in-law.

"Why not? Did they put you into a prison camp or didn't they?" he says, referring to the time when my uncle, then a Polish soldier, fled from the Nazis, only to be captured by the Soviet Army on the border and sent to Siberia.

Uncle Abraham's face darkens, "That's *my* business. We're here to celebrate, not to read the burial service." He shakes his head, stretches his narrow lips into a smile, and winks, "Entertainment time!"

My cousin Sima slowly gets up from the table and walks to the piano with the expression of a martyr about to be thrown to the lions. She opens her instrument and attempts to play Mozart's Turkish March. The adults—the lions—reward her with intoxicating clapping.

Then hot tea makes its steaming appearance, and—finally!—my aunt reaches inside the cupboard behind the table. When she turns around, the smile on her face is as broad as her hips, and a box of chocolate is in her hands. The box is tied up with a bow like a red rose. Aunt Raya unties the rose and, with the flair of an experienced magician, pulls off the lid. Rows of candy, wrapped in thin white paper, are revealed to our eyes. Aunt Raya turns to her son and gently hands the treasure to him, "Sweet wishes!"

With everybody's eyes fixed upon him, Roma, who has been unusually quiet during dinner, carefully pulls one white ball out of the box and holds it in his hand.

"Open it!" His mother says, beaming.

Roma does not move but stares at the piece of candy as if it is a grenade rather than the epitome of sweetness.

"What are you waiting for?" Aunt Raya says. "Go ahead, open it! It's not going to bite you."

She puts the box down and, still smiling, grabs the white ball from Roma's palm. The wrapping paper collapses under my aunt's fingers like a dry flower, and the smile on her face dies.

"This is strange," she says, bringing the wrapper closer to her face and unfolding it. I crane my neck as much as I can, but see no chocolate.

"It's ... empty!" My aunt cries, dropping the rumpled piece of paper to the floor. Then she grabs another white ball—with the same result. Feverishly, she squishes one paper ball after another, mumbling to herself, "Empty, empty, empty ..."

As the last piece quietly falls, Uncle Abraham rises from his chair. His face is red, his eyes are like bonfires, and his white hair stands on end, which makes him look a head taller.

"Can you explain this?" He growls to his son, whose face has taken on the color of the wrapping paper that now covers the floor like snowflakes.

Instead of answering, Roma starts shrinking before our eyes. When he reaches the size of Hans Christian Anderson's Thumbelina (he never becomes as cute as her), I turn to my mother and whisper, "Where are the chocolates?"

"Good question," my uncle says loudly. "Where are the chocolates?"

"I don't understand," Aunt Raya says, perplexed, gazing from one face to another and finally stopping at her husband's. "Who gave you this box?"

"What don't you understand?" My uncle barks. "I think it's rather clear!"

I pull my mother's sleeve and whisper again, "Is this a magic trick?"

"This is a trick, all right," Uncle Abraham announces to his quiet audience, and an ominous expression flashes across his face. "Let's ask the magician how he did it. Tell us, you, louse!"

At this, Aunt Raya emits a weak "Ah!" and slumps into her chair. My mom emits a loud "Ah!" and jumps to her feet. Uncle Abraham cries, "I'll show you!" He pushes his chair away and, with the speed of a cobra striking its prey, grabs his son by the collar with both hands and begins vigorously shaking him, as if hoping that the vanished candy would fall from Roma like ripe apples from a tree. "How dare you eat the chocolates?!!"

The room explodes. Everybody is pushing chairs and shouting. "What's the world coming to?" "Abraham, that's enough! It's his birthday!" "If *I* did something like this when I was young, my parents would've killed me!" And, over all that chaos, I hear Roma's wounded-rabbit-like scream, "I'm sorry, I'm sorry, I'll never do it again!"

Roma, 1959

"How did Roma eat the chocolate?" I ask my mother on our way home, still hoping that some of the long-awaited candy could be recovered. "Wasn't the box tied with a ribbon?"

Mom sighs, "Well, he took the ribbon off, I guess, and, at first, he ate just one piece. He thought nobody would notice. Then he ate another piece, and then another, and before he knew it, he finished them all." Here Mom stops, crouches in front of me, and says, looking straight into my eyes, "Let that be a lesson to you. This is what happens when children start doing bad things. They think that nobody will notice, but it never works that way. The best you can do ..."

I stop listening. I understand the only thing that really matters to me. *There is no hope of getting any chocolate*. Not today, not tomorrow, not the day after tomorrow. Not until New Year's. And that is a long wait.

CHATER FOUR

HOW MANY LANGUAGES DOES ONE MAN NEED?

"… *Gai kaken oifen yam*!" (Go shit in the ocean, Yiddish.)
"*Shvaygn*, Raphail!" (Be quiet.)
"*Zi farshtey dos nit*." (She doesn't understand.)

Both of my grandparents grew up in the Pale of Settlement (where the Jews in imperial Russia were required to live), in a Ukrainian *shtetl* (village) called Monasterishche. The place was relatively prosperous. It had two plants—one produced sugar and the other plows and other agricultural equipment—two synagogues, two orthodox churches, several Jewish schools, and a gymnasium. Half of Monasterishche's population was Jewish and the other Ukrainian or Russian, but almost everybody knew Yiddish. The Russians and Ukrainians worked in the nearby fields or at the plants, and the Jews—who were forbidden to own land—as shoemakers, tailors, tinsmiths, and such.

My grandfather's father had a small leather-currying business. He was a hard-working and strong man who, according to family lore, could bend an iron poker with his bare hands. He was also religious. He went regularly to synagogue and presided over Sabbath dinners with a *yarmulke* on his head and a *tallit* over his shoulders.

Together with my great grandmother he had five surviving children: three sons and two daughters—my grandfather the oldest. When the time came, the sons went to a *cheder* (a traditional Jewish school), where boys—but not girls—studied the Torah and the Talmud, as well as learned some Hebrew under the supervision of the Rabbi.

Later, my grandfather went to a government school, which was taught in Ukrainian but offered Russian as well. There he perfected his Ukrainian, improved his Russian, and developed good penmanship. The latter especially came in handy when, during World War I, he was drafted in the Tsar's Army. He served as a military clerk—a rare job for a Jew—which may have saved his life, although it did not prevent him from being captured by the Germans and spending a year in a German POW camp.

The good thing was that, in those days, the Germans treated all their prisoners, including Jews, equally. So my grandfather survived the camp and, after the war ended, came home dressed in a European-style suit and hat. That hat impressed many young women in Monasterische, including my grandmother and, more importantly, her parents, and soon my grandparents were married.

Of course, the *shtetl* my grandfather returned to was not the same *shtetl* he left before the war. It had undergone pogroms and revolutionary changes. The pogroms alone left half the town dead. During one of them, several drunken men burst into my great grandparents' house demanding money. My great grandfather and two of his children were out of town. My great grandmother, with her youngest daughter on her lap, was at home fixing dinner. She got up and offered the marauders some food. They shot her in the chest, and they threw the toddler out the window. The youngest son rushed to his fallen mother, and they shot him, too. The middle daughter tried to escape, but the bandits caught up with her and raped her. Everywhere around them, hundreds of people were murdered, hanged and tortured, and their possessions stolen while the police did nothing.

Despite such recent violence, the beginning of my grand-parents' life together was no different from the lives of any young Jewish couple in the Pale of Settlement. They worked. They went to synagogue. Their only ambition was to start a family. They could have been supporting characters in Shalom Aleichem's "Fiddler on the Roof"—neighbors or distant relatives of Tevye, the milk-man. They spoke the same language, wore the same clothes, and had the same problems. Besides, my grandfather was a good musician, although he poured his heart out through the guitar and not the fiddle.

The difference was that Shalom Aleichem sent his characters to America, while my grandparents stayed in Russia. That forever changed their lives, for shortly afterward, the October Revolution of 1917 swept across the country.

When my grandfather returned home after the war, he first joined his father and younger brother in the family's leather tanning business. Soon, however, the new Soviet government introduced taxes so high that no matter how much they worked, they could hardly break even. The family decided to close the business and leave Monasterishche.

They moved to a Jewish collective farm, Frayheyt (Freedom), near the Black Sea where my grandmother's parents had settled earlier. There they were given a place to live and a job as dairymen. For a while, life seemed good. They worked hard, but the work paid off. Their children were born, and my grandmother's parents, who lived nearby on a small farm, helped to care for them.

This relative tranquility did not last long. The power-hungry Soviet authorities began a campaign of *raskulachivanie*—expropriation of the property of independent farmers. The better-off farmers, most of whom did not have much land and never employed anybody outside their immediate families, were branded *kulaks* and pronounced "class enemies." Arrests, deportations to Siberia, and executions were commonplace.

At the same time, the Soviet government, led by Stalin, began another assault on the peasantry—forced collectivization of all agricultural workers into government-ruled *kolkhozi*. This new action, designed to build "socialism in the countryside," brought all Soviet agriculture under state control while greatly decreasing its efficiency. All in all, in 1930-1937, Stalin's policies led to the starvation and death of 15 million peasants, including 5 million in the Ukraine alone.

As for my own family, in 1931, four of my great grandparents were arrested and sent to a *kolkhoz* in Kazakhstan, where they starved to death within two years. My grandfather and his brother managed to hide from the authorities and flee Frayheyt during the night. They headed for Moscow—their wives and children would join them later.

Nobody in my family talks about any of this, and I will not learn about our history until much later. They do not talk much about their life in Moscow under Stalin either. Or, if they do speak about it in my presence, they use Yiddish, a language which I don't know.

My relatives do not teach me this language for two reasons: one, they can say anything they want without my understanding them; and two, they have no fear that I will repeat something dangerous on the street. This is crucial in a country where children are taught at a very early age to love their country first and foremost, even to the detriment of their families. Also, maybe even more importantly, they do not want me to stand out among other children. Like immigrants everywhere—and they *are* unwanted immigrants in their own country—they want their offspring to fit in. Speaking Yiddish will betray me as Jewish, and Russians do not care for us Jews.

My uncle, my aunt, and my mother as children

Whether my family is right or wrong, I grow up monolingual. The only language I know is Russian. The only tales I hear are Russian fairytales. My toys have Russian names, and my own name, Sveta, is Slavic. In fact, it was Grandma who named me, for she wanted my life to be different from hers: bright and full of light—*svéta*—and that is what my name means in the Russian language.

It never bothers me that adults in my family speak a funny language that I do not understand, the name of which I will not know until I am older. I grow up believing that speaking two languages is what adults do, like going to places they call "work" or making boring jokes, or drinking vodka. In my world, there is one language for everybody and a secret code for adults.

When I go to school two years later, I will learn that not every adult speaks two languages, and, in fact, that is one of the things that separates us from the families outside our door.

CHAPTER FIVE

MOSCOW NIGHTS

I spend long hours on my little sofa going through Russian folktales with images of a burly *Ded Moroz* (Grandpa Frost) and his lovely granddaughter *Snegurochka*, Snow Maiden—both in felt boots, puffy red coats, and hats with white trim. I examine pictures of the hook-nosed *Baba Yaga* who is peeking from her wooden cabin perched upon a chicken leg. I know many of these tales by heart—my parents have read them to me many times, so I can repeat them aloud to Grandma. Also, I can count to twenty and back, I know the alphabet, and I can read several simple words. I can even scribble my name on a piece of paper that Grandma hands me on the condition that I give her "some peace and quiet for at least half an hour."

I am very proud of my writing, but Grandma does not have much time to admire my unsteady scrawls. She's as busy as ever. Grandma and I have just returned from a rented summer house, a *dacha*, outside Moscow, and now Grandma has her hands full with unpacking and washing and, of course, cooking.

"I wonder what your grandfather ate when I was away," Grandma says, suspiciously eyeing her kitchen. I do not care about that. I want to know where my parents are. This past month, I did not see my father at all, and I saw Mom on Sundays only. She wasn't much fun, though. She didn't even play with me.

She would say, "I'm tired. Find something else to do." She had to get up early in the morning, take a bus and the metro to the train station, and then spend two hours on the train, loaded down with an array of heavy string bags containing a week's worth of produce for Grandma and me, since nothing but milk and bread can be bought locally.

Life at the dacha was so-o-o boring. Grandma and I mostly took walks around the block and listened to the radio, which was boring, too—a lot of talking, a lot of stormy music, and annoyingly long songs. There was just one song that I liked. It had a smooth, slightly drawn-out and warm melody—just like the summer evenings that sneaked up on us shortly after supper.

In fact, that was the song's name, *Podmoskovnye Vechera* (Moscow Nights), and it had words like "I will never forget a friend I met in Moscow." That song was everywhere in 1957. I heard it pouring from our neighbors' houses as Grandma and I walked toward the train station to meet Mom. It was sung on the platform by young people waiting for a train. And Mom, when she arrived, hummed it, too.

Podmoskovnye Vechera became popular because of the Sixth World Festival of Youth and Students. Mom talked about it a lot. It was the first international festival held in Moscow or anywhere in our country. Thousands of young people came to us from abroad, and all the Soviet republics sent their representatives to meet with the foreign guests. Government-sanctioned events and festivities took place all over the city. Music—even officially ostracized bourgeois jazz!—sounded everywhere, and young people of all nationalities danced in downtown Moscow, which, according to Mom, was "thoroughly cleaned."

Most of what Mom talked about went over my head. Yet I understood her last remark, and in my mind's eye, I immediately pictured a detachment of bearded, hoarse-voiced *dvorniki* (men who take care of the city streets and sidewalks) fiercely sweeping the pavement with long-handled brooms, while raising thick clouds of dust and scattering lazy pigeons.

"Did the *dvorniki* clean the streets for the dancers?" I asked.

Mom just sighed and winked toward my grandmother. The "cleaning" had nothing to do with the *dvorniniki,* or dust, or pigeons, but with Moscow's "unreliable elements"—criminal and political—who were moved 100 kilometers away from the city during the festival.

Besides their bourgeois music, the foreigners shocked the Soviet people with their easy manners, broad smiles, and never-before-seen tight blue pants called "jeans." Every time Mom visited, she described a new and exciting detail of the festival, including the fact that, for the first time in ten years, Soviet people were allowed to mingle with foreigners.

"Not alone, you understand," she said, giving Grandma a meaningful glance.

"With a teacher?" I asked.

"You can call it that, I suppose," Mom said and then added, to me, "Why don't you go out and play."

As I was slowly putting on my shoes, I heard Mom telling Grandma about somebody's daughter, Nina, who came home with a large lock of hair shaved off, and how she was going to "pay for her behavior dearly." That sounded so interesting that, despite my mother's order, I immediately took off my shoes and returned to the room to find out more about Nina's hair and her payment. Mom just rolled her eyes and switched to Yiddish, so I had to resign myself to putting my shoes back on and going outside.

My mother, of course, was not talking about teachers' supervision but about a ban that Moscow authorities imposed on Soviet youth to prevent them from meeting with foreign delegates unofficially. Yet curiosity, a post-war lack of men, and the hasty love that saturated the warm air of Moscow's nights overcame the strict rules, and unsanctioned encounters took place all over the city.

The foreigners thought nothing much about it, but the Russian women who were caught by the Soviet security services during raids of city hotels and parks had part of their hair shaved off. This made it easy for their college or work authorities to spot them and promptly "deal" with the women's "amoral behavior." Still, nine months later, more babies were born in Moscow than usual—some of them strikingly non-Russian in appearance.

Now, with the boredom of the *dacha* and the excitement of the festival safely behind us, I am looking forward to seeing my parents.

"Your mother will come tonight," Grandma says, chopping a large onion and wiping her tears with the back of her hand.

"You'll soon move to your own apartment, you know."

No, I do not know. Nor am I sure that I like this news.

"Are you moving with us, Grandma?"

"I don't think so. Your grandfather needs me here. Besides, you'll have a nanny."

That is another thing I am not sure about. A strange nanny? I have never spent much time with strangers, and the mere thought that I will be left alone with one of them for a long time makes my heart sink. Besides, what if the nanny is like *Zolushka's* (Cinderella's) stepmother—fat, greedy and mean? Or even worse, like ugly *Baba Yaga*? (*Baba Yaga* is never far from my thoughts, because, as every Russian child knows, if you don't behave, she'll come and get you!)

With trepidation, I pull out a book of Russian Folktales, find a picture of *Baba Yaga*, and carefully examine it. If my book is any indication, my future is grim. The old woman who stares back at me with an ominously crooked smile showing her only tooth definitely does not like children. In fact, she tried to bake some in a wood stove and eat them for dinner!

When Mom appears in the doorway, I jump off the sofa, scattering books and pieces of paper with my name all around the floor, and blurt out, "Are we leaving now?"

"No, no," Mom laughs, bending over to give me a kiss. The apartment is not finished yet, and when it is, they will first move our furniture, and only then will I leave my grandparents.

"Is my nanny there? What's her name? Will she beat me?"

No, the nanny is not there and, in fact, they haven't found her, yet. I sigh with relief. Hopefully, they'll never find anybody, and I will stay at the grandparents', where life is not exciting but predictable, and where I do not have to worry about strange nannies, *Zolushka's* stepmother, or *Baba Yaga*.

CHAPTER SIX

DON'T TELL ANYBODY

I get my wish. For what seems a very long time—two years, by my recollection, and two weeks, according to my parents—I am left with my grandparents. Most of the day, I play with my old companion Masha, who by now has lost some of her blond locks and whose formerly blue eyes have turned gray. I like her all the same. She looks like girls in our neighborhood, with straw-colored hair and limpid eyes. I myself am dark-haired and my eyes are so dark that Grandma claims she cannot see my pupils. No kid on our street looks like me, nor do the characters from my favorite books. Even *Zolushka*, who appears dark and smudgy on the cover of my book, turns into a beautiful blond by the time she arrives at the king's ball in her pumpkin carriage!

On the weekends, despite the cold Moscow winter, Grandpa takes me for a walk. Grandma helps me put on *valenki s galoshami* (felt boots with black rubber overshoes), a threadbare gray fleece coat and hat, and a pair of thick mittens—all hand-me-downs from my cousin Sima. With a jerk that shakes my whole body, Grandma ties a scarf underneath the coat's collar, and off we go.

Our destination is a big city park nearby—Sokolniki. We cross several streets blanketed with fresh puffy snow and edged by wooden houses with white swollen roofs until we find ourselves at the park's gate. The park is large, with broad alleys, a pond, soccer and hockey fields, as well as several amphitheaters that are used for holiday concerts and special events.

I love this park. In the summer, it looks like a green island where trees and bushes spread free and untamed, where wind plays with the hair of the promenading public, and where a few mischievous squirrels make their exciting appearance. In the fall, maple leaves swirl in a melancholy dance before becoming a multicolored carpet that rustles under my feet. And springtime brings clusters of lilacs showing off their fragrant petals against heart-shaped leaves.

Now, in December, the park is a winter wonderland. Snow-dusted trees, benches, and ice-cream kiosks sparkle under the frigid northern sun. White snow showers, set in motion by a fussy sparrow or a cawing crow, stream down from the stately pine trees. Sounds of a waltz pour from the loudspeakers of an ice rink, where young couples skate in elegant unison and single skaters perform fancy pirouettes.

Grandpa and I stroll along the main alley past the skating rink and the ice-cream kiosks. We breathe the invigorating cool air, admire the graceful skaters, and enjoy the music, accented with the crisp sounds of skates cutting the ice. Our route is well established. Not far from the rink, behind a patch of tall pine trees, sits a small beer stall surrounded with a crowd of men even on cold days. This is where we part. Grandpa joins the enthusiastic crowd, and I head to a playground by the pine trees.

Today, the playground is empty. Everybody has moved to an amphitheater nearby. There, in the middle of the stage, towers a tall fir tree—we call it *elka*—topped with a large shiny red star and decorated with multicolored garlands and shimmering glass balls. In front of the *elka*, stands a *live* white-bearded *Ded Moroz* (a Soviet version of Santa Claus) in a long red coat and a red hat. He leans on a long magic staff, and a large sack hangs over his right shoulder.

Next to *Ded Moroz* poses his granddaughter *Snegurochka* in a sparkling blue coat with a white furry collar. A pointed ornamental *kokoshnik* (a traditional Russian woman's headdress) crowns *Snegurochka's* straw-colored hair, a thick braid falls down to her waist, and a white puffy muff hides her mittenless hands. I stop, rooted to the spot. This is the first live performance I have ever seen, and I am immediately drawn into its magic.

Despite the decorated fir tree, this play has nothing to do with Christmas. We live in a country of atheists that does not celebrate religious holidays. Our festivities are secular or political, and the only holiday we celebrate in December is New Year's. As for the *elka* with the star on top and the burly *Ded Moroz* with the sack of presents, these are a mixture of Russian legends and the long gone traditional Russian Christmas, which the Russian Orthodox Church and its few elderly followers celebrate on January 7.

Of course, nowadays the old symbols are given new meanings. The fir tree no longer evokes the Christian faith, but symbolizes New Year's. The star on top does not recall Bethlehem, but represents the Soviet flag; and, in fact, the summit of the Kremlin's main tower, whose chiming clock heralds the arrival of a new year, is also crowned with a large red star. Santa Claus becomes *Ded Moroz*, and presents—mostly fruit (a rare delicacy at this time of the year), hard candy, and small toys—are just presents. For what parent does not enjoy a smile on his child's face?

The story unfolding before my eyes is a standard New Year's tale. In it, *Ded Moroz* and *Snegurochka* are making their way from the frigid vastness of the North Pole to Moscow on a *troika* (a sleigh drawn by three horses). They are in a hurry. They carry New Year's presents for the children, and, more importantly, *Ded Moroz* and *Snegurochka* must light the *elka*, which sits on the stage entwined with numerous strings of unlit bulbs. If they are late, the new year will never come; and, although nobody ever explains what that would mean, all children understand this would be a catastrophe.

As the performance progresses, *Ded Moroz* and his granddaughter get separated, and they face countless obstacles and Russian folktale villains on their long and dangerous journey to us. The story is breathtaking and full of suspense. Will *Ded Moroz* and *Snegurochka* find each other? Will they deliver the presents? Will they light the *elka* on time?

Ded Moroz looks down at his anxious audience: "Children, help me!"

We jump up and down and shriek and shout: "Oh, look, *Baba Yaga* is just around the corner! Don't go there! Don't go to the other side either! A wolf is hiding behind the tree! Ru-u-u-n!!!"

I strain my voice in the cold crisp air. My freezing breath merges with the breath of other excited children and hovers above our heads like steam from a geyser.

Ded Moroz and *Snegurochka* finally reach the *elka*. "Children, do you remember the magic word?"

The frantic crowd explodes in mighty unison, scaring off every wild creature left in the park: "One, two, three, *yelochka gore-e-e!!!"* (Pine tree, light up!)

A myriad of little stars spark in the thick greenery.

"*S novym Godom*, children!" (Happy New Year!)

And then … the story is over.

The crowd breaks into small fragments and recedes from the amphitheater, like the tide ebbing from the shore. *Ded Moroz*, *Snegurochka*, and the other characters pick up their props, load them on the sleigh, and start moving.

"Is this the last performance today?" A young woman with a bellowing toddler asks.

"No, we just started," *Ded Moroz* says.

To my surprise, his voice sounds young, younger than my father's and much younger than his silvery-white beard implies.

"There'll be several more. Not here, though. We're going to another stage."

"Don't cry," the woman turns to the toddler, "We can watch it again!" And they trail behind the fairytale group.

As if pulled by an invisible cable, I follow them, too; all my emotions focused on the anticipation of more magic. Together, we reach another amphitheater, and the performance starts all over again—less suspenseful than the first one, but no less exciting. In fact, it is even better, because now I do not have to worry about the evil forces!

I do not remember how many times I move from one stage to another. Twice? Three times? I am not sure, and I do not care—until, suddenly, the rules change, and instead of starting a new act, all the characters walk toward a small wooden building and disappear inside it.

I wait. In a little while, several strange men and women come out of the building with large string-bags in their hands, animatedly talking to each other. The tallest of them, a young man with somewhat familiar gray eyes, locks the door, and then they are gone.

I am still waiting. No sound comes from the wooden building. This is strange. Where are *Ded Moroz*, beautiful *Snegurochka*, and ugly *Baba Yaga*? I shift from one foot to the other and look at the sky. The sun, now low on the horizon, is ready for its evening dive, and shadows spread their blue wings on the snowy ground.

Suddenly, I remember—Grandpa told me to wait for him on the playground! But … where is the playground? Where is the beer stall? Where am I?

"Grandpa!" I try to shout, but my thin voice barely penetrates the chilly air, while quick tears rise up to my eyes. I look around—a few people still walk along the darkening alleys. I follow them, hoping somehow to end up in a familiar place. Useless. People scatter in different directions, none of them recognizable.

Tears begin to roll down my cold cheeks, and a lump in my throat sends a shock of panic down to my weakening legs. Also, icy needles tickle my fingers inside the mittens, and my feet feel painfully numb. I am like that poor stepdaughter from a Russian folktale. She was sent by her wicked stepmother to the "wide, wide fields in the crackling frost," where she would have died if not for the help of *Morozko* (a younger version of *Ded Moroz*). If I do not find Grandpa soon, I will freeze to death here, and no *Morozko* will save me …

"What's wrong?"

I have never before seen this woman in a gray wooly kerchief bending over me.

"Are you here alone?"

"I don't kno-o-o-w," I sob loudly. "I lost my grandpa-a-a. *Ded Moroz* and *Snegurochka* went into the house and never came out … And *Baba Yaga*, too … And I don't know where my grandpa is ..."

Through my tears, the woman's face is blurry and sallow. Her kerchief is pulled down to her brows, from under which peer deeply sunk pale blue eyes.

"What's your name?" She says.

"Sve-e-t-a-a-a …"

The woman gives me a triumphant look, as if somehow she knew that all along.

"Didn't they just call you over the loudspeakers? Listen!"

Distant metallic sounds cut through the quiet of twilight:

"Sveta, your grandfather is waiting for you at the main entrance. I repeat. Sveta, your grandfather …"

"It's me! It's me!" I shriek and tug at the woman's sleeve so frantically that she shrinks back. I don't care. Grandpa is waiting for me! At the main entrance! Then another wave of panic washes over me. Where is the main entrance? I look around the darkening haze and start weeping again.

"Well," the woman says, straightening her back, "Let's go and find your grandfather."

She takes my hand and pulls me along a darkening alley, all the while questioning me.

"How old are you? Where do you live? Where are your parents?"

Her questions fall on me like rain drops, quick and unnerving, and I am too exhausted to answer. The woman stops and looks at me disapprovingly.

"A girl your age shouldn't be in the park alone. I bet your grandparents are gonna teach you a lesson!" I say nothing. No punishment can be worse than this.

Another turn around a corner and—oh, miracle!—I see my grandfather pacing back and forth between the glowing globes of the street lamps marking the park's entrance.

"Grandpa!" I scream as I yank my hand from the woman's grip and run towards him, stumbling and falling in the snow and picking myself up.

"Sveta! *Dankn Got*! (Thank God! Yiddish) Where have you been? I've been worried sick!" Grandpa folds me in his arms, and I smell beer and tobacco on his breath. Even through his thick coat, I can feel his racing heart. Or is it mine? I don't know. I am flooded with tears of relief.

Grandpa carries me through the dark streets dotted by window lights. He puts me down only when we reach our house.

"Don't tell anybody that you got lost. Especially your grandma. Okay? It'll be our secret," he says.

"Okay," I exhale, relieved that nobody will punish me for my misadventure.

CHAPTER SEVEN

CAVIAR

I do not know what other parts of Moscow look like at the end of the 1950s. All I know is our new working class neighborhood *Marina Roscha*, which is gloomy all year round but especially in the spring, when dirty snowdrifts stubbornly cling to the ground, sometimes until May, and in the fall, when ubiquitous puddles reflect a morose sky endlessly drizzling rain.

We now live in a two-family wooden house. On the outside, the house is weathered by frequent rains and winter storms, and on the inside, it is rotted from old age, dampness, and the misery of its occupants, past and present. Still, here we have our own room. The other room belongs to a family of three, an elderly woman with a married daughter and her husband. Between the rooms are a communal toilet, a sink, and a kitchen where several *kerosinki* saturate the air with thick smells of food.

Most of our furniture comes from the grandparents' place. The new additions are a bookcase and a dining table. The bookcase is divided into three clearly defined areas. Technical books for Dad are perched on the top shelves, medical books for Mom fill the middle, and picture books for me are placed on the bottom, where

I can easily reach them. The dining table, covered with a flowery vinyl tablecloth, sits in the middle of the room. It also serves as an ironing board and a desk.

The room is so crowded that when my parents get angry with me and send me *v ugol* (order me to stand in the corner—a common way of punishing small children), the only corner they can use is the one with a coat rack. For this punishment to be fully effective, the corner is supposed to be dark. Yet that would require turning off our only light which dangles from the middle of the ceiling and, at night, paints fleeting circles of light on the dining table beneath it. When that fixture is off, my parents are in the dark, too, so the best they can do is make me face the drab pile of coats and think about my *plochoe povedenie* (bad behavior).

I never think about that, though. Instead, I brood about how unjust my parents are. Often, they put me in the corner because of my "terrible" eating habits, which are definitely not my fault. The food Mom gives me is gross. *Mannaja kasha* (semolina boiled in milk) is covered with a wrinkled skin of burnt milk. Chicken soup is coated with yellow lumps of grease and thickened with pimpled chicken skin. And *gogol-mogol*, a concoction of raw eggs beaten with sugar and diluted with boiled milk—a supposedly nutritious drink—makes me sick to my stomach even as I watch Mom make it.

My other problem, according to my parents, is that I am sluggish, and it requires "the patience of a saint" to wait for me to dress. Yet there are so many layers I have to put on before walking out in the cold! Grandma always helped me, but Mom does not. She says that I am "a big girl," and I have to learn how to do things on my own. Also, she adds, she is not feeling well, and she cannot squat down the way she used to.

Nobody has explained to me that she is pregnant, so I do not understand why she gets impatient with me while *I* am squatting on the floor, putting on heavy wool socks, *valenki,* and galoshes. Besides, it is not my fault that she's always in a hurry!

Mother and me before my sister was born

The way I see it, the only reason my parents are so mean to me must be because they are my *adoptive* parents. And if I have learned anything from Russian folktales, stepparents—and especially stepmothers—*never* love their stepchildren, no matter how good they are. (I firmly believe that I am good.)

Every time I find myself in the corner, contemplating the events that brought me there, I come to the same conclusion: *these* parents will *never* love me. I spend some time grieving about that and then, inevitably, arrive at another conclusion—my life is not worth living, and the only solution to my suffering must be my early death. I am not sure how I should die, but that never stops me. I quickly skip over that detail and concentrate on how sorry my parents will be when I am dead.

I lean against the rough fabric of the heavy coats, inhale the dusty smell of the old wool and moth balls, and, in my mind's eye, watch a small coffin being carried out of our house. The coffin is open and, inside its shallow interior lined with puffy white blankets, I see my slim body in a dark-blue dress. My hands are crossed on my chest, my face is morbidly pale, my eyes are shut, and my feet are covered with a pile of artificial flower wreaths.

A small crowd of grieving relatives surrounds the coffin: my parents, grandparents, aunts and uncles, and all my cousins. Everybody is dressed in black, and a small military orchestra plays heart-rending funeral marches. These details come from the only funeral I have ever seen, the funeral of one of our neighbors, an elderly naval officer whom we never met when he was alive and whose funeral procession was departing from the house next door as my family was moving in.

All my relatives are wailing, especially Grandma. She pulls a black kerchief off her head, points her index finger at my mother, and exclaims, "What did you do to my poor *bubala*? I babysat her for years, and she was just fine!"

Here my mother screams, "I didn't want her dead! I am so so-o-o-r-r-y-y!" and faints into the coffin beside me, while my dad mumbles, defensively, "If only we had known …."

I work myself up to such a profound sense of grief that soon I begin sobbing in my corner—first softly, then loudly. Unfortunately, I never know how to end the funeral scene in a satisfactory way, for I never can figure out how I—motionless and silent—can let my parents know that I will *never* forgive them for their cruelty.

This makes me cry even more, and my weeping—which my parents perceive as a sign of repentance—finally attracts their attention, and they let me out of the corner, still reprimanding me for my transgressions.

Today is one of those days. Mom has just bawled me out for not eating my dinner. Yet instead of sending me *v ugol*, she rummages in her large bag and pulls out a tiny tin can with a bright label that depicts a fat fish swiveling its tail over a small pile of reddish grains. My heart sinks. This is caviar, a true Russian delicacy. Mom opens the can, cuts a thick slice of white bread—her knife hits the cutting board with the mournful sound of a hammer driving nails into a coffin—smears it with caviar, and hands it to me.

"This is good for you," She says. "Make sure to eat it till *posledni kroshki* (the last crumb)!"

I fix my gaze on the sandwich. I hate caviar! When I bite into its colorful pellets, their skins break with a tiny pop and thick reddish liquid seeps out of them like the mushy innards of a squashed caterpillar. And the taste … it is bitterly salty, whereas the only taste I like is sweet. Besides, if caviar is so good, why don't my parents eat it themselves?

I sit in my chair and count the tiny eggs, wishing that they had been given a chance to metamorphose into young fish and swim effortlessly into a vast sea far from our house. Also, it occurs to me, these tiny red balls might still possess the power of life, and if I slip them into a glass of water, one by one, they may turn into tiny slippery minnows and fill the glass with their aimless swirling.

"Are you going to take a bite?!" Mom's voice breaks through my daydreams.

I stare at the sandwich as if *it* is going to bite *me*. I am powerless. Life is awful when you are a child. Behind me, Mom explodes, "Take your sandwich and go eat outside. I can't see this anymore. *Ti mne vse nervy istrepala!*"(You have frayed my nerves!) Then she adds, "And don't you dare come back before you finish the sandwich!"

This is not good. Mom believes religiously in the positive effects of fresh air, but it is April, and it is still cold. Besides, we just moved into this neighborhood, and the world outside our door is largely unknown to me. With a heavy heart, I leave the table, put on my warm clothes, and, holding the wretched sandwich in my bare right hand, cross our threshold.

Immediately, my lungs choke from a gust of cold air, and it takes me a minute to recover from coughing. After I do, I timidly look around. Our house is one of the six shacks crowded around a circular *dvor* (courtyard) connected to a city street by a narrow entrance. There is a bench in front of every house, but only one of these outposts is occupied at the moment. There, two middle-aged women in woolen kerchiefs and winter coats with rabbit-fur collars—one gray, the other black with white spots—are chatting excitedly under the weak sun of early spring. In the middle of the courtyard, several kids are making a *snezhnaja baba* (a snowman).

I watch the children from afar. I know no one here, and, besides, these kids are older than me. The snowman is almost finished: three snowballs are piled up, two sticks with woolen mittens poke out from the snowman's middle, and dull pieces of coal indicate his eyes and mouth. All he needs is a nose.

A boy in an unbuttoned short coat with mittenless hands steps toward me, "Do you have a carrot?"

"No," I shake my head.

"Then get out of here!"

I shrink back—the boy sounds as if he is about to hit me.

"Don't be rude to the new girl, Vanya," the gray-collared woman says. Then she gives me an appraising look, "What'cher name, honey?"

The saccharine in the woman's voice makes me feel uneasy, but my parents have taught me to answer an adult.

"Sveta."

"Ah. And what's that in yer hand, Sveta?"

"It's a caviar sandwich," I say quietly, squirming under the woman's glare.

Both women exchange glances. Caviar is expensive, and it is usually served on holidays and other festive occasions, and not just an ordinary day.

"Whatta yer parents do?" The woman with the spotted collar chimes in.

"My mom is a doctor" (a low-paid profession in the Soviet Union) I say, deeply regretting not eating the sandwich at home. "And my dad goes on business trips."

The women exchange glances again. "Ah, trips ... And where's yer Mama now?" The light-collared woman does not let me off the hook.

"She's at home. She sent me outside to eat the sandwich."

"Oh, did she? So, why ain't cha eating it?" Both women scrutinize me with their eyes peeping below their kerchiefs.

"I don't like caviar."

"You don't?!" The women echo each other, looking at me as though I am a two-headed midget.

"Throw it away then!" The spotted-collar offers after a brief pause.

I look at her, confused. Is she joking? The woman's face reveals nothing. I shift my gaze to my right hand. It is red from the cold, but as long as I hold the sandwich, I cannot put on my mitten. Suddenly, getting rid of the sandwich seems like the right solution. No, wait. Mom said, "Eat it to the last crumb ..."

"Mom will be mad at me. She'll put me *v ugol*," I say.

"How would she know? We won't tell 'er. Right, Zina?" The light-gray collar says, winking at her friend.

"Right, Lida," Zina says and winks back. Then she turns around and points somewhere behind her. "You can dump it right there!"

Following her finger, I turn and look at the snow-covered gap between our house and the house next door. Then I study my hand again. My fingers barely bend now, and if I do not do something very soon, I am going to lose my grip on the sandwich anyway, so I fling the sandwich into the crisp cold air as far as I can. It dives into the deep white powder, leaving behind a shallow whirlpool of snow.

"Ah!!! Are you stupid or something?!" Zina exclaims, clasping her hands in her bulky woolen mittens. "We was just jokin'!"

"What's yer Mama going to say?" Lida joins in, her face shining with the pleasure of unexpected entertainment.

I look at them without comprehension. How would Mom know?

"Well, we have to tell yer mother," Zina proclaims. "Don't we, Lida? Children must learn not to throw money *na veter* (into the wind)."

The two women get up from the bench and walk towards our house. I stand rigid. If there has ever been a moment when I wished that the earth would swallow me up or that I would never see my parents again, this is it. Unfortunately, the earth does not split open, and as for running away from my parents, where would

I go? I do not even know how to get to my grandparents' place. All I can do is stay here and wait for my inevitable execution.

Soon, both women come out of our house and walk to their bench—neither one giving me another look. I catch fragments of their conversation: "I don't know about those 'business trips.' Just one room. Nothing special."

"Sveta, come home immediately!" Mom's voice is as sharp as a kitchen knife.

Stumbling at every step, I drag myself to our house. Mom meets me in the doorway. Her face is flushed, and she holds her hands on her protruding belly as if trying to calm something inside it.

"What's wrong with you? Why did you do that? We spend our last kopeks for you! Deny ourselves everything! Whom do you take after …"

Once again, I find myself in the corner. But why? I did what the women said! How was I supposed to know that they were joking? I am so mad at Mom that I cannot even cry. Instead, I feel like digging my teeth into the rough fabric of the coats in front of me, tearing them with my fingers, and screaming from the top of my lungs, "I hate you! I hate both of you! And you know what? I'll just die here, in this dusty corner with the moth-eaten coats and cobwebs hanging from the ceiling, and *everybody* will know how cruel you are!"

There I stop. Who is going to tell everybody about what happened today if I'm dead? I think for a minute and, suddenly, it comes to me. I won't die immediately. First, I'll go into a coma, like that woman Mom and Dad were talking about the other day. Everybody thought she was dead, but when they started nailing her coffin shut, they heard some scratching noises inside it. They opened the coffin and saw that the woman's eyes were wide open, her hands raised, and her cheeks wet with tears.

Yes, that's it! I'll go into a coma, and, when they carry my coffin out, I'll open my eyes, raise myself on my elbows, and, looking straight at my parents, tell everybody about the caviar, the ghastly women, and the unfair treatment my parents *always* subject me to. Then I'll fall back on the flower wreaths and die for good!

As I imagine this scene, tears of self-pity stream down my cheeks, but the sweet taste of revenge curls snugly in my heart and makes me feel better.

CHAPTER EIGHT

GIVING DIRECTIONS

It has been several months since we moved to *Marinaja Roshcha*, yet I still miss my grandparents, the little garden in front of their house, and Sokolniki, my favorite park. In our new place, greenery is at a minimum, and life is centered on the dusty courtyard surrounded by small wooden houses. Here, women chatter on rickety benches, men smoke *papirosi* (pungent Russian cigarettes), and kids scare sparrows with their games and shouting.

Our schools are organized by neighborhoods, so all the children from our *dvor* go to the same school. After classes, they often play together, but they do not include me in their games. I am *maljavk*a, too young to go to school yet, and no self-respecting school-age kid plays with me. They tease me a lot, though. By now, everybody knows that I am a bad eater, I am easily scared, and even more easily driven to tears. Also, my mom, a doctor, religiously believes in a midday nap for children. This makes me a laughingstock in our working-class neighborhood, which likes nothing more than mocking the wimpy habits of the *intelligentsia*.

When the neighbors' kids have nothing better to do, they climb on a bench and recite, with one of them swinging his arms like a conductor:

Sveta has a lot of fears,
Sveta pours a lot of tears.
She can't sleep, she can't eat,
She hates kasha, she hates meat!

I turn away, pretending not to hear the singing, but treacherous tears quickly fill my eyes, fueling more laughter and enthusiasm from the mischievous choir.

The only child who plays with me is Igorék, a boy from the house next door. He is a year older than I, but we both will start school next September, and, chances are, we will be in the same class together. Igorék is short and skinny, with long curly eyelashes and sad hazel eyes. Despite being older, Igorék is clumsy and weak, which makes him a perfect playmate for me. Our parents are friendly, too, and sometimes I sense that we all have something in common, although nobody tells me what it is.

Today, Igorék does not come out. He is sick, Mom tells me. Igorék is sick a lot—one more thing we have in common—but that is no consolation to me. In his absence, I am condemned to loneliness and boredom in our small courtyard world. I am too old to ask my busy parents to play with me, and I am too young to venture into the city streets on my own.

"Don't ever leave our *dvor* alone," my parents warn me.

Alas, there is only so much I can do here on this first warm day of May. Several girls are skipping rope by the house next door, but as soon as I get closer, they shout, "First, learn how!"

I retreat and watch from afar as they jump over swooshing ropes, rhythmically raising clouds of dust with their feet and chanting a businesslike, "One, two, three …"

My doll Masha and me, 1956

It is not true that I cannot skip rope, but I cannot do it as well as they do, alternating their quick feet, crossing their skinny arms, drawing fleeting figures with their ropes in the glowing spring air. So, as often happens, I am alone with my old doll Masha. We sit on a patch of sickly grass in the middle of the courtyard, and I show her the chirping sparrows and the friendly blue sky with clouds dappling its infinity. In doing so, I am imitating my mother, who is very enthusiastic about the beauty of nature.

"Ah! See how blue the sky is!" she proclaims, and her hands fly up like two exclamation points. "How high! The clouds are so light, just like dreams! And the air … can you smell the air? It's so fresh! Look up, both of you! Isn't it wonderful! Are you listening to me, Natán?"

Dad nods in agreement, but his expression is vacant. The sky and the sun do not impress him. His world is a black and white world of engineering textbooks, with no space for smells, colors, or the "oohs!" and "aahs!" of his easily excitable spouse.

My parents before I was born

The truth is, my parents are very different. It starts with their looks. Dad has a Mediterranean complexion, unruly black hair, serious dark eyes, and a prominent nose that descends immediately from his thick eyebrows. Mom's complexion is light, her soft hair is chestnut-colored, and her eyes are deep green with yellowish speckles floating in their smiling depth. Also, unlike Dad, Mom can strike up a conversation with nearly anybody: strangers on a bus, women in grocery stores, even a *militsioner* (a policeman) on the street.

I wish I could be like Mom, smiling and easygoing, so the kids in the neighborhood would like me and play with me. Unfortunately, I am more like Dad. I have a hard time making friends, and I am easily embarrassed. On a playground, I never talk first, much less ask children to play with me. I just stand there, quietly watching, until Mom grabs a girl by the shoulder, turns her toward me, and says, "This is Sveta, my daughter. She'd love to play with you. Right, Sveta?"

Also, I am afraid of thunder and lightning, stray cats and dogs, dark rooms, and, according to my cousins, even flies. My parents do not have to worry about me leaving our small courtyard and venturing into the big outside world. I am afraid of that, too. Today, though, with nothing to do in our *dvor*, I edge toward the entrance and look out into the street.

Big cottonwoods border the sidewalks on both sides of the street. The trees are still bare, but new leaf-buds are already popping up in their crowns. I walk up to the nearest tree, lift my head, and study the scrawny branches set against the sky. The clouds above my head are as puffy as the cottonwood tree balls that will fill the air later in the summer. And the aroma ... Mom is right, it is so fresh, so tempting …

I am not supposed to go any farther, but the spring sun caresses my face, and a playful breeze whispers something sweet into my ears. I take several steps forward and find myself on the street. Across from me, a group of men in drab shirts and pants cluster around a telephone pole, talking loudly in deep hoarse voices and smoking *papirosi*. On my side of the street, two men in black work uniforms and cloth caps walk toward me, perplexedly turning their heads right and left. I watch them approach. They must be looking for something or someone. What if they ask me a question? Mom warns me against talking to strangers. I'd better go back to our *dvor*.

I start moving backwards, to the courtyard entrance, but before I escape, the men stop and one of them shouts across the street, "Hey, fellas, where's the fire station?"

The smokers on the other side stop talking. "The fire station? You're almost there," says one of them, screwing up his eyes against the bright sun and letting a large white cloud of out of his mouth. "See that filthy *zhidovskoe otrodje* (kike's spawn) on the corner?" He nods in my direction. "Turn right of her and you'll see the fire station on the left." With that, the man puffs again, turns back to his friends, and their dissonant conversation continues to disturb the quiet of the street.

I look around, confused. Who was he talking about? It couldn't have been me. For one thing, I'm not filthy. Mom had washed and ironed my dress. It's not new, of course, but it's not filthy either. I glance at Masha, drooped in my hand. Masha does not look good—her colors are peeling, her straw-colored hair is tangled, and her dress is faded and wrinkled. But she's just a doll, not a person. Is there anyone else here?

I turn around. The men seeking the fire station have disappeared around the corner. The smokers are still by the telephone pole, and a vague silhouette of a woman appears off in the distance.

There isn't anybody else on this street, which is lined with the budding cottonwood trees and splashed with the golden glow of spring. Then … he must've been talking about me! What did he say? What is a *kike's spawn*? I've never heard these words before. Do they have anything to do with my leaving our *dvor*? Does he know that I shouldn't have been here? Will he tell my parents?

Questions without answers rush through my mind. Nobody is looking at me now, but—I suddenly realize—that man was not looking at me then either! He looked *through* me. He just stated a *fact*, like it's sunny today or it's raining.

The light wind, which I enjoyed so much a short time ago, now feels cooler and stronger, and in its gusts I suddenly hear muffled screams: Go back! Back! Before it's too late! I turn around and run as fast as I can. I run past the cottonwood trees, the kids skipping rope, and the women gossiping on the bench. I do not understand what has just happened, but an acute sense of shame coils inside my chest like a snake ready to strike.

I reach our door and, breathless, grab the handle the way a drowning person grabs a life vest. Then I look back. Everything is the same. The sun is still glowing and the sparrows are still chirruping as if nothing is changed. As if the world is, and always will be, a warm and friendly place. As if the words I just heard were never spoken, and I will never hear them again.

That night, I ask my mother, "Is Igorék a filthy kike's spawn, too?"

"Where did you hear that?" she says.

"On the street. This man said 'filthy *zhidovskoe otrodje*.' But I wasn't filthy! Why did he say that?"

"How many times must I tell you? Don't *ever* leave the *dvor* alone! You hear me? Ever!"

"But Mom …"

"Never!"

And yet, in just a few months, I will leave our *dvor* to go to school, where I will hear such words time and again.

CHAPTER NINE

WHERE DO BABIES COME FROM?

My sister is born on a cold and windy January day in 1958. I do not know she is coming until my father takes my mother to the hospital. Neither of them tells me what is about to happen, and I haven't thought much about the changes in my mother's appearance or to what those changes will mean for me.

Pregnancy, of course, is not a topic people talk about freely and certainly not with children—not because of the sublime mystery of it all, but because of a vague sense of shame and, especially, superstition, so prevalent in our country. Unlike our Western counterparts who do not hesitate to express their happiness, we, builders of the great kingdom of communism, are afraid of saying anything positive. In those rare cases that we do, we cross our fingers, knock on wood, or spit over our left shoulders three times, "*tfu, tfu, tfu.*"

As for the future, we never jinx it with irresponsible prattling; we avoid talking about it altogether. Only close adult relatives are initiated into the detail of a pregnant woman's condition or (God forbid!) informed about her due date. And what does it matter? We have no custom of throwing baby showers or bringing presents for the newborn. In fact, even future mothers' parents do not buy anything in advance; or, if they do, they keep it a secret.

Even after the baby is born, the cloud of superstition does not dissipate. New parents never blab out that things are going well, and they do not invite anybody but the immediate family to see their newborn until it is several months—better yet, a year—old. Nor do they take the baby's picture before it is at least six months old. As they say, better safe than sorry. The world is full of malevolent people who are more than happy to cast an evil eye on you and your family.

I am very puzzled when Dad comes home with the news that I now have a sister. Where did she come from? What do we need another girl for? Can I have a brother instead? Dad never answers my questions, but on the next day he takes me to the hospital to visit my mother and new sister.

Packed crunchy snow lies everywhere, and snowdrifts pile up to the first floor windows of the hospital. Visitors are not allowed into the maternity ward beyond a small reception room, where a reticent nurse collects small parcels and letters for the patients.

Like everybody else, we give her our offerings: some fruit and a letter that we wrote together the night before. My father did the writing, and I supplied names for my new baby sister. Not having any preferences, I listed all the female names I knew, starting with Tanya, and my father diligently wrote them down.

Dad asks the nurse about Mom and the baby and, after her indifferent "Everything's the way it should be," he pulls me outside. There, we join other visitors who are attempting to spot familiar faces behind the dull, double-layered windows of the maternity ward.

Lucky visitors have their women on the first floor, and they can see their pale faces pressed to the frosted glass, which is sealed for the winter with patches of dusty cotton. Mom's room is on the third floor, and I can barely make out her features. Dad puts me on his shoulders, and, at the top of my lungs, I shout into the freezing air that I want Mom to come home. She can't hear me, though, and just waves at us from up high—a ghost-like silhouette framed by the frozen window. I burst into sobs, and Dad takes me home.

Mom and Tanya come home in five days. Tanya is no bigger than my doll Masha, although unlike Masha, she has a reddish face, no hair, and a piercing voice. She also has the undivided attention of my parents, especially my mother, so I quickly realize that bringing her home is a mistake. For a week, I beg my parents to take her back to the hospital, but they never do. In fact, I am not even sure that they hear me. Tanya is a nuisance. I myself will never have babies.

For the first six months of her life, Tanya sleeps in a small zinc washtub that is also used for her bath. This makeshift bed sits in the corner by the bookcase, making it hard for me to get to my books. Of course, nobody has time to read to me anymore, so the first thing I have to master after my sister's arrival is reading.

Then, as if that is not bad enough, another newcomer enters my life—a long-feared nanny. The nanny appears just before Mom goes back to work, and, as was the case with Tanya, no one warns me about her coming. One day, the door of our apartment squeaks open, and a small, snub-nosed woman with light thin hair and a broad Mongol face simply steps into our room.

"I'm Tosja," she says and gives me a hesitant smile showing her small, slightly crooked teeth.

I hide behind Mom's back. The woman puts her suitcase down, looks around, and her face takes on a worried expression. As small as she is, there is no space for her here—not unless she agrees to sleep in another, bigger, zinc washtub kept under Mom and Dad's bed.

Luckily for Tosja, it never comes to that. During the next week, my father and uncle put up a thin partition on one side of our room—big enough for Tosja's narrow bed and suitcase—and Tosja moves there, increasing the number of people in our apartment to five.

To my relief, Tosja is not a bad person; nothing close to Baba Yaga or our mean neighbors Lida and Zina. She is a young, twenty or so, provincial woman from the Ural Mountains. She comes from a village that is connected to the outside world by a dirt road, where nobody has a car or a truck, where hard work is the only way of life and heavy drinking the only way of escaping it.

All able-bodied women in Tosja's village work at a local *kolkhoz* (communal farm) for almost nothing, and they survive, as well as feed their children, by growing vegetables in their small yards and milking their scraggy goats. As for entertainment, at night, they sit on the benches in front of their houses, gossiping, cracking sunflower seeds, and spitting out the husks.

Another important characteristic of Tosja's village is its lack of men. The majority vanished during the war. Those who avoided death and returned home have a hard time staying sober, and their wearily patient wives have to continue performing both female and male duties—including those at the *kolkhoz*—exactly the way they did during the war. The only marriage-worthy men in Tosja's village are the *kolkhoz* chairman and his deputy. Those two drink less, but they never do any heavy lifting either, for they have enough work to do ordering the women around and attending functions of the district Communist Party.

Had Tosja stayed home, she would have been single. Or, if by some miracle she had married, she would have repeated the fate of many generations of female villagers, who are overworked, abused by their drunken husbands, and old by their early thirties. Tosja, like other young Russians from the provinces, has come to Moscow in search of a better life. Yet here she has a problem—she has no official permission to leave her village and, consequently, cannot obtain a legal job or, for that matter, a residence.

This is nothing to sneeze at. Nobody over sixteen years old can move around in our country for more than thirty days without official permission and an obligatory passport—which in rural communities is kept at the local government offices. Typical grounds for obtaining permission for exit are getting married, going to college, or bribing a government official.

The first requires securing a candidate for marriage beforehand, which is difficult to achieve for someone who has never lived anywhere else. The second involves excellent grades and recommendations from teachers, and, by its very nature, is available to very few. The third, bribery, should have been the easiest, considering the corruption of the government officials, but it requires money, which Soviet people do not have. As a result, very few people venture anywhere, and those who do have to do it at their own risk.

Getting married to a Muscovite must be Tosja's cherished goal. This does not mean that she neglects taking care of my baby sister and me. She does what she can: feeds us (not a small job in my case), changes Tanya's diapers, and absentmindedly listens to my reading. I guess she is supposed to read to me, but that never happens. When Tosja first came, she told me several folktales that were popular in her homeland, but she quickly exhausted her repertoire, and I stopped asking for more.

The thing that Tosja likes doing the most is taking us for a walk. She cheerfully helps me put on my clothes, swaddles up my little sister, puts her into a bulky perambulator, and off we go. Tosja's affinity for spending time outside the house could be a remnant of her past life in the Urals, where she invariably had to travel long distances on foot, but I suspect that it has a more important motive, too.

How else can you explain that no matter where we are heading—to a grocery store, a pharmacy, or just around the block—we inevitably end up at the red brick building of our local fire station? There we spend a long time doing absolutely *nothing* interesting except talking to thickset and hoarse-voiced firemen dressed in mustard-colored padded jackets, squeaky high boots, and earflapped caps. Tosja does most of the talking, while my side of the conversation is a repetitive: "I want to go home!" and my sister squeals loudly.

With the exception of a local school and a dye factory, our neighborhood consists of small one-story wooden houses, so having a fire station here is important. Still, fires are rare, and when they do occur, they are quickly extinguished. For one thing, the overcrowding guarantees a quick discovery of the disaster; for another, the size of the dwellings does not allow for large and protracted conflagrations. In my memory, there has been only one serious incident—a fire at the dye factory.

That fire started early in the evening, and by the time Tosja and I got there, a huge glow already consumed the building and exploding cans of dye flew across the dark sky like shooting stars, causing mild panic in the crowd of spectators. Animated Lida and

Zina were there, too, gasping and informing anyone willing to listen that the fire must have been a terrorist act by Western spies.

Most of the time, the firefighters seem bored, and they are more than happy to entertain a young provincial nanny, despite her annoying charges. And who can blame them? They are demobilized soldiers who spent two years marching in *portjanki* (foot-binding cloths used in the Soviet army instead of socks) and obeying the mindless commands of their officers.

As for Tosja, she is just a lonely young woman. Her home and family are hundreds of miles away, and here in Moscow she has nobody to help or protect her, nobody to tell her what to do, and nobody to teach her to be careful. Besides, thirteen years after the war that killed and injured tens of millions of men, young males are hard to come by, even in a big city, and a fire department seems as good a place as any to meet some.

It is a Sunday morning. I wake up to the sounds of Tanya's whimpering and women talking. I open one eye and look. Mom is sitting at the table with Tanya in her arms—a bowl of kasha in front of her.

"Tosja," she says. "We're going to my parents. Could be back late. If you go out, please, don't forget to lock the door."

This is Mom's frequent request. In Tosja's small village, where drunken fights often ended in mild—and not so mild—injuries, theft was rare. A scarcity of material goods accounted for much of that and everyone's familiarity with everybody else accomplished the rest. Here in the big city, theft is common, and Tosja's repeated failure to lock the front door disturbs my parents and angers our neighbors.

"Sure, Firochka Raphailovna. (Mom's first name is Fira, and Tosja's 'Firochka' gives it a childishly endearing quality.)

Don'tcha worry," Tosja says, her voice ringing with excitement, unusual at this relatively early hour.

I open my second eye and look at her. Tosja's thin straight hair is arranged in cascading waves exactly like Mom's, and she is ironing her dress on the side of the table opposite to Mom's.

"I'll be visitin' my aunt today. I may be back late, too," Tosja says a little bit too casually. Then she lifts a large aluminum cup from the table, sucks a mouthful of water from it, and liberally spews it out on her wrinkled dress.

"Your aunt? I did not know you had an aunt here."

"Oh, ya know. I wasn't quite sure I'd find 'er, so I didn't tell ya. It's my mother's sister."

"Really? I thought that your mother didn't have any sisters!" Mom's voice is laced with suspicion.

"That's my father," Tosja says, lowering her eyes and firmly landing the iron on the flowery fabric, which responds to the heat with gurgling sounds. "*His* folks didn't have no girls."

"Uh huh," Mom says, knitting her brows.

As a streetcar carries my family to my grandparents, I overhear my parents' conversation.

"I'm not senile! She told me that her mother has no sisters!"

"We're not her family, Fira, and she's not a child. She can do whatever she wants."

"I know that. But don't you see she's headed for trouble?"

"And what do you suppose we can do? First of all, you don't know for a fact that she's lying. Secondly, let's say she is. Are you going to lock her in her room?"

Time goes by. Every Sunday afternoon, Tosja dresses up and goes to visit her newly discovered relative.

"How's your aunt doing?" Mom asks her at night.

"Good. She's alone, ya know. She needs me." And at that, the conversation ends.

One Sunday, Tosja stays at home.

"Are you going anywhere, Tosja?" Mom says.

"Nah," Tosja says in a morose monotone.

"Are you sick?" Mom says.

"Nah."

"Well, we'll have guests over. You're welcome to join us, but you might be bored."

Tosja says nothing. When the guests arrive, she goes to her closet-room and closes the door.

"Is something the matter with your nanny?" My Aunt Raya whispers to Mom.

"I'm afraid so," Mom whispers back and gives her sister a meaningful glance.

"Ah," Aunt Raya says. "I knew it would end like that."

"I did, too." Mom says, and they switch to Yiddish.

More time goes by, and one day I suddenly notice that Tosja is getting fat. Kind of like Mom before she had Tanya.

At night, I report my observation to my parents. "She's not fat," Mom says, glancing at Dad. "She's going to have a baby."

A baby!? With the exception of Sundays, which are Tosja's days off, Tosja and I spend lots of time together. If Tosja is to have a baby, I will likely have one, too!

I have nothing against babies—besides my bothersome sister, that is—but being fat is a different matter. In fact, being fat is the worst thing that can happen to a kid in our neighborhood. There is a fat boy in the house across the street, and nobody *ever* plays with him. Even worse, they all tease him until he runs home, spreading tears all over his round face with his fists.

I dash to the mirror and inspect my reflection—a scarecrow-skinny girl stares back at me.

"Will I have a baby?" I say in a thin voice.

Dad looks at Mom and says, "Eventually, I guess."

And Mom says, "What nonsense! This has nothing to do with you. Children can't have babies."

CHAPTER TEN

THE COLOR OF WATER

One month before school starts, we are going to the Black Sea. "We" means Mom, Tanya and me; Dad is staying in Moscow. I am not sure whether going to the sea is bad news, like Tanya's arrival, or good news, like going to visit the grandparents.

"Mom, is the water in the Black Sea black?"

"Not at all. It's as blue as the summer sky."

"Why do they call it 'black' then?"

"I'm not sure."

"Is the Black Sea bigger than Sokolniki's pond?"

"It's much, much bigger, and it has real nice sandy beaches and mountains around it."

I have never seen sandy beaches. I have only seen sand on playgrounds and around the pond at Sokolniki. As for the mountains, they appear in pictures in my fairytale books, the ones about heroes who go "far away and over the mountains" in search of a treasure or a princess they want to marry. Do regular people go there, too?

On the day of departure, Mom, with Tanya in her arms, and I board a train at bustling Kazanskaja station. Behind us, Dad carries a large, heavy suitcase. He brings it to our sleeping car compartment, kisses us good-bye, and leaves. Mom lowers the compartment's window, and as the train jerks, groans, and picks up speed, we wave good-bye to my father who stands on the platform waving back at us and quickly growing smaller. When I can no longer see him, I turn and look around.

The small compartment is furnished with four narrow bunk beds—two on the right for us and two on the left for our new neighbors—a small built-in table by the window, and a sliding door. The door keeps slamming: a black-mustached conductor peers in with a pile of linen, a young woman searches for her companion, a vendor offers *sosiski* (Russian hotdogs), and our new neighbors, an elderly couple, walk in and out.

Mom asks me to hold Tanya and begins organizing our possessions. Then she positions herself on the lower bunk-bed, turns sideways, and, trying to be inconspicuous, uncovers her breast to feed Tanya. The neighbors exchange glances and politely leave. After Tanya is fed, Mom assembles our dinner: bread, pickles, and pieces of boiled chicken.

A loud knock on the door announces the arrival of hot tea, and the conductor walks in with two large amber-color glasses, which tinkle in heavy metal glass-holders. He puts the glasses down on the table, counts out two lumps of sugar per glass, and leaves. I hear his hoarse "Tea anybody? Tea?" fading down the corridor.

After Mom and I finish our dinner, we go to the corridor and our neighbors return to the compartment to eat their dinner. The corridor is busy. People walk up and down, talking, laughing, looking for the conductor, or heading to the bathroom. Mom unfolds a narrow built-in seat beneath a window, sits down, and begins rocking Tanya to sleep. I stick to the window next to her and watch the scenery fly by: streams, birches, power lines, and unkempt villages with dark figures of people and animals.

At night, Mom and Tanya settle together on the bottom bunk, and I climb to the top. The train rocks rhythmically underneath me, and, for a while, I listen to the night sounds of the compartment: Tanya's weak moaning, the elderly neighbor's snoring, and Mom's breathing. Soon, in time to the choo-k-choo-k—choo-k—choo-k—choo-k of our train, I fall into fitful sleep, interrupted only by the whooshing of passing trains.

In the morning, we have a breakfast of bread, boiled eggs, and cheese, which we wash down with more hot tea. Mom and the neighbors talk about our destinations. We, Mom says, are going to Adler (a little town by the Black Sea), where she will look for a place to rent. Our neighbors, on the other hand, are going to a sanatorium in Sochi (a much bigger town in the same area), where they will receive medical treatment.

"You're a doctor, right? Let me ask you a question." And they break into a long and tedious monologue about their ailing health.

I take my observation post by the window. Overnight, the landscape has changed. Pines, birches, and cedars have disappeared, and now our train rumbles through green fields and orchards. At the train stops, tanned, loud-voiced women in headscarves bring apples, cherries, and grapes to the idling train and sell them in paper cones made out of torn newspapers.

Mom orders me to take care of Tanya and joins other passengers hurrying outside to stretch their legs and buy some goodies. I try to protest: "What if you miss the train? What will we do then?" Nothing bad happens, though. Mom comes back with a paper cone full of cherries so sweet that I forgive her for the fright she has given me and savor the cherries, one by one.

Late in the afternoon, the train takes a wide turn and an immense glimmering turquoise surface opens up before our eyes like a mirage. Yet unlike a mirage that can deceive human vision but not our sense of smell, this surface emanates a mineral fragrance I have never inhaled before. Exclamations of "Look, look! That's the Black Sea!" sweep through the train, and everybody rushes to the windows to look at the wonder.

Two hours later, our panting train comes to a halt and passengers begin unloading. A small crowd of women in dark clothes and headscarves hurries toward the newcomers:

"Do you need a place to stay?"

Deals are made quickly, and the platform empties in no time. We follow an old woman with a stooped back and crow-like features.

"Did you bring your passport, my dear?" She says to my mother—her black eyes looking out sharply from under her headscarf.

"Yes," Mom nods. She knows better than to leave Moscow without her passport.

For the next ten days or so we stay in a dark six-by-nine-foot room with a small window whose deep sill serves as a dinner table. Days pass, each indistinguishable from the next, like the envelopes Mom uses to mail letters to Dad. After breakfast, we walk to the beach, which looks like a huge quilt patched with numerous blankets in a variety shapes and colors. The blankets stake a one-day claim to a small piece of southern luxury. The earlier the vacationers bring their blankets, the better the places they get—closer to the water, with finer sand, and, if one is really lucky, in the shade of one of the tall wooden umbrellas that stick in the ground like enormous mushrooms. The only spaces left for late sleepers are the rocks at the edge of the beach.

There is just enough space between the blankets to walk among sunburned bodies—some tiny and resilient, others saggy and misshapen—to the water's edge, where playful waves call vacationers to the depths of the sea. We maneuver toward our blanket—which Mom takes to the beach early in the morning while Tanya and I are still asleep. Here we spend most of our day. Like everybody else, we breathe the intoxicating sea air, sunbathe, bury each other under the hot sand, and wade in the water. I have not learned how to swim yet, and Tanya is just a baby. Mom sometimes goes for a short swim, still keeping an eye on us even as her body sinks into the clear water.

Me, Tanya, and Mom in the Black Sea

When Mom and I are hungry, we snack on *vobla* (dry and salty Caspian Roach fish, a perennial favorite of our countrymen), and at noon, Mom opens a can of Spam and makes us sandwiches. For supper, we go to a nearby diner.

Mom goes first to take a place in line, and I stay on the beach with Tanya. An hour or so later, when Mom's turn seems close, she comes back and gets us. The food in the diner is always the same—*solyanka* (a soup made with pickles and tomato paste), *kotlety* (hamburgers), and *compot* (a sweet drink made of dry fruit). I mostly drink the sweet *compot*, Mom eats her dinner and the rest of mine, and little Tanya squeals in Mom's arms.

At night, before going to sleep, we join a crowd of vacationers strolling along the town's promenade, which is bordered by the shore on one side and blooming acacia and chestnut trees on the other. Here, the sultry smell of the sea mixes with the light aroma of the acacias and the heavy perfume of the vacationers, who enjoy a warm southern evening and watch distant ships lingering in the harbor.

Everybody is dressed in their summer best: men in light shirts and pants and women in light summer *saraphan* that reveal their bronze skin peeling from too much harsh sun. A small orchestra sends whirling waltzes into the darkening air, and their sounds reverberate from the calm surface of the sea and the still-warm asphalt of the promenade. Also, the bewitching baritone of a popular singer Leonid Utesov, who himself was born and raised beside the Black Sea, pours seductive, nostalgic melodies of lost love out of the loudspeakers.

Time seems to stretch, easy and warm, and I no longer think about Moscow or going to school, or even about my grandparents and my favorite park Sokolniki. Yet one day everything changes.

That afternoon, as Mom slowly submerges her body in the sea, squatting, splashing turquoise water, and exclaiming something between "Aaaaah" and "Uuuuuh," I bring Tanya to the water's edge. I sit her on my lap, and point to Mom, so Tanya can join in Mom's excitement with her favorite "goo-goo." When my little sister does not respond, I jokingly slap her on the back. Suddenly, Tanya's little body becomes rigid, and she begins jerking—once, twice, three times. She shakes harder and harder, as though she had been wound up inside by an invisible hand and cannot stop until she is completely unwound. Her head falls back, her face goes blue, and her eyes close, just like the eyes of a dying bird I once saw.

"Mom," I scream at the top of my lungs, making a desperate attempt to hold shaking Tanya in my arms but inadvertently dropping her onto the sand, where she writhes and twists as if in a frantic dance.

"Doctor, doctor! This baby needs a doctor!" I hear people nearby shout, and I see Mom—her wet hair glued to her scalp and her eyes wide with terror—jump out of the sea and run toward us, spraying those in her way with water and sand. She kneels in front of my sister and tries to feel her pulse. Then she clasps her to her chest, but Tanya continues to struggle in her arms, almost slipping away from Mom's embrace.

"Mom, stop her, stop her!" I cry, as if I am the only one who knows that this mad dance needs to be interrupted.

The rest of that day is gone from my memory. All I remember is walking over numerous railroad tracks. Why or where, I do not know. One day later, we take a train back to Moscow.

"It's all your fault!" Father spits at my mother in a hoarse whisper. His eyes are red, as if he had not slept for many nights, and his usually shiny hair is dull and disheveled.

"How could I have known? I wanted the best for both of them …"

Mom speaks in a low voice, rocking Tanya to sleep. "Sea air is supposed to be good for children."

"I told you she's too young to take her there!"

Father's voice reaches a strained falsetto that sounds like a stifled cry. Mom's shoulders quiver, and when she looks at me, I see tears streaming down her cheeks. She carefully lowers Tanya into her zinc bath-tub bed, covers her with a blanket, and motions me to leave the room. Dad walks behind us.

When we reach the kitchen, he opens his mouth as if to say something else, but instead, he grows pale, clutches at his heart and, gasping for air and moaning something about Mom's "stupid" stubbornness, sinks to the floor. Terrified, I look to Mom—What's wrong with Dad?—but she is already kneeling in front of my father, feeling his pulse, the way she knelt on the hot sand of the Black Sea before my little sister not long ago. Then she lifts her wet face to me—"Get a cup of water. Hurry!"—and rushes back to our room.

When she comes back, I see two tiny blue pills on her open palm. She brings them to my fathers' half-open mouth and pushes the pills inside it. "I'm sorry, I'm sorry, I'm sorry," Mom repeats in a tired monotone—the way nuns and monks chant their endless prayers—until her husband's breathing becomes normal and the color returns to his face, which still wears an expression of someone unfairly betrayed by the world.

Time goes by. Doctors come and go. Tosja comes back—thin as ever. Yet my home is never the same—more like a front-line hospital, with its smells, cries, and sounds of a raging war nearby, than the warm and comfortable place it used to be. In this new home, I am alone with my fears: What's wrong with Tanya? What's wrong with my parents? Will things ever be the way they once were?

There is nobody to ask. Tosja will not talk about it. As for my parents, they keep fighting. In fact, their fights will never stop.

They will go through their lives—and ours—arguing and complaining about each other. The reasons will be numerous—parenting and money, relatives and jealousy, and other ordinary miseries of life. Still, no matter what the reason, most of their disagreements will end up the same way: Dad sinks to the floor, Mom kneels in front of him, and I—and later Tanya—run for water.

For now, though, all I can do is spend as little time at home as possible, which is easy, since I finally start school.

CHAPTER ELEVEN

WHAT'S IN A NAME?

September 1st is a very special day in our country. Not because summer has already faded, and the trees have turned red and yellow. And not because September marks the enchanted time of the year we call *babiye leto* (woman's summer), known as Indian summer in America. The thing that makes September 1st special is that on this day students all over the country—from first graders to PhD students—start a new school year.

Rain or shine, the streets light up with streams of school children carrying bouquets of pink, white, and purple gladiolas or sun-splashed chrysanthemums. Young children, excited and apprehensive, walk with their parents, nestling their small hands inside the adults' big ones. Older students stride on their own, chattering, scanning faces around them, and laughing out loud. All of them move toward their schools the way brooks and rivers flow toward the sea. The rest of the school year is commonplace and dull, but the first day is fresh with expectations mixed with the fragrance of flowers—a short-lived triumph of hope over experience.

I walk to school with Mom. She is wearing her best dark-maroon woolen jacket, which Dad brought her a year ago from one of his business trips, and I am wearing a brown woolen dress and a white satin apron with wing-like gathers along the shoulder straps.

My dress uniform for school, 1958

"Just like an angel," Grandma sighed when she first saw me try on my new uniform. Later that day, she took me to a photo studio. There, a tired photographer, overwhelmed with energetic first-graders and their parents, seated me on a high chair and placed my right hand on the armrest and my left hand on my right elbow. Then he hid behind his tripod and said: "Look into the camera! A little bird is going fly out of it!"—and took my picture "*na dolguyu pamyat*" (as a remembrance).

Despite my festive appearance, I do not feel festive. For one thing, going to a new place, even if it is only two blocks away, feels to me like jumping into a strange lake. For another, my best friend and next-door neighbor Igorék will not be in my class as we both expected.

"There will be two first grades," Mom said to me when I asked her about it. "You'll be in First Grade A, and he will be in First Grade B. I'm sorry. There's nothing we can do about that."

By the time Mom and I get to my new school, the school yard looks like a small parade ground. Rows of children are drawn up on one side, a crowd of adults on the other, and officially dressed women scurry between the two. Mom hesitantly lets go of my left hand, and a strange young woman in a white blouse and black skirt immediately grabs my hand and pulls me away—as if I am a baton passed on in a relay race. I turn and give Mom a desperate look—Where is she taking me?—but Mom just waves at me and smiles encouragingly.

In a minute, I find myself in a line of other first graders. The boys in my class wear dove-gray woolen suits and white shirts, and the girls have uniforms just like mine, with large white bows clinging to their heads. Too bad Grandma cannot see us now—a flock of angels waiting for their first assignment.

As soon as I get used to my surroundings, I look for Igorék. I spot him in the group next to mine. Shriveled among other gray-suited boys, he seems thinner than usual, and his face is almost as white as my new apron. I wave at him and smile, wanting to encourage him the way Mom tried to encourage me. Igorék looks at me and casts his eyes down. I understand. He does not want other boys to think that he is a *devchatnic* (a boy who keeps company with girls).

Several more minutes pass by. Then a small middle-aged woman in a black suit walks to the center of the school yard and raises her hands. Despite her size and civilian clothes, this woman has the presence of a military commander. For a minute or two, she studies our faces, as if trying to decide whether we are worth her effort. When the noise and excitement subside, she claps her hands and presses them to her bosom in a gesture of urgency:

"Dear children! Today is the most important day of your lives. Today you're joining thousands and millions of children all over the country in the pursuit of education …"

The woman is our school principal. She talks about the importance of learning, discipline, and making good grades—not just for our future or our parents' satisfaction but, more importantly, "for the prosperity of our country." The principal's speech is long and her voice is monotonous, so gradually our attention flags, and we shift from one foot to the other. Yet just before we get openly restless, the principal's voice raises to a high C, and she pushes her hands forward like an opera singer who is about to break into a final aria, "Remember, children, all of this is available to you because of our dear Communist Party!"

The speech is over. Led by our teachers, we head to the school's front door, which is decorated with a banner, "Thank You Our Dear Communist Party for Our Happy Childhood!" One by one, we walk underneath these words of gratitude and into the school building, while our parents wave at us and brush away tears.

Before we enter the classroom where we will study for next three years, we are sorted into pairs— one girl and one boy—and told to take seats in the order of our arrival. The classroom is filled with several rows of black *party* (wooden student desks for two) with folding front panels that make loud noises every time we get up or down. In front of the room sits a teacher's desk. Behind the desk, just above a blackboard, hang large portraits of two men: one with high temples, piercing eyes, and a short pointed beard; the other with a bold head, small eyes, and an almost simple-hearted expression on his round face.

The first man is Vladimir Iljich Lenin—or rather *Dedushka* (Grandfather) Lenin as we children are taught to call him—a great revolutionary and the most important person in the history of our country. The portrait next to Lenin depicts our current leader Nikita Sergeevich Khrushchev.

I have seen numerous pictures of Lenin in my ABC book: *Dedushka* Lenin by himself, *Dedushka* Lenin surrounded with young workers, *Dedushka* Lenin giving a speech in front of revolutionary soldiers, and others. In fact, there are two more portraits of him in the classroom. On the wall to the right, Lenin, in a cloth cap, one hand in his pants pocket, is talking to a group of children. On the wall to the left, he stands on the roof of an armored car—his coat flies open, his hand points forward, and a sea of people crowd around him on all sides. As for Khrushchev, his pictures do not appear in our ABC book, but his face is also familiar to me—his photos fill our newspapers and adorn tall city buildings during government holidays.

Everybody is seated, and our teacher, a large woman with deeply-set, suspicious eyes, opens a class roster.

"Hello, children," she says, forcing an official smile. "My name is Maria Ivanovna and I am your teacher. Now, I need to know your names. I'll read the roster, and when you hear your name, I want you to get up, so I can see you."

She goes down the list, and the children stand up one after another—some look straight at the teacher and some carefully study the surface of their desks. When my name sounds, I get up, too, and whispering sweeps through the classroom like the rustling of falling leaves. I turn around—Is something wrong with me?—but I can see no answer. I am dressed like all the girls in my class. My hair is arranged into two coiled braids, the way many of them wear theirs. My briefcase, my cotton stockings, and my shoes are almost identical to everybody else's. And yet, I must be different. I feel it with my skin and in my suddenly aching teeth. What is it?

The explanation is simple, and it has nothing to do with my appearance. The thing that makes me stand out is my family name—too long and characteristically Jewish. I am not aware of that, yet, but the children in my class are. There are twenty-four of them around me. Some know each other, some do not, but all of them know that I am a stranger who will never be like them.

Roll call is over and the class begins. My classmates open their ABC books and start repeating after Maria Ivanovna, "A—alphabet, B—babushka …"

My heart is still pounding, and my eyes are filled with tears. I bite my lips and breathe deeply—the way Grandma tells me to do when I have coughing fits or cannot stop crying. I try to follow the class, too, but the pace of the lesson is too slow, and, despite being the youngest student here, I already know how to read. In fact, that is why my parents sent me to school a year early. That, and also Tosja's claim that it is too hard to babysit both of us, especially now that Tanya is sick.

I furtively look around again. I know no one here, and Igorék, my only friend in this school, is in a classroom down the hall. I sigh and quietly pull a slim volume of Russian Fairytales out of my new briefcase, open it under my student desk to the page titled "Vasilisa the Beautiful," and read "Once upon a time in a distant kingdom, there lived a merchant …" And that makes me feel better.

CHAPTER TWELVE

WHY I WILL NEVER BE A HERO

As soon as my first school year is over, we are going out of town. Despite the bad experience we had at the Black Sea, my mother still believes that, in the summer, children—especially sickly children like Tanya and me—should be taken away from the smog and dust of a big city to places where clean air, fresh milk, and eggs will perform miracles for our health. This time, we follow Dad, whose job takes him to a distant provincial village on the border with Ukraine.

The village consists of barely twenty single-story, run-down wooden huts built along a dirt road, muddy when it rains and dusty when it's dry. The house where we are renting a room with a *pechka* (fireplace) sits by a wide circular lawn formed by a bend in the road. Like other village dwellings, it is surrounded by a wooden fence that contains a small vegetable garden, a chicken coop, and a cowshed. One thing that the fence does not contain is smells—from the bitter aroma of garlic to the pungent odor of chicken and cow manure.

Life in this house is monotonous. Chickens kill time digging in the dirt, while a dozen cheeping chicks fuss cutely around them. A cow and her offspring spend most of their days in the pastures, and one can set one's watch by their drawn-out bellowing, which sounds early in the morning as they leave their shed to join the village herd, and in the evening, when they come home tired from the serious business of feeding. As for our elderly *khozyaika* (proprietress), her existence is as routine as the lives of her animals: chore after chore, day after day.

My life is not exciting either. No children my age live nearby, and I spend most of my days reading books and watching the chickens. I am supposed to watch Tanya, too, but at the age of one-and-a-half, she can play on her own and does not require much attention. Nor am I willing to give it to her anyway. Tanya has passed the constantly crying stage, and she has gotten over whatever illness she caught at the Black Sea. Yet I cannot forgive her for the changes her arrival has brought into my life, and I believe more than ever that I am an adopted daughter. What else can account for my parents fussing over Tanya's every move and not exhibiting any interest in me?

Twice a day, Mom makes us drink fresh cow's milk. She sends me to the shed where our proprietress milks her cow. While I wait, I watch the elderly woman forcefully pull the long teats of the melancholically ruminating animal. I inhale the tangled smells of hay, milk, bread, manure, and sweat and listen to the sounds of liquid squirting into the bucket. The milk I bring home is thick and warm, and, even outside the shed, it smells like a wet cloth. The fact that it has just come from somewhere inside a cow and not from a grocery store bothers me. Yet, as usual, there is nothing I can do about that but contemplate the unfairness of life and hope that the future will be better than the present.

It is a warm summer evening. Tanya and I are sitting on a pile of sand thrown in the middle of the lawn, about fifty yards away from the house. I am reading a book and Tanya is digging in the sand with a trowel. The setting sun illuminates the tree tops of a distant grove, and the low moos of the returning cows signals their owners to get ready for the nightly milking.

By now, I am used to these sounds, and I am no longer afraid of the slow-moving beasts. For one thing, they seem to be indifferent to everybody but their cowherd and owners. For another, they are too busy chewing to be bothered by anything but horseflies and mosquitoes.

I put down my book and watch the herd gradually disperse and move toward their respective homes. There are three cows heading in our direction—one in front and another with a calf behind. The latter two belong to our proprietress, but the animal in front of them is not familiar to me. I watch the strange cow approach. It is black with white spots, while ours are solid brown. It is also bigger than them, and it is moving faster, rapidly shaking its head from side to side.

Why is it coming here? It does not belong to our house, nor does it belong to our neighbors ... Wait, didn't Mom talk about a village bull yesterday? That he got away from the herd and gored some village kid? Could this be *that* bull?

A pang of pain tingles in the pit of my stomach. I get up from the sand and pick up my book, all the while glaring at the animal running directly towards me, growing bigger and bigger by the minute. Unsure of what to do, I take several steps toward our house, first slowly, then faster and faster, until I get to our gate. There I take a deep breath and, relieved, look back. The cow—or is it the bull?—is still galloping toward the sand pile I have just left, where—to my horror!—I see my little sister diligently digging in the sand.

My legs go limp and the rest of my body goes hot and cold. Oh, no … I forgot about Tanya! For a short time, I stand still by the gate inhaling the oxygen-depleted air. There is absolutely *no way* I want to run back to get Tanya. But … there is absolutely *no way* I can leave her there alone either! Not because *I* care for her very much, but because my *parents* certainly do. In fact, if something bad happens to Tanya, they will kill me! This thought flashes through my mind as clearly as if I were reading it written on a page. Yet this crazy cow could kill me, too! What should I do?!

"It's your fault!" My father's voice sounds in my head like a kick, and I quickly look around but see no one. Then, trying to minimize the view of the approaching danger, I screw up my eyes and, with my heart pounding and my legs collapsing under me, I make one tiny step toward my sister, then another. Walking has never been so hard, and, to make any progress, I must push myself forward the way a swimmer pushes herself against a current. Still, despite my laborious movements, the distance between Tanya and me does not seem to diminish, and her small figure in a red dress appears as far away as ever. I will *never* reach her in time!

"Help!" I try to shout, "Help!" No sound comes out of my dry mouth—all my energy is spent on advancing myself.

Finally, after what seems to be eternity, Tanya is next to me. I grab her by the hand and pull her away from the sand pile toward the safety of our house. But instead of following me, she drops her trowel and screams at the top of her lungs as if *I* am the villain she needs to be protected from. She digs her heels into the warm sand and, with unexpected energy, struggles to extricate her hand from mine while I squeeze her tiny fingers with all the strength I have left and drag her through the lawn as her screams fill the air.

The cow is so close now that despite the loud wailing of my sister, I can hear its ominous breathing and the sounds of its stamping hoofs behind us. Yet—Oh, goodness!—I am not the only one who hears it now. Tanya's cry has awoken the neighborhood. Doors and windows are opening everywhere, and I see our father rushing out of the house toward the gate. And the last thing I register before collapsing on the ground behind our gate is the crashing sound of horns hitting the fence.

I do not remember how we get into the house or what the adults say to me or to each other. And I am glad I don't. I do not want to relive the recent terror—not now, not ever. Not even in the safety of my urban neighborhood, where cows and shepherds appear only in pictures, and milk—watery and cold—comes from grocery stores. Also, more importantly, I do not want to admit to anybody—even to myself—that I wasn't *really* saving my little sister. I was saving *myself* from the wrath of my parents.

In September, our teacher Maria Ivanovna asks the class to write about our most memorable summer experience, and I write about the chickens and their fussy offspring. As for the incident with the cow, I bury that memory under a pile of other things I am not proud of. It only comes alive in my nightmares, mercifully melting away at daybreak. And when I wake up in the morning, I am not even sure if the whole thing really happened, or whether I just dreamt it while dozing on a pile of sand on a warm summer evening.

CHAPTER THIRTEEN

BEETS

In the fall, my family moves again—this time to a four-story apartment house made of unpainted cement blocks, not far from our old apartment. Our new building is an exact replica of countless other faceless gray boxes that have sprouted all over Moscow during Khrushchev's era. In fact, that is what we Muscovites call them—*Khrushchevki*.

Our new apartment has been granted to us by the furniture factory where Mom works at the medical clinic. Housing is still scarce, so some institutions try to improve their workers' living conditions. The catch is that the workers are plentiful but construction is limited, so it takes years of waiting to "receive" a new place.

To be put on a waiting list, a person has to be in good standing with the authorities, and he also has to prove that his family has less than two square meters (about two square yards) per person in his current location. These requirements are less stringent for members of the Communist Party.

My parents have waited for their new apartment since I was born, and, if not for Tanya's arrival, they would have been waiting still. Yet, here we are, in a place that, to me, is as grand as the castle where Cinderella met her prince and as desirable as the prince himself.

Of course, unlike the royal couple, we occupy only half of a two-room apartment on the fourth floor without an elevator. The other half belongs to our new neighbors with whom we share a kitchen and a bathroom. Still, everything here is new, with no signs of mold or smell of kerosene. In fact, we now have a gas stove, a toilet, running water, a heavy metal bathtub, and only two strangers to share this luxury!

Our new neighbors are a middle-aged couple: Klavdia Petrovna and her husband Naúm Vasilievich. Klavdia Petrovna is large, with flabby cheeks, cascading double chins, and a skinny gray braid coiled on top of her head. Naúm Vasilievich is also large, with a wisp of light baby-thin hair and the cheeks of a drinker, red enough to strike matches on their burning surface.

Klavdia Petrovna and Naúm Vasilievich do not have children. At first, I expected this to change any day, since, in my limited experience, women as big as Klavdia Petrovna were about to give birth. Yet four months later, Klavdia Petrovna's size remains constant and, in fact, the number of people in our apartment diminishes. Tosja, our old nanny, finally leaves us for good.

Whether Klavdia Petrovna has anything to do with it, I cannot say. I did notice, though, that Tosja and Klavdia Petrovna became very friendly, and I once overheard Klavdia Petrovna telling Tosja that "it is a shame for a young Russian woman to wipe Jewish asses." Whatever the reason, one day, Tosja packs her cardboard suitcase, tells my parents—in the old-fashioned Russian way—"Forgive me if I did something wrong," and walks out, leaving Mom in a quandary over my sister's childcare.

"I found a new nanny for Tanya," Mom announces after dinner, while collecting dirty soup bowls and plates to take to the kitchen. "Her name is Zoya Ivanovna. She'll come here in the morning and stay with Tanya until you come home from school."

"Fine," I say indifferently, pulling my textbooks and writing pads out of my briefcase and settling down to do my homework.

After Tosja's departure, Tanya had gone through two babysitters. The first one agreed to look after Tanya together with three of her own grandchildren. Unfortunately, the woman was so overwhelmed with four children to mind that, on her first day, Tanya slipped out of the woman's third-floor apartment and, being her usual over-energetic self, tumbled down a steep staircase. When Mom came to pick her up that night, Tanya's knees, elbows, and forehead were bandaged sloppily, and her face was scratched and bruised.

The second babysitter, a reticent childless woman of uncertain age, was taken to the hospital at the end of Tanya's second week with her. Not being there myself, I cannot say for certain that there was a connection between my sister's unpredictable behavior and the poor woman's stroke, but the thought definitely crossed my mind.

Zoya Ivanovna, then, is Mom's third attempt to keep Tanya at home until her turn at a daycare center comes up. The wait was not supposed to be long—the daycare is run by Mom's factory, and her boss, the head of the factory's medical clinic with whom Mom is on good terms, promised to *zamolvit za neio slovechko* (put a word in for her). However, two years later the daycare still has no space for her.

The next morning, two sharp rings announce the arrival of Tanya's new babysitter, and I rush to open the door for her. A gaunt woman in black walks in. She is tall and flat, with no hint of a bosom or other features of female anatomy. She is also the oldest woman I have ever seen. Her narrow lips reveal a toothless gaping mouth. Her thin white hair covers her scalp like cobwebs, and her deeply wrinkled face resembles a dried mushroom wasting in the woods. In other words, Zoya Ivanovna looks like a mummy I once saw in a museum; the main difference is that instead of peacefully lying in her sarcophagus and contemplating eternity, Zoya Ivanovna walks among the living with small and unsteady steps. Mom must have been desperate to hire this shadow of a woman. Surely, this babysitter will not last long.

I am wrong. Three months later, Zoya Ivanovna is still around. When I come home from school, she is the first person I see. Her shriveled dark figure stands out against the doorway, her coat is buttoned up, her headscarf hugs her ancient face tightly, and her pale eyes, hidden under beetling white brows, are filled with the eager anticipation of a soldier waiting to be relieved from her watch.

"Good day, Zoya Ivanovna," I say, holding back the urge to click my heals and salute her, like one service man to another, for I know firsthand what her time with my sister must have been like.

"Well, I think I'll go now," Zoya Ivanovna replies—her shuffling feet already polishing the cold stones of the staircase behind our door.

I never blame her for the quick retreat. I wish I could go, too. In fact, I am amazed that Zoya Ivanovna has tolerated this long Tanya's mercurial temperament and her rare knack for getting into trouble. It is difficult even for me, and I must be a hundred years younger than Zoya Ivanovna.

One morning Zoya Ivanovna does not come. Instead, Mom takes Tanya to her place. After school, I go to pick up Tanya from Zoya Ivanovna's house—a decrepit structure near my school. I ring the bell of her apartment, and my sister opens the door to a dim, cave-like room.

A strange smell stops me in my tracks. I look around. Everything in the room is old and worn out, including its owner, who is sinking into the sofa, looking ominous with exhaustion—as *Baba Yaga* might look near death. For a minute I stare at Zoya Ivanovna's wasted figure, trying to identify the source of the odor. Is it mold? Spoiled food? Or Zoya Ivanovna's body? I am used to modest circumstances, but it suddenly hits me that this is true *poverty*. This is what it must look like, and this is what it must smell like.

But it cannot be! Not according to my teachers, my textbooks, or our radio and TV. Poverty is a sign of rotten capitalism, and it does not exist in our country! Our slogan is "From each according to his ability to each according to his needs." As for old people, every school age kid knows that they deserve a "happy old age"!

I am staring at Zoya Ivanovna. Her face shows no signs of happiness. As for this smell, I do not know what "rotten" capitalism smells like, but it cannot stink any worse than Zoya Ivanovna's apartment. And, despite everything I have heard and learned in school, despite all the slogans, I realize that poverty, unvarnished and ugly, *does* exist in our country. What else pulls Zoya Ivanovna off her broken-down sofa and makes her babysit my fidgety sister? The little money she gets from my parents makes her struggle for survival easier, if not bearable. For what can be bearable about living on a miserable pension after long years spent serving one's people and country?

I help Tanya put on her coat and we head home. "You'd better listen to Zoya Ivanovna, Tanya," I say to my sister who is paying as much attention to my words as she does to the clouds in the sky. And when we walk into our apartment—which suddenly seems as luxurious as the Russian tsars' palace—I feel as lucky and privileged as I have ever felt.

Two weeks later, I get sick, and Mom takes Tanya to Zoya Ivanovna's once more. When they come home at night, Mom's cheeks are flushed and Tanya is trailing behind her, whining.

"Tanya, don't bother me now and don't bother your sister either," Mom says very loudly, elaborately sucking air through her dilated nostrils. Ordinarily, this statement would make me very happy, but there is something in Mom's voice that does not feel right. Besides, she does not look at me, does not put her medicine-smelling hand on my forehead in a gesture of concern, and does not ask me if I feel any better.

"Is something the matter?" I say, but Mom just glances at me—her face like a storm cloud about to erupt with lightning—and goes to the kitchen. Soon, I hear the loud staccato of a kitchen knife hitting the cutting board with the fury of a guillotine chopping.

Not until Dad comes home do I learn—overhear, really, for how can I not hear my parents whispering four yards away from my bed?—what has happened. Both Mom and Dad sit at the table—Dad eating his dinner and Mom, next to him, talking.

"I left early today," Mom starts, first slowly, visibly looking for words, but then faster and faster. "And I thought that before I picked up Tanya from Zoya Ivanovna's, I'd go get some cabbage for *shchi* (soup made of green cabbage). So I go to the vegetable store on the corner, get in line, and look around. And who do you think I see?" Mom takes a deep breath, as if she is about to dive into unfamiliar waters. "I see Tanya! She's standing at the counter next to a woman buying beets and potatoes, just as if she were that woman's daughter."

Dad's spoon freezes in mid-air, "What was Tanya doing there?"

"That's what I want to tell you!" Mom bursts out, forgetting to whisper. Then she lowers her voice and continues. "Tanya's standing there, but because she's short, the saleswoman can't see her on the other side of the counter. The woman customer is busy arguing with the saleswoman over spoiled potatoes and trying to take them off the scale, and everybody else, you know, is watching them."

"Did you call Tanya?"

"Well, I opened my mouth to call her, but she suddenly stretched out her hand, grabbed a beetroot from a pile on the counter, and hid it under her coat!"

Dad's spoon swoops into his bowl and splashes the vinyl tablecloth with bits and pieces of his dinner.

"I thought I'd fall through the floor!" Mom whispers theatrically, leaning toward my father who looks as if he is about to follow her on her way through the scratched planks of our wooden floor to the core of the earth.

"And where was Zoya Ivanovna?" Dad says after a pause—his angular face distorted and his thick eyebrows knitted together.

"That's the thing!" Mom exclaims, throwing up her hands and, once again, forgetting to speak softly. "She was right there! Standing in the corner and *waiting* for Tanya to give her the beetroot and who knows what else!"

Here Mom looks around and notices me, half-thrust out from under my blankets with my ears pricked up. "And you're supposed to sleep off your cold and not eavesdrop on the things that have nothing to do with you!" She says. Then she turns back and continues talking in a hushed voice, while the expression on her face speaks loudly of her feelings.

Insulted, I pull back. It's not *my* fault that Tanya steals beets from the store, is it? Why is Mom angry with me? My parents keep whispering for some time, but all I can decipher is "just like an experienced thief!" which Mom accompanies with a jerky movement that, apparently, imitates Tanya's grabbing the beetroot. I turn toward the wall, and soon heavy dreams transport me into a kaleidoscope of feverish scenes in which Tanya and I are running from an angry crowd headed by a saleswoman in soiled oversleeves and a dirty apron.

My sister spends the next couple of weeks at the grandparents, and when she comes back, Mom tells me that Tanya's long-awaited turn at the daycare center has finally come up.

I never see Zoya Ivanovna again. She disappears from our lives the way wilted autumn leaves disappear into the void, swept by the cold winds of the winter. For a while, I keep asking Mom about her. What is she doing now? Why did she teach Tanya to steal? Was she a bad person or was she just hungry?

Mom's only answer is "Stealing is stealing. They can put you in prison for that. And don't you talk to your sister about Zoya Ivanovna. Understood?"

Several months later, I do break Mom's ban and ask Tanya what Zoya Ivanovna told her to do in the store and what else Tanya stole for her. Tanya looks at me under her long eyelashes and tilts her head to one side, the way she does when puzzled,

"Who's Zoya Ivanovna?"

CHAPTER FOURTEEN

LIFE LESSONS

Another summer announces its approach with a show of pop-up showers, washed blue skies, and flowers in city parks. School is over and, once again, we follow Dad to his summer job—this time in a provincial village located near the old Russian city of Novgorod, some 500 kilometers from Moscow.

The village is bigger than the one we went to last year, but life here is still nothing like it is in Moscow. No street cars or buses run along its main drag, which is bordered by one-story wooden shacks. No Metro stations wink at pedestrians with their neon signs. And the only sounds that disturb its provincial quiet are produced by hoarse dogs, farm animals, clamorous domestic disputes, and, once in a while, trucks and farm machinery that strain their engines in a fight with the ubiquitous mud and ruts in the road.

The trucks and machinery belong to the local *kolhoz*, where peasants work together, and where profits are divided equally among them—that is, after the lion's share has been sent to the central government. Another vehicle that rumbles through the village, raising clouds of dust or splashing mud, is the jeep of the *kolhoz* chairman, who is also head of the local Communist cell. The rest of the time the road is empty, for nobody here—as in any

Russian village—has any personal transportation, not even a horse.

There are no grocery stores here either, and the residents have to take a bus to the next village to buy baking flour, salt, sugar, vodka, and matches. Anyone whose needs stretch beyond these basic necessities must travel to the nearest town. As for delicacies like bologna, mayonnaise, herring and such—not to mention clothes nicer than *telogreika* (a working-style padded jacket) or *rezinovie sapogi* (black rubber boots)—these require a journey to a regional center or even to Moscow.

The bus stops here only twice a day, so Mom, when she has to buy groceries, does not even ask me to come along. This is fine with me; I hate standing in lines anyway. And the lines are very long in 1960. The country is at the height of Khrushchev's corn fiasco. Everybody talks about it: people in grocery store lines, babushkas (old women) on the benches by our house, and, of course, my parents at home.

From what I gather, last year, our leader Nikita Sergeevich Khrushchev traveled to America, a country located so far away that no Soviet high official before him had ever been there. During his visit, Khrushchev learned that corn grows everywhere in America—which, apparently, is a great thing. Nikita Sergeevich was so impressed with all that American corn that when he returned home, he set his heart on increasing the corn production in our country. Before his trip, we mostly grew corn to feed cattle, but now we were going to feed corn to people, too, and every collective farm was given a command to plant more corn.

I do not know much about growing corn. In truth, I do not know much about growing anything besides medicinal *aloe vera* whose bitterly stinging sap Mom uses as nose drops. I do not know much about America either. I only see it on the map in my geography class, and that map does not show anything growing there anyway.

Most of my American knowledge comes from Mark Twain's *Adventures of Tom Sawyer*, which never mentions growing corn, but painting fences, getting lost in a cave, and other things like that. It is a great book, though, and when I first heard my parents talk about Khrushchev's visit to America, I immediately asked them if he had met Tom Sawyer, which would be the first thing I would do had *I* gone to America. My parents said that they did not think so and asked me to find out if Tanya needed my help.

In any case, something went wrong with Khrushchev's corn project. Unlike our *aloe vera* that needs little attention—we just water it once a week and watch it sprout its prickly branches over our windowsill—corn needed something that most of our country could not provide: hot summers. As a result, the corn that did so well in faraway America stubbornly refused to do the same in our northern country. That happened to be very bad news indeed, since by the time our authorities realized their mistake, the collective farms had already eliminated a lot of wheat—which does very well around here—to increase space for corn.

To make a long story short, this disaster resulted in Khrushchev's earning the ironic nickname "*kukuruznik*" (the corn man) and in severe food shortages. The one exception is an abundance of canned sweet corn, turrets of which fill the shelves of our otherwise empty grocery stores as monuments to Khrushchev's ingenuity. Dad put it this way: "You reap what you sow." This, I thought, was a strange thing to say, since we surely sowed much more than we reaped. Yet Dad never explained to me what he meant.

The food shortages, which are bad even in Moscow, are especially bad in the provinces, where lines for flour, macaroni and such—never mind meat and other delicacies—are almost as long as the distance between our country and the corn fields of America. In our village, many are unhappy with Khrushchev, and everybody is suspicious of "capitalist America" which "must have planned" the whole thing all along to undermine our country.

The good thing is that, unlike city dwellers, the peasants have something going for them. Outside their collective farms, where they work long hours for very low pay, they are allowed to plant vegetables and fruit trees in their small yards. Had they owned some land, they could have grown wheat or other grains, too. That, however, ended a long time ago with the collectivization of Soviet agriculture, during which small farms were eliminated and their owners—my textbook call them *kulaks*—were imprisoned or shot. Now peasants have to buy flour, buckwheat, and other grain at a store, the same way town folk do.

They *are* allowed to keep a few farm animals, though. Our proprietress Evdokia Nikolaevna has several chickens and two mean geese, which I am told to watch "*v oba*" (vigilantly) since they might attack Tanya. She also has a cow that I watch *v oba* on my own account because I am terrified of cows after my misadventure last summer.

Once, Grandma, who stayed with us for a couple of weeks, took Tanya and me for a walk in the woods, and we ran into several grazing cows. The only thing that kept me from fleeing and possibly never seeing my grandma and sister again was that I was scared of running into even more cows that might have been grazing nearby.

Grandma, on the other hand, stayed very calm. "There's nothing to worry about," she said to me when one cow started trotting toward us. Then she picked up a long twig lying on the ground and fearlessly shushed the cow away. That was the most impressive thing I ever saw her do—almost as impressive as a magician swallowing fire at the Moscow Circus. And during the rest of our walk, Grandma talked about *her* parents (Grandma had parents, too!) who lived on a small farm by the Black Sea and had a vegetable garden, chickens, a horse, and two cows.

"If not for Stalin," she said, her voice quivering, "You could've been born there."

"Grandma, were your parents *kulaks*?!" I said.

"Nonsense," Grandma said, "My parents had a small piece of land and they worked it themselves. My younger siblings helped them, too."

"You had siblings, Grandma? How many?"

"Six, but let's not talk about that."

I could hardly believe this. Not only did Grandma have *kulak* parents, but she also had *six* brothers and sisters I never knew anything about! How can I not talk about that?

"Where are they?"

"Passed away," Grandma said, averting her eyes.

"How? Did they have whooping cough?" I said.

"No," Grandma said, speeding up her pace. "Two of them were killed during a pogrom, and one died later of typhoid fever."

"And the others?"

"One brother died before you were born, and one sister died of an illegal abor… Well, you don't need to know about that." Grandma said, her voice trailing off.

"Grandma, what happened to the sixth?" I insisted, having done quick math in my head.

"Well, one sister left for America, but don't you tell this to anybody!"

That she did not have to tell me. What kid would like people to know that her great-grandparents were *kulaks*, the very "enemies of the people" every school child is taught to hate? As for relatives in capitalistic America, that is at least as bad, if not worse!

Tanya and me (front row);
Grandma and Mom (back row)

"How did *you* survive, Grandma?" I said, suddenly realizing how little I knew about my grandparents.

"I had no choice." Grandma smiled a sad smile. "I *had to* survive so one day I would have grandchildren." Then she looked straight into my eyes and added, "We're all survivors, *bubala*. You, too."

Here, Tanya began whining that she wanted to go home, and we turned back to the village. I kept questioning Grandma about her family and about why we are all survivors, but she never explained that.

Another farm animal found in this village is rabbits. In fact, they are as common around here as badly groomed cats and dogs. Our proprietress has rabbits, too. They are fascinating to watch—fluffy, with large watery eyes, twitching noses, and a sweetly apprehensive expression on their little faces. Evdokia Nikolaevna keeps them in a rabbit-hutch that is divided into several sections.

"Just like a miniature apartment house," Mom says, but to me the hutch looks like a rabbit prison.

For one thing, the rabbits are never allowed to go outside; for another, nobody comes to play with them. True, Evdokia Nikolaevna brings them food, cleans their cages, and gives them water, but she never stays with them for long or speaks to them in a baby-talk voice. I am the only visitor the long-eared inmates ever have, and I do my best to compensate for that. I, too, bring them fresh grass and push it inside through the wire netting. I give them names and tell them about the events of the day while they move their long ears, blink their dark eyes, and wiggle their whiskers—always interested in what I have to say, more so than my own family.

The more time I spend around the rabbits, the more I am mystified with their lives. Some days Evdokia Nikolaevna keeps them in cages in pairs, while other days I find them alone. Pairing the little animals makes a lot of sense to me—clearly, everybody needs a playmate. Yet she never keeps them together for long.

Also, the "temporary" playmates are always the same, as if Evdokia Nikolaevna does not have enough space for them in her rabbit-hutch, so she has to move them from one cage to another.

Gradually, I notice that the rabbits that lose their temporary playmates grow fatter, until one day I find four tiny bunnies in a cage with a formerly obese rabbit.

"The rabbits have babies, too!" I report to my mother at night. "They're the cutest little things you ever saw. Would you get me some?"

"I don't have the time for rabbits," Mom says. "With all this housework, I hardly have the time for the two of you."

"I'll help you, Mom," I beg. "I'll take care of the rabbits myself. I'll spend more time with Tanya, too. Mom, please! Just two!"

After a lot of beseeching and promising on my part, Mom finally gives in, and a cage with two rabbits appears next to a strawberry patch that I have solemnly promised to weed every other day. I rush to the cage and something inside me melts, as if I have swallowed a whole box of chocolates in one go. Not only do I have two wonderful creatures all to myself (Tanya does not count, she never pays attention to anything for more than a day), but also *my* rabbits are the most beautiful rabbits in the whole rabbit world! Their puffy coats are snow-white, their long ears are exquisitely-translucent, their glimmering eyes are full of naïve curiosity, and best of all—something that Mom does not yet know—they are going to bring me the cutest rabbit babies known to man!

The next week must be the best week of my life. Every morning, I run to the fields to gather fresh grass and clover. In the afternoon I beg Mom to spare some of our cabbage and carrots for my rabbits, and every evening I clean the rabbits' cage. I also take care of our strawberry patch and play with my little sister—all without getting tired or bored.

By the end of the week, I walk up to Mom, who is bent over a one-burner portable propane stove with a ladle in her hand, and ask her for another cage. Mom stops stirring *borscht* and looks at me.

"What do you need another cage for?" she says.

"I have to separate the rabbits," I answer, proud of my insider's knowledge.

"Separate for what?"

It is appalling how little Mom knows about country living in general and the propagation of rabbits in particular. Does she even realize that, if not for Stalin, I would have been born on her grandparents' farm? And, although I was not, I am still excited about recapturing my secret rural heritage. "For babies, of course!"

"What babies?"

"You have to separate the rabbits so they can have babies," I tell Mom in a voice she herself reserves for talking with little Tanya. "Ask Evdokia Nikolaevna! She always does that."

The ladle slips from Mom's hand and falls on the scratched wooden floor, splashing me with hot reddish liquid and pieces of chopped beets. Yet, instead of inquiring if I am okay or, at least, picking up the ladle and cleaning the floor, my mother stares at me as if I just told her that my rabbits have grown horns or I am going to America to visit Tom Sawyer.

"I'll talk to your father," she says after a minute of dead silence.

The next day, Dad brings another cage and transfers one of the rabbits there. All I need now is patience. First thing in the morning, I run to my cages and look the rabbits over. I am not quite sure which one of them will have bunnies, so I carefully examine both. Yet, day after day, my rabbits look exactly the way they did when I first saw them—white and fuzzy, and cute— but they are no bigger.

A week later, I ask Mom to bring the rabbits back together. She does not mind. After several more days, we separate the animals once again, and my feverish observations continue—to no avail. Finally, after a series of separations and happy reunions, my rabbits become nervous, while I become deeply disappointed.

My parents will not buy me another couple, I realize that. I have to give up my idea. The last time I pull a trembling rodent from its cage, I clasp it to my face and, despite a nagging premonition that no earthly effort will bring about a change, I whisper into its silky ear, "Please, please, please, bring me little bunnies!" And then I kiss it on its wet, sniffing nose.

This time, the change does come. It is not the one I hoped for, but it is definitely a change. In size, too. Not in the rabbits, though, but in my face. By next morning, it swells like the risen dough for Mom's *pirozhki*, while my eyes turn into two hardly visible slits, as if, instead of coming from a long line of Diaspora Jews and Ukrainian *kulaks*, I come from the stock of Genghis Khan. I also feel feverish, and my body itches as if ants were crawling all over it.

Several days later, after Mom brings me home from a local hospital where I have been treated for allergic shock, the rabbits and their cages are gone. I open my mouth to ask about them, but I look at Mom and bite my tongue. I have learned my lesson. Sometimes, the very thing you long for so much can hurt you. Besides, as Mom tells me—her hand stroking my hair—there is a little one in our household already. Not as cute as bunnies and definitely much more troublesome—it is my sister Tanya, who, according to Mom, needs my attention "even more than the rabbits."

Tanya proves the truth of Mom's statement the very next day. While playing in the kitchen, she finds a kernel of sweet corn and, for nothing better to do, pushes it deep inside her left nostril. The kernel, which suddenly finds itself in a warm and moist environment, apparently starts growing there—unlike the corn our whole country tried so hard to grow—and the next morning, Tanya wakes up screaming in pain.

Mom rushes her to the same hospital, and the same doctor treats her. When they return home, Mom's green eyes are dark-olive and fulminating. Just before Tanya was released, the doctor asked Mom how many *more* children she has. This may have been a very innocent question, but Mom took it very hard, and I quickly find myself grounded for the offence of not watching Tanya "*v oba glaza*." By the time I am finally forgiven, golden spikes of fall begin penetrating the summer greenery, the evenings cool off, and we move back to Moscow.

Years later, I ask my mother if she remembers the summer in the village where everybody had rabbits.

"Sure," she says. "They raised them for meat."

"They did?!" I say, making a belated connection between the 1960's food shortages and the number of rodents in the village. What else did I miss?

"What about *my* rabbits?" I ask. "Why didn't they have bunnies?"

"I had no time for rabbits," Mom says. "Grocery shopping took hours, not to mention cooking on a one-burner stove. We bought you two females."

CHAPTER FIFTEEN

I REMEMBER THEM

"For as long as we live, they too will live,
For they are now a part of us, as we remember them."
Reform Judaism Prayer Book

"A great achievement of Soviet Science!" An announcer's voice pours breathlessly from the radio, "The first in world history!" The voice reaches a state of ecstasy: "Soviet human spacecraft *Vostok* 1 orbited the Earth in 108 minutes!" Victorious sounds of a military choir conclude this breaking news, affirming the gravity of the event.

Wow! Just this morning, while I was still asleep, Yuri Gagarin, our first cosmonaut, flew into outer space! How great is that?!

"This is really amazing!" my father says, as if reading my mind. "We're the first! *Eto vam ne zhuk nachikhal!* (This is nothing to sneeze at!)."

"Oh, sure," Mom says, putting away breakfast plates and bowls, no trace of triumph in her voice. "I personally wouldn't mind if things were that amazing on the ground, too. With our salaries for one thing. Apartments for another."

"Well, Fira, you must admit. This is a great achievement! Things like this don't happen every day."

"Neither do the things I just mentioned," Mom says. Then she looks at her watch. "Don't forget that Tosja's going out tonight, so you have to come home earlier."

I stare at Mom. What is she talking about? What does our apartment have to do with anything? Of course Dad is right. It is great that we are first! Naturally, I am not surprised. Maria Ivanovna, our teacher, says that our country is first "in everything," and we "must be proud" to be born here. I sure am. Yet it is not clear to me where exactly "outer space" is. In my nine years, I have never boarded a plane, although I have seen planes gliding through the silky blue sky, leaving behind slowly widening white tails. I have also seen war movies with droning bombers and screeching fighter planes—five-pointed stars painted on the wings of our planes and ugly Swastikas on Germany's.

I guess outer space must be just above where all those planes fly—somewhere between them and the sun. Still, why is it so amazing? It's just higher, that's all, isn't it?

"Dad, didn't we already fly into outer space?"

"You're thinking about *Sputnik*," Dad says. "That was four years ago, and there was no human there."

"Really? What was it for then?"

"Well, that was the first time anybody in the world launched a spacecraft into orbit."

"And what did it do?"

"It flew around the earth and transmitted signals."

"That's all?"

"Oh, that was very important," Dad says, "But it's hard to explain. When you're older, you'll understand."

Everything ends with "when you're older." I cannot wait to be older! First of all, I won't have to go to school. I am not a bad student, but I have only one friend there, my next-door neighbor Igorék, whom I have known since I was five. Still, Igorék and I are enrolled in different classes, so we mostly meet after school anyway. Igorék is Jewish, like me, which is no secret to anybody in school, since it is written on the back of our class registers.

Every time Maria Ivanovna has to leave the classroom during a lesson, several kids spring from their desks, crowd around the teacher's table, and quickly go through the register. At first, they check out their grades and then, inevitably, progress to the last page—the page that reveals our addresses, the names of our parents, and our ethnic origin—which in our country is called "nationality."

In Moscow, the city located in the heart of the Russian Federation, almost everybody is Russian, so in my class of 25 and Igorék's of 24 we are the only non-Russian children. And there is always somebody in the mischievous crowd who enjoys reading the "nationality" column aloud—as if they had not memorized it already—quickly chanting the names of Russian origin and relishing Igorék's or mine.

Another good thing about being older is that I won't be required to babysit my sister Tanya, since she will be older, too. Babysitting Tanya is a drag. Every time she falls and cries, it is *my* fault. And Tanya falls a *lot*! Unlike me, she is never static, and I cannot remember a time when she walked like a normal kid. It seems that as soon as Tanya learned to stand upright, she just took off like a little tornado. She is so fast that despite being six years older, I sometimes have a hard time keeping up with her.

Unfortunately, Tanya never notices sharp corners and obstacles in her way, so it is only a matter of time before she plops down howling, with her knees bleeding. On top of that, my sister likes getting into my things, and I have to tolerate that because she's younger and, according to my parents, I "should be smarter." It is as if my parents punish me for being born first, which wasn't *my* choice!

Most importantly, when I am older, I will be able to do something exciting, maybe even become a cosmonaut! When I was little, I wanted to be a doctor, like Mom, but I had to give that up because I'm afraid of blood. Then I wanted to tame wild animals. That started the day Mom took me to the Moscow Circus. For two hours, we watched impossibly slim acrobats in sparkling tights glide above our heads at the top of the circus dome, a magician in a black cloak pull doves and rabbits out of his top hat, and two white-faced clowns in clumsy shoes make the audience die laughing with their jokes and tricks.

Yet the act that struck me the most was a group of trained Siberian tigers. The tigers ran out onto the brightly lit stage through a cage-like passage—their large bodies moving in a loping stride, their heavy heads shaking from side to side, their sharp teeth bare, and their thundering roar bouncing off the circus walls. Behind the tigers appeared a tamer—a tall, handsome man with a whip in hand. At his command, the tigers rolled over on the stage, stood up on their hind legs, and jumped through large multicolored hoops.

At the end, the tamer put his head into the biggest tiger's mouth, and loud drumbeats sounded from the orchestra pit, while astounded "aahs" swept through the audience. My heart began racing in time with the drums, and I closed my eyes with my hands, so, if the tiger bit the tamer's head off, I would not have to see it. But nothing bad happened. The drums gave way to rousing music and deafening applause, and when I took my hands away, the tigers were retreating from the stage, and the smiling tamer was blowing kisses to the audience.

The tamer was accompanied by a young woman assistant who was dressed in a beautiful suit decorated with spangles and rhinestones and also sparkling high boots. So I immediately decided I would become a tamer of wild animals, or, at least, a tamer's assistant.

All of that seemed childish now—no comparison with being a cosmonaut. Just look at Yuri Gagarin. His broadly smiling, likable face appears on the pages of *Pravda* ("Truth," the main Soviet newspaper) and other newspapers and magazines, and everybody talks about him: TV and radio announcers, teachers in school, and even kids in our *dvor*. What could be better than that?

Of course, my dream depends on whether a girl *can* be a cosmonaut … but why not? Nobody says that cosmonauts have to be men. In fact, they even sent a dog into space some time ago. I was little then, but I remember. Her name was Laika. She was a Siberian husky, and everybody admired her then almost as much as we admire Yuri Gagarin now. I remember seeing her picture. She was so cute—with pointed ears and dark curious eyes, and a kind of harness put over her furry body for the flight.

"Dad, is Laika still flying?"

"Who?"

"Laika, the dog they sent into space, remember?"

"Hmm … *That* Laika … I don't know. Maybe."

"Does she still have enough food? She's been up there for a long time."

Dad gives me a careful look, "I guess so."

"Do you think Gagarin brought her back?"

"Well, I didn't hear anything, but that's possible," Dad says and then quickly adds, "Don't you have some homework to do?"

Later that week, after school, I report to Igorék about my decision to become a cosmonaut. We stand in front of our building. The snow drifts that covered the ground during the long winter are sagging from early springtime melting and refreezing, and their surfaces, blackened by air pollution, look like burnt cake icing.

Not far from us, neighborhood boys are engrossed in a war game: one group pretends to be Russian soldiers, the other German—we call them *Fritzes*. The enemies hide behind our building from where they make short offensive charges, shouting excitedly, "Hurray!!!" or "Hände hoh!" and firing "Rata-tat-tat-tat!" into the damp air.

"Girls can't be cosmonauts." A boy's voice sounds behind me. I turn and face Liosha Mironov, my classmate and one of the students who enjoys reading the nationality column in our class register. Unlike Igorék, who is quiet, small, dark-haired, and dark-eyed, Liosha is loud, tall, and tow-headed, and his almost white brows curve above eyes as light and transparent as if they were made of ice.

"How do *you* know?" I say.

"I know. You have to be a pilot first, and pilots are always men."

I turn away from Liosha. This could be true. Every book I have read about the last war portrays women only as telegraphers, nurses, or doctors. In fact, my Mom, a doctor, says that if there is another war, she will be drafted to work in an army hospital.

"I'll be a pilot after school," Liosha says and gives me a look of contempt. He does not add anything else, but I understand his meaning. *He* has a chance of becoming a cosmonaut while *I* do not. Then Liosha spits on the darkened snow near my feet and shouts to the boys playing the war game, "Hey, wait for me!" And he is gone.

Too late though. He has already spoiled my mood, and I no longer feel like talking about my new calling. Besides, Igorék is not feeling well. He keeps coughing, and soon he says that he needs to go home and leaves me alone.

I am often alone. When I come home from school, my parents are still at work and my sister and Tosja are usually out. That is fine with me, since I have the freedom to do whatever I want, which, most of the time, means reading everything I can get my hands on. The bookcase in our apartment is full. I have already read "Adventures of Tom Sawyer," "Twenty Thousand Leagues Under the Sea," and I even started on "War and Peace," but it proved to be so boring that I switched to "King Solomon's Mines."

Today, though, I do not feel like reading. I keep thinking about Laika. Nobody says that she is back, so she must be still up there—a little furry ball of life, flying around the earth all by herself, looking through the window at the world beneath her.

"Maria Ivanovna, how long will Laika fly?" I ask my teacher the next day.

"Who? Laika?" Maria Ivanovna takes off her glasses, the way she always does when she is not happy with us, and looks at me intensely, her lips pressed together into a straight line.

"She'll fly as long as it's needed," she says after a pause, and her voice sounds as self-assured and important as the voices of radio announcers. Yet she turns her gaze away from me.

"Needed for what?" I want to say, but I know better than to annoy Maria Ivanovna.

At night, I lay in bed, wondering about Laika. It's a pity that nobody asked Yuri Gagarin to bring her back to us. If I ever meet him, I'll ask him. But where can I meet him? Well, there is a good chance that I'll spot him one day standing in line for groceries, as all adults do. Or Mom and I may run into him at Minaevskij marketplace near us. No, that's not likely. Mom says that the market is way too expensive, so we rarely go there. Then, maybe, he'll come to visit our school?

That's it! He will come to tell us all about his flight and what he saw from his spaceship. With this happy thought, I quickly fall asleep, and, in my dream, I see sad little Laika. Her black round eyes are wet, and she is looking sorrowfully at me, as if begging for help or asking me not to forget her, still orbiting in the cold nothingness of the cosmos.

Several weeks have gone by since I talked to Igorék about becoming a cosmonaut, and I have not seen him since. He has not been going to school, and he has not been coming over to play after school either. Last weekend, Mom sent me to visit the grandparents, and after I came back, I thought that I would see him for sure, but I did not.

Every day I ask Mom about Igorék, and every day she tells me that he is still sick. This is really annoying. How long can Igorék be sick? Even my sister Tanya, who is ill often, recovers faster than he does, and she is much younger!

By now, the snow has melted and the asphalt around our house is dry. After school, kids pour outside to skip rope, kick balls, or play *klassiki* (hop scotch). I mope around, waiting for somebody to ask me to join, and, when nobody does, I draw hop scotch squares with a piece of white chalk and hop by myself.

"Training to be a cosmonaut?" Liosha appears in front of me, his shirt half-buttoned and a soccer ball under his arm.

I know he is mocking me. I won't pay attention.

"Not a chance. You can't even hop good," Liosha comments, scornfully observing me awkwardly frozen on one leg.

"Leave me alone," I say and put my bent leg down. "I don't want to talk to you."

"Eh, who do you want to talk to? Igorék? He's gone."

"He's gone? Where?" (Why didn't Mom tell me?)

Liosha's bleached brows rise above his icy eyes, "Are you stupid? *Everybody* knows."

I look at him uncomprehending, but already something heavy begins swarming inside my chest.

"You're stupid yourself!" I scream and push the ball under his arm as hard as I can. The ball falls on the asphalt and bounces happily down the sunlit street and away from Liosha.

"*Idiotka*!" Liosha shouts. "Crazy Jewish *idiotka*!" And he takes off after the escaping ball.

I rush in the opposite direction. What was he talking about? What is it that everybody knows?

As I open the door of our apartment, I hear the rhythmic sounds of a knife hitting the cutting board. Mom is cooking, and potato peels are piled up on the kitchen counter in front of her.

"Where has Igorék gone, Mom?" My heart is pounding so fast that I have a hard time getting the words out.

Mom slowly puts the knife down, looks at me, and wipes her hands off on an apron tied around her waist.

"I'm sorry, Sveta. I should've told you. Igorék … he … he …" She puts her hands on my shoulders and pulls me closer. "He's died."

Died? What is she talking about? I remember that he was coughing the last time I saw him, but nobody dies of that! I had whooping cough when I was little, and I had to stay at home with Grandma for a long time. Is that what Mom means?

"Can we go and visit him?"

"Well, he's buried in the cemetery. We can visit him there … if you want."

In the cemetery? Kids don't get buried in cemeteries. They play games, they do things! Cemeteries are for old people. Like that woman from the house next door, who died several months ago. She must have been ancient and I only saw her once or twice, but I've known Igorék for years!

I know birds can die. I found one once under the tree not far from our house. It was just a chick, with yellowish colors around its beak and neck. I picked it up and held it in my cupped hands. It was chirruping, turning its head right and left, and opening its beak wide. I ran home with it. I thought I would make a cotton nest for it and feed it until it learned how to fly. But when I got home, the chick no longer moved or made sounds. Its eyes were closed and its head was dangling down like the head of a broken dandelion. I dropped it to the floor and burst into tears. My father picked it up and took it outside, and I never asked him what he did with it. I didn't' want to know.

But I can't imagine Igorék with his eyes closed and his head dangling down. It's just … just … stupid! It is so stupid that it's even funny, isn't it? And I start laughing. I know that it's wrong, but I cannot stop. I am laughing and laughing, and the more I laugh, the harder it seems to stop.

I feel Mom's hands on my shaking shoulders. She is saying something about water and going to bed. I want to answer, "No! I don't need water and I don't want to go to bed!" But I cannot talk either. I am still laughing and my teeth are chattering against the cold glass.

The next day, Mom allows me to stay at home. Both Mom and Dad are at work, and Tanya and our nanny Tosja are taking a walk. I am alone. I pull "King Solomon's Mines" from the shelf and try to read it. Useless. Even reading is no help. Without Igorék, I am as lonely down here as Laika is up there in outer space. I put the book down and go outside.

A light wind caresses the world with faint smells of grass and budding leaves. The sky is clear. I throw my head back and look up, intensely. There is a tiny dot up there, so tiny that I can only see it if I cover one eye with my hand and strain the other.

"That must be Laika's spaceship." I think to myself. "Hi, Laika!"

I must have said that aloud, because suddenly, I hear a familiar voice, "Who are you talking to *now*?"

I shift my gaze. It is Liosha. Again. Why is *he* not in school?

"None of your business."

"Did you say Laika? That dog? You're even stupider than I thought. Wake up! She's been dead for years. She burned!" And he pushes me, hard.

I fall on the warm asphalt and scratch my elbow. Drops of blood appear on my skin, but I feel pain in my chest.

He's lying! Of course, he's lying! I won't believe him, and I won't cry. He knows nothing! He's the worst student in our class. Besides, Grandma says that nobody is gone as long as we remember them. That memory gives us a hope.

"She's not dead, you creep!" I shout at the top of my lung, my voice breaking. "I wish you were dead! I wish you were burned! You don't know anything, anything … I *remember* her!"

And then tears start pouring from my eyes the way water flows from an open faucet. I cry for Igorék, for Laika, for myself, and for everybody I love who may leave me one day.

Many years later, I run into Igorék's mother, a skinny elderly woman with a full head of snow-white wavy hair who tells me that her son had galloping consumption. Also, around the same time, during a casual conversation, I finally learn that Laika died a few hours after her launch. Sputnik 2, the spacecraft that raised her to the sky, was not designed to be retrievable, and from the very beginning, Laika's fate was to be sacrificed for the sake of Soviet Science.

Laika
photo by Bobbie Johnson, Flickr, CC by 2.0

Yet even now, both Laika and dark-eyed Igorék are still a part of me, and with all the pains and losses of an adult life, I remember them, and their vague images still come to me—if only in my dreams. Grandma was right, for as long as I live, they live, too.

CHAPTER SIXTEEN

YOUNG PIONEER

It is near the end of my third year of school, and we are preparing to become Young Pioneers.

"It's an honor," our teacher Maria Ivanovna tells us, "And it is a very important stage in your progress toward becoming conscientious Soviet citizens!"

Everybody in my class is excited, but I feel anxious. Young Pioneers are supposed to be ten, but since my parents sent me to school a year early, I am still nine, and I may have to wait till next year. My only hope is that Maria Ivanovna will make an exception for me—that is if, as she puts it, I "take it very seriously and study hard."

I am eager to do that. Joining the Pioneers is much more important than joining the *Octyabryata* ("Children of October," an organization for young school children), which took place two years ago. Two classes of first-graders were lined up in the school gym—girls in festive white aprons and boys in freshly starched white shirts. The principal made a speech about the importance of being good students and how becoming *Octyabryata* was our "first step toward evolving into conscientious Soviet citizens." Then the teachers pinned *Octyabryata* badges with a portrait of *Dedushka* (Grandfather) Lenin on the girls' aprons and the boys' jackets, and the meeting was over.

This time, we are told, good and well-behaved students will get to go to Red Square, where thousands of students from all over Moscow will join the Young Pioneers in a festive ceremony. So, if I do not become a Pioneer this May, despite being a good student, I will be left behind with the hooligans and *dvoeshniki* (pupils with the lowest grades). That would be awful, since I am already a pariah in my class.

I am the only Jew there and, as if that is not bad enough, I am a hopeless athlete. I must be the worst runner in our school's history and the clumsiest gymnast in the whole school district. When I climb a rope, I grab it with both hands and, after a short struggle, place my feet on the knot at the end and gradually straighten my body. Then I clasp my hands above my head as far as I can reach and hang there, unable to pull myself any higher, to the roaring laughter of my classmates.

Also, every time I try to jump over a pommel horse, I land exactly in the middle of its slippery, black leather back—as if on a saddle—and make my way to the far end of the beast by wildly wiggling my whole body while wishing I had never been born. Failing to become a Young Pioneer would be my final catastrophe, from which I might never recover, even if I made nothing but A's for the rest of my school life.

There are many things I need to learn to achieve my cherished goal. The first is the Young Pioneer Oath, which goes like this:

"I, a Young Pioneer of the Soviet Union, in the presence of my comrades, solemnly promise to love my Soviet Motherland with all my heart and to live, learn, and struggle as the great Lenin bade us and the Communist Party teaches us."

There are also songs we rehearse during our music lessons, like "The Young Pioneers March," "Our Land," and "Gaidar Marching First." And, most importantly, we study the history of the Pioneers movement.

Much like the Boy Scouts and Girl Scouts of the West, the Young Pioneers wear uniforms and neckerchiefs, go on campouts, and declare the importance of loyalty, honesty, and being prepared. In fact, Scout groups existed in our country even before the Russian Revolution, and a few of them soldiered on for a short time afterward. Yet since many Scouts fought against the Red Army, their groups were quickly eradicated after the Revolution, and the Young Pioneers sprouted in their place. The goal of this new organization is to take Soviet youth to a higher level of ideological consciousness.

We don't learn any of this. All we learn is that the Young Pioneers movement started in May 1922, and its first member, whom our textbook calls "Hero-Pioneer of the Soviet Union Number 001," was a peasant boy named Pavlik Morozov. Maria Ivanovna has already told us about him, and we have read a story of his short life. Now we are discussing it in class:

"Masha, tell us what you have learned," Maria Ivanovna says, crossing her arms across her ample bosom.

"Pavlik Morozov lived in a small Siberian village near Yekaterinburg, and he was thirteen, and he was a good student and a leader of the Young Pioneers in his school, and he overheard his father talking to *vragi naroda* (enemies of the people), and …" Masha recites breathlessly, her two scrawny braids bouncing off her narrow shoulders in time with every "and."

"Very good, Masha," Maria Ivanovna interrupts her. "You can sit down now. Seryozha, continue."

"Pavlik Morozov learned … that … his father hid … um … several sacks of … wheat from … from the authorities … and … and then sold them to … to the enemies," Seryozha slowly carries on, peeking at the open book in front of him.

"Well, Seryozha, what else?" Maria Ivanovna uncrosses her arms, takes off her glasses, and gives Seryozha a piercing glance.

"Pavlik was a good Pioneer." Seryozha is gaining speed now, happy to have arrived at the part of the story he actually remembers. "And he reported his father to the NKVD (Stalin's secret police)."

"Sit down, Seryozha. Nina, go ahead."

Nina gets up, adjusts her black apron, and studiously concludes the story. "Pavlik's family were all *kulaks*. They retaliated by killing him and his little brother while they were picking berries in the woods. But later, the murderers were caught and convicted."

Maria Ivanovna gives Nina an approving nod, and Nina sits down.

"Well, children," Maria Ivanovna says, slowly lifting her large body from the chair. "Do you understand the significance of Pavlik's heroic act?"

The room is still; only Maria Ivanovna's eyes roam from face to face like searchlights scanning the night sky during an air strike. Then, as if shrapnel has hit the room, Maria Ivanovna's clenched fist hits her desk, and her voice reaches its highest pitch, "Pavlik was a patriot! He sacrificed his life for the flourishing of communism and for the prosperity of our country!"

The class breaks into a discordant, "Yes, we understand." But Maria Ivanovna is not done yet.

"Pavlik is an example for all of you. Being loyal to your Motherland is more important than you, or your families, or anything else! Remember this!" With that, Maria Ivanovna puts her glasses back on and sinks into her dolefully protesting chair.

There is no way we can forget this lesson. The Hero-Pioneer of the Soviet Union Number 001 is ubiquitous. His image appears in museums, on postcards, and postage stamps. Stories and poems describing his courageous and tragically short life crowd the shelves of our bookstores. Songs, cantatas, and even operas eulogize his exploits. Streets, ships, and libraries are named after him. And his bronze statue, holding a stiffly streaming banner, looks forward to posterity from a tall pedestal in the park bearing his name less than two miles from the Kremlin.

Too bad Maria Ivanovna did not ask me a question. I know Pavlik's story by heart. I have even dreamed that *I* am Pavlik Morozov, risking *my* life by informing the authorities about enemies of the people. It happens to me often that stories I hear, books I read, or movies I watch come back to me at night as dreams. Some of them are nightmares really, like the ones about the Second World War.

Actually, it is often the same dream, which plays itself out like this: Moscow is being bombed. Screeching sirens split my head, thundering explosions raise geysers of dirt all around our house, and shrapnel flies outside our windows. I am under the dinner table, which seems to be the only safe place in this world gone mad. I try to shout. Where are my parents, where is my sister? But somebody puts a palm over my mouth, and I see a forefinger pressed to dark-purple lips, shushing me. Be quiet. Don't make a sound.

Through blinding tears, I cannot see the person's face; all I see is a figure hidden under a black, hooded gown. I strain my eyes, trying to discern the stranger's features, and, to my horror, I realize that it has no face! No face at all! Just dark-purple lips floating in a gloomy shadow under the hood. I scream, loudly and hopelessly.

It's Death! Everybody's dead! I am all alone! And then … I wake up, sweaty and moaning, to Mom's "Wake up, wake up! It's just a bad dream, honey."

My dreams about Hero-Pioneer 001 are different, though, not agonizing, but angry and decisive. I am in a two-room apartment where I have never been before. There is a group of people in the next room, whispering conspiratorially. At first, I can hardly hear them, but when I get close to the doorway, I recognize familiar voices, although I cannot place them.

The voices are talking about now much they dislike our country, our leaders, and even our school teachers, who teach children "nonsense." They talk about "corrupt communists," the good life in America, travel documents, and other things I do not understand. I *do* understand, though, that these people are against us! They are against my school, against our government, against everything Maria Ivanovna calls "holy for every Soviet citizen." Who knows what could happen if these people succeed? They might enslave us, they might bomb Moscow, they might even kill us all! How dare they?! I have to stop them. I have to let somebody know!

I carefully walk out of the apartment and quietly close the door behind me. I'm going to inform the NKVD. This is my sacred duty and my destiny—even if I must die. And I think I will die. For a little while, I feel sad about that, but I tell myself that my death will be remembered. People will write books and compose songs about me, and my statue will be erected in a city park. I wipe away tears, take a deep breath, and continue my journey to the NKVD and into posterity.

When I wake up in my bed with my heart pounding, I feel disappointed. Although I am still alive, I am just a school girl and not a hero. Besides, it suddenly hits me, I do not even know where the

NKVD is, and, if I ever need to find "the authorities," I have to learn that first.

"Mom," I say casually when my mother hands me a semolina-kasha breakfast smelling of burnt milk, "Where is the NKVD?"

"The NKVD? It doesn't exist anymore. We have the KGB now," Mom says. "What do you need them for, anyway?" she adds in a moment, nudging my sulking sister towards the table. "Just eat and go to school. I'm busy with Tanya. We'll talk later."

Well, here are my parents in a nutshell! Do they ever have *any* time for me? No. Do they ever do *anything* for me? No. Not even *today*, the day I am becoming a Young Pioneer! *Everything* is about Tanya. Or, it's about *them* being tired. What about *me*? Choking, I shove the kasha down my throat and moisten it with a glass of hot tea. Then I put on my new Pioneer's uniform (a white shirt and a dark-blue skirt that Mom ironed for me last night), slam the door of the apartment, and leave, carrying with me a new flaming-red silk Pioneer *galstuk* (neckerchief) and a Pioneer *znachok* (badge).

As soon as I find myself on the street, the May sun bestows its warm embrace upon me, and a light wind playfully caresses my cheeks. I forget about the injuries my family causes me, my angry pace slows down, and my lips stretch unconsciously into a smile. After all, this is the day I've been waiting for. And we won't spend it in the classroom, but at Red Square, which, as *everyone* knows, is the most important place in the whole country and, quite likely, in the whole world!

Even before I approach the school building, I spot two buses. We third-graders board them with our teachers, and the buses carry us from our gloomy neighborhood to the taller buildings and wider streets of the city center. Everybody is cheerful, and laughter and singing spill from the open windows like foam from a bottle of champagne on New Year's Eve. About an hour later, we reach the red brick Kremlin walls. We get off, form two columns, and march to Red Square, where other festive columns of children are waiting to become troops of Young Pioneers.

Red Square is the focal point of the city, and the major streets of Moscow radiate from here like arteries delivering blood to all parts of the body. Numerous visitors come to Red Square to express their awe or satisfy their curiosity, and military parades and civil demonstrations roll over its ancient cobblestones in a display of our country's power and solidarity.

Today, the square is taken over by school children: boys and girls whose impatient hearts beat under their freshly starched white shirts. The day could not be any better: the sky is silky blue, the sun is aglow, and the air is filled with excitement and the sound of children's voices that echo through the square and bounce off the Kremlin walls and the marble stones of Lenin's Tomb.

After a while, silence falls on the disorderly formations—the ceremony has begun. A tall man with a red Pioneer neckerchief and two young drummers behind him goose-step to the center of the square.

"Today is the most important day in your life," the man proclaims—his amplified voice soaring high above our heads. "You are becoming members of the Young Pioneer Organization of the Soviet Union. From this day on, your life is dedicated to our great Motherland!"

The man stops and a group of young men and women in Pioneer neckerchiefs approach the columns of students to perform the initiation. The drums sound, and we take turns stepping forward. A scarlet neckerchief is wound around each skinny neck and a badge with Lenin's profile and the inscription "Always Ready!" is pinned to every white shirt.

When everybody gets back in line, the master of ceremonies raises his hand above his head in a Pioneer salute, and everybody follows his lead.

"Repeat after me!"

And hundreds of voices join him in excited unison: "I, a Young Pioneer of the Soviet Union, in the presence of my comrades, solemnly promise to love my Soviet Motherland …"

"Be ready!" The Master of Ceremony calls to us at the end.

"Always ready!" resounds mightily through the square as our assurance and energy rises to the blue sky.

My heart pounds inside my chest like a bell delivering great news. I'm a Young Pioneer! And now we are going to Lenin's mausoleum!

The line to the glossy red-and-gray mausoleum is long, but everybody is bubbling with excitement and a sense of self-importance. We are laughing and talking nonstop. In thirty minutes or so, our laugher weakens and the boisterous conversations die out. We shift from foot to foot and glance impatiently at the head of the line—feeling more tired with every shuffling step. For a while, apathy takes over, but then the animation picks up again. We are getting closer. We are only a few yards away from the entrance. We can almost touch the two armed guards standing rigidly on both sides of the entrance in full dress uniforms. Now it's our turn!

Having waited in the bright sunlight for about two hours, I am struck by the dimness of the interior.

"Like a grave," I hear somebody say behind me.

We *are* in a grave, I feel like responding, the most important and sacred grave of them all!

As soon as my eyes get used to the low lights, I spot more armed guards who keep the line moving. Several more steps, and we approach a large glass sarcophagus. I stand on tip-toes, trying to make out the dark-suited figure that lies there. From behind the people in front of me, I can see Lenin's silhouette, strangely small for somebody Maria Ivanovna calls the "father of our country" who "changed the course of world history." I try to get closer to discern the familiar features, but the crowd keeps moving, and a bright spotlight that illuminates Lenin's face makes it look like a papier-mâché mask. Also, this smell … the smell of chemicals and a hospital room, and … what else?… death? All of a sudden, I feel lightheaded and my stomach begins to turn.

"Move on, move on," I hear a voice say, and the force of the crowd picks me up and spits me out into the bright sunlight outside the mausoleum. It is over. I am still nauseated, but the fresh air makes me feel better. Then it hits me—I have missed my big moment! Maybe forever! Back there, behind the heavy doors, lies the man whose face I know as well as my own, whose life I studied in school and read about in books, and to whom, according to Maria Ivanovna, I owe my very existence. And I have barely seen him! How terribly unfair! What am I going to tell the neighborhood kids or my family?

I do not remember how I get home. In my mind, I keep going over the events of the day, getting ready to describe them to future listeners. Yet, as soon as I open our door, my mother shushes me and points to my sister's bed. Tanya is lying there. Her eyes are closed, her cheeks are the color of my new Pioneer neckerchief, and Mom's left hand holds a white compress on her forehead.

"It was really great!" I begin, but Mother interrupts me. "Quiet! I put your dinner on the table. You can eat it in the kitchen, if you want." Mom's voice is a whisper, and her posture, huddled on the chair by Tanya's bed, speaks of weariness and frustration.

"But Mom …"

"You'll tell me later."

"I just …"

"Later, later," Mother waves me off.

This is too much! Tanya is *always* sick. Does this mean that I will *never* get any attention? I was sick at her age, too. So, what did my parents do? They left me with Grandma! They "had to go to work." Is that fair? When is it *my* turn? Nobody ever talks about things that are important to *me*. They just demand that I make good grades, that's all. Just recently, Dad didn't want to speak with me about Pavlik Morozov. What did he say? "*Ne zabivay svoyu golovu chepukhoy*." (Don't take that nonsense into your head.) What's that supposed to mean?

Dark waves of anger flow over me. Blood rushes to my head, which, suddenly, is very clear, and a strange voice speaks from somewhere inside it.

"You *know* what that means. It means that your parents and grandparents, and your aunts and uncles are 'enemies of the people.' That's right. And this is why everything dear to the Soviet people is 'nonsense' to them. And now that you're a Young Pioneer, you *must* do what Pavlik Morozov did. You *must* report them to the authorities!"

I almost stop breathing. It's true! Those voices I heard in my dreams about Pavlik Morozov were not just *familiar* voices. They were *their* voices! And the conversations about corrupt communists, "this damn government," and life in America—I didn't just dream about them, I heard them! In fact, I hear them every time my relatives get together for birthdays or holidays. And I can prove it, too! Grandma herself told me that her parents owned a farm, and then there are those photographs in the top drawer of her dresser—pictures of relatives who live in New York, wear silky clothes, and have fancy haircuts.

No, maybe I shouldn't inform on my grandparents. I stay with them during my school breaks. Besides, Grandpa plays the guitar and sings sad songs, and Grandma makes my favorite strudel. If they are in prison, I won't have a place to go. Still, my parents are really awful! They're never happy with anything I do. They make me babysit Tanya, they force me to eat all that gross food, and … I *definitely* should turn them in!

I take a bowl of soup and storm out of the room, not willing even to look at Mom bending over Tanya's bed. I walk straight to the bathroom, pour the soup into the toilet and flush it. I don't need her food! And I don't want to talk to her *ever* again!

For a while, I mope around our small kitchen. Unfortunately, I cannot spend much time there. The neighbors, Klavdia Petrovna and Naúm Vasilievich, are already eyeing me suspiciously. I head back to our room.

"Sh-sh," Mom says again. "Did you finish your dinner?" Then she beckons me closer, puts her arms around my shoulders and whispers, "Congratulations! Did you have fun?"

I do not answer. Too late now! They think I'm stupid. They think I don't understand what's going on. But I'm a Young Pioneer now! I'm a patriot! I know that being loyal to our Motherland is more important than my family, especially such an awful family.

"Svetochka, what's wrong?" Mom says, peering into my eyes.

You are wrong! All of you!—I want to say, trying to extricate myself from Mom's embrace, nourishing my anger.

"Are you sick, too, honey?" Mom's palm lands on my dry forehead.

Her voice sounds so concerned, and her arms envelop me so tenderly that, for a moment, I feel like cuddling on her lap and telling her all about driving through Moscow, about Red Square, the ceremony, and my disappointment in the mausoleum. But … I won't! She's just *pretending*. She's *never* interested. Pavlik's father must've pretended to be nice to him, too, but Pavlik didn't let himself be fooled. He did what he had to do, and so will I, and no "Svetochka" will stop me!

A short cry comes from Tanya's bed, and we both turn to look at her. Tanya's breathing is laborious, but her eyes are still closed, and she appears to be sleeping. Suddenly, the thought goes through my head, what will happen to Tanya when my parents are gone? She could be put into an orphanage. Well, she's a pain. Why should I care? Of course, she's sick now. I'd better wait till she's better and *then* turn my parents in to the authorities.

But … what will happen to *me*? I guess I could live with my grandparents. No, wait. Will they want to kill me? That's what Pavlik's relatives did. My heart skips a bit, but I shake off the scary thought. *My* grandparents would not want to kill me. They love me! Still, what will they do when they find out about my deed? Will they take me in then? What if they won't? I can't live alone, can I? I have no money and I don't know how to cook. Also, who will buy me clothes or take care of me when I am sick? If my parents are taken away, I'll have *nobody*. It'll be the way it is in my war nightmares. I'll be under the table, scared and alone.

The room is quiet, and everything stands still, except Mom's hand stroking my hair. Her hands smell of medicine, and they are as soft and comforting as sun-rays breaking through the clouds after a long cold winter. I don't remember a time in my life without my mother's hands. These are the hands that cuddled me when I was little, these are the hands that woke me up from my nightmares, and these are the hands that ironed my new Pioneer uniform last night. How am I going to live without them?

Something starts to melt in my chest, dissolving my anger into streamlets of tears. Of course, being loyal to our Motherland is more important than my family, and of course my parents are not the kind of people Maria Ivanovna would hold up to us as an example. But, they're the *only* parents I have, and I do love them!

I wipe off my tears, bring my face closer to Mom's, and whisper, sniffling, into her ear, "I won't report you."

Mom looks at me blankly, "What are you talking about? Report? To whom?"

At this moment, another moan comes from Tanya's bed and, once again, Mom turns to my sister, forgetting about me. I follow her with my eyes, and my heart grows heavy. I recognize that I'll never be the center of Mom's attention, nor will I be a true Soviet patriot. Because, to my shame, all I can say to my mother's bent back—as well as to myself—is: "To anybody."

Tanya and me, 1961

CHAPTER SEVENTEEN

DESDEMONA AND SUGAR

Another winter melts in the warm embrace of spring, which, in its turn, gives way to rising temperatures, clear skies, and the irresistible temptations of summer. School is over and all of us, except Dad, are going to a summer Pioneer Camp sponsored by the factory where Mom works—I as a camper, Mom as the camp doctor, and Tanya and Grandma as members of the doctor's family.

On a warm June morning, prospective campers and their parents head to the factory building. When we arrive there—sacks and suitcases weighing down our arms—we hardly recognize the place. Buses line up on the street in front of the factory like giant caterpillars. Flags, posters, and flaming-red Pioneer scarves fly in the wind, and young voices mix into a cacophony of sounds, like an orchestra tuning up before a performance.

The camp's *vozhati* (leaders), with Pioneer scarves around their necks and large notebooks in their hands, check newly arrived children against their lists, sort them by age into *otryadi* (detachments), and send them to their buses. Before the children are swallowed by the vehicles, their parents kiss them, instruct them to behave and write letters home, and, as the motors start coughing and growling, wave good-bye. The next time they will see each other will be in twenty-four days.

After several hours of riding along curvy gravel roads, our caravan arrives at a fenced-off cluster of one-story wooden barracks hidden in a thinned-out coppice. The biggest of the barracks is the camp cafeteria, the smallest Mom's clinic with a four-bed infirmary and, in the back, a room for Mom, Tanya, and Grandma. The rest of the barracks are wards for the campers, lodging for the staff, and one more for the office of the camp director, a small library, and rooms for *kruzhki* (hobby groups).

The heart of the camp is a square with a tall flag pole that rises to the sky like the mast of a ship. Every morning, we wake up to an energetic bugle call, "Tatá-tatá-tatátatá-tatá"—which, according to the long-established camp tradition, translates into "Get up, get up, put on your underwear!"

Yawning and shivering in the fresh morning air, we half-heartedly pour out of our barracks and perform compulsory physical exercises. We bend our stiff bodies, flap our arms, squat, and run laps. Then we head to the outdoor zinc *umivalniki* (wash stands) lined up beside the building like a row of metallic cow udders. We quickly splash our faces with cold water, brush our chattering teeth, and head inside to groom ourselves. In fifteen minutes or so the bugle sounds again, and we form a line to march to the camp square for the *lineika*—the raising of the flag.

The *lineika* is a vital part of our day. Every detachment takes turns reporting to the Chief Camp Leader, a young strawberry-blond woman with cold blue eyes who wears a Pioneer scarf on her neck and a no-nonsense expression on her face. She, in her turn, reports to the camp director—a misshapen middle-aged man with a balding head and the unnaturally rosy cheeks of a heavy drinker.

The reports touch on sickness and discipline issues, and they are followed by a short discussion among the camp leaders at the end of which every detachment receives a detailed schedule for the day. Then a drumbeat breaks the morning calm, sending local crows into a panic, and one of the children hoists the camp flag. The rest draw themselves up and salute. The day has officially started.

And what a full day it is! Under the vigilant supervision of our leaders, boys play sports and girls do crafts. Children with good voices rehearse songs about our happy childhood, like *"Ah, chorosho v strane sovetsky zhit! Ah, chorosho svoyu strany lubit!"* (Hey, it's great to live in the Soviet Union. Hey, it's great to love our country!) And those few without athletic abilities, hobbies, or performing talents—in short, children like me—head to the library and lose themselves in imaginary worlds.

If the weather permits, we swim in a small lake nearby—twenty minutes every other day—and older kids go on hikes. Once a week, we go to *banya* (bathhouse), from which the boys emerge with red cheeks and the girls with heads wrapped in towels, looking like African Queens.

Also, every detachment, except the youngest one, takes turns helping in the kitchen: setting up tables, collecting dirty dishes, and serving food. Our common dinner dish is *makaroni po-flotsky*—macaroni with boiled ground meat, often mixed with small bone fragments that get stuck between our teeth if we are not careful. Our common drink is *compot*—dried fruit boiled in a large quantity of water.

Every evening before dusk, we march to the camp square for the lowering of the flag. It is an honor to be chosen to hoist or lower the flag. The usual recipients of this honor are good athletes or kids with talents. With their cheeks blushing and their eyes fixed victoriously on their friends or enemies, they get to bask in everybody's attention and feel important, if only briefly.

I am terribly jealous of them. I myself have nothing to offer to society at large or to my detachment in particular. I do not knit or sew. I do not like singing. I am terrible in track and field, and my swimming technique—desperate thrashing in the cool water of the lake while trying to feel its bottom with my toes—never gets me farther than three yards from the shore.

My only talent—if I have one—is reading. Unfortunately, I have not read any ghost stories, and ghost stories are big in our barracks. As soon as the drawn-out evening song of the bugle—"Tá-tá- tatatá-ta" (Go to sleep to your wards, boys and girls)—sinks into the shadows behind our windows, and our *vozhati* Evgenia Vladimirovna turns off the lights, somebody whispers loudly in the dark, "Anyone know a ghost story?"

Olga Fedorova, a tall girl with a freckled snubbed nose and large round eyes that never lose the expression of utter surprise, often responds first. She sits up in her bed and begins weaving a story.

"This woman lived alone in a village not far from here. Every day, just before nightfall, her neighbors saw her walk toward the cemetery on the edge of the village—always in black, with her eyes lowered. Early in the morning, people saw her again, walking back to her house. Nobody knew what she did in the cemetery, but they all wanted to find out … "

The room is still: no squealing of springs under our thin mattresses, no whispering, not even breathing disturbs the silence.

"One night, a village drunk decides to follow the woman. She walks and he walks, she stops and he stops. In thirty minutes or so, the woman enters the cemetery with the drunk behind her. The woman kneels by a grave near the entrance and starts digging with her bare hands."

We are frozen in our narrow beds. Our hearts pound, our pulses race, and our hair stands up on the back of our necks.

"And as the drunk watches, another woman, all in white, rises from the grave, moaning and howling. She points at him and screams, 'Die, die, die!'"

At this pivotal moment, something hits our barracks window from the outside, as if a ghost were trying to reach us from its unquiet grave, and we scream with one terrified voice, "Aaaaaah!!!"

It was probably a large moth that lost its way in the depth of the starless night. Yet long after the scare is over and everybody falls asleep, I am still awake, too frightened to close my eyes—watching shadows crawl in the corners and listening to howls from the woods.

In the morning, I have a splitting headache and Evgenia Vladimirovna sends me to see the doctor. Despite being in the same camp, I rarely see my mother. She is busy taking care of campers scratched by a variety of objects, struck by footballs, suffering from indigestion caused by eating raw mushrooms or camp food, or afflicted by other ailments.

Every morning Mom and her two nurses walk from one detachment to another checking for cleanliness of the campers' hands and nails, and, after *banya*, they inspect children's hair for lice. On top of that, Mom is responsible for the sanitary condition of the camp and the quality of the cafeteria food.

Even before I open the squeaking door of the clinic, I hear Mom talk to Grandma. Mom's voice is high with excitement, Grandma's low and worried.

Mother with her nurses

"Wait, wait, Fira. I don't get it. Why did you decide to check up on him?"

"Lida, his assistant, told me that he steals food from the cafeteria," Mom says.

At this, I open the door ever so slightly to see Grandma say, "She told you that? Why?"

"What do you mean, why? Because she's an honest person!" Mom tosses her head like a horse champing at the bit. Then she adds, "Well, I did see them argue a couple of days ago... Anyway," Mom speeds up again, "She came to me today and said that she saw him hide something in the teakettle."

"Oy vey, what if she lied?" Grandma says.

"But she didn't! When he was leaving the kitchen, I stopped him and asked him to bring me tomorrow's menu. I said, 'I'll hold the teakettle while you're looking for the menu.'"

"Did he give it to you?" Grandma asks.

"He had no choice. And when he turned around, I 'accidentally' dropped the teakettle and sugar poured out of it!" Mom says, half-triumphant, half-disgusted.

"So, what now?"

"I told the director. I hope they'll fire him. Maybe even sue," Mom says.

"I don't like it, Fira. The cook won't forgive you. You shouldn't have crossed him. We don't need any more *tsuris* (trouble, Yiddish)."

"What can he do to me, that thief? I'm just doing my job!" Mom's voice is like a breaking violin string. "He was stealing from children who get the bare minimum as it is!"

"Oy vey, you shouldn't have done it. And what if ..." Grandma's voice trails off, and I can no longer discern her words. No matter. I have heard enough. My headache is forgotten, and my imagination takes off like a plane. In my mind's eye, I see the whole scene as if I had witnessed it myself: Mom crouched over the teakettle spilling sugar on the floor, and the angry cook bent over her. This is almost as exciting as a story I recently heard about a man who stole a valuable violin and wanted to sell it abroad for American dollars.

I have never seen American dollars, nor have I, or anybody I know, ever traveled abroad. Still, I have a vague feeling that American dollars must be worth more than our rubles, which surprises me, since, according to our teachers, the Soviet economy is—and always will be—the best in the world.

In any case, the *militsiya* (Soviet police) were looking for the violin, so the man hid it in the coffin of his stepdaughter, who had just died under mysterious circumstances. The man's wife, however, suspected that her husband had something to do with her daughter's death. After the funeral, the wife went to the police and told them all about it. The *militsiya* men drove to the cemetery, dug up the coffin, opened it, and found the violin where the girl's body was supposed to be. Unfortunately, just as they arrived to arrest the husband, he pulled a Swiss army knife out of his pocket and stabbed his wife to death!

This last detail suddenly sends a pang of pain through my body. The knife. While it is true that hiding sugar in a teakettle is not the same as hiding a valuable violin in the coffin of your stepdaughter, it is also true that there are lots of knives in the camp kitchen. In fact, the last time our detachment was assigned to kitchen duty, I looked them over, and I vividly remember seeing a butcher knife with a long sharp blade and a thick handle. Is that what Grandma is thinking about, too?

Blood abruptly rushes to my head and invisible needles begin pricking my fingers. I push the door open. Grandma is gone and Mom is sitting at the table, writing one of her numerous reports about the sanitary state of the camp.

"Mom, he might kill you!" I blurt out, breathless.

"What are you talking about?" Mom says, lifting her green eyes from the report and fixing them on me.

"You have to call the *militsiya*!" I mumble hurriedly, already picturing the grim scene of Mom's funeral in my head: a cold and rainy day, Tanya and I in black dresses and Dad in a black suit, his hair gone gray overnight.

"Did you eavesdrop?" Mom says, interrupting her funeral scene and giving me a "look"—as if *I* were the one who hid sugar in the teakettle. "You know you shouldn't do that."

"But, Mom, he'll seek revenge!" I say in a melodramatic whisper as I nervously look around to make sure that the cook is not hiding somewhere in Mom's office with the butcher knife raised.

"Oh, stop that nonsense. Nobody is going to kill me," Mom says. Then she puts her pen down and gives me another "look."

"What are you doing here?"

Of course! I'm trying to save her life and all she can say to me is, "What are you doing here?"

I turn around—my hands crossed on my chest and a "soon-you'll-be-very-sorry" expression on my face. I head for the door, while Mom's voice trails behind me, "Don't you say anything to anybody, you hear me?"

For the next several days Mom rushes around the camp as if nothing has happened, while I have trouble sleeping, eating, and even reading. Had my mother recognized the degree of danger and reported the cook to the *militsiya*, she would have taken the burden of worries off my narrow shoulders. Had we had a phone in our Moscow apartment, I would have called my father and asked him for help. Unfortunately, Mom has no intention of contacting the authorities, and my family—like every family I know—has no telephone. So all I can do is try to keep track of the cook's whereabouts. But he spends most of his time in the kitchen and rarely walks around the camp. I, on the other hand, must attend camp activities, therefore I have no time or excuse to hang around the kitchen.

I am not quite sure what I will do if the cook attacks my mother—besides screaming at the top of my lungs and pounding his thick back with my fists. Yet I must do something! For now, I resort to declaring a variety of ailments for which I can be sent to the doctor's office, so I can check up on Mom. This is not technically lying—I am sick with worries. But for Evgenia Vladimirovna, I have to come up with something more substantial, like a bad headache, an upset stomach, or sudden dizziness.

Soon, Evgenia Vladimirovna gets impatient with my poor health and tells my mother to keep me in the infirmary or send me back to Moscow, so she, Evgenia Vladimirovna, will not have to keep track of my comings and goings. A week goes by uneventfully, and I gradually relax and almost forget about the threat to my family. Besides, another exiting event has come up—our detachment is going on an overnight trip to watch the sunrise!

In the evening, contrary to the bugle's plaintive command, "Go to sleep ...," we form a column and, chuckling and giggling, march into the twilight shrouding the woods outside our camp. Evgenia Vladimirovna walks at the head of the column lighting the way, and Victor Gerasimovich, our male *vozhati*, brings up the rear. Both *vozhati* carry large backpacks and we, the campers, rolled-up woolen blankets. In thirty minutes or so, we stop at a hilly clearing with a tall pile of tangled sticks and twigs in the middle. The pile is laid for a bonfire, but in the shimmering moonlight, it looks like a giant anthill or a mound built by mysterious inhabitants of the woods for a ritual sacrifice to the sun god.

Of course, I do not actually believe in the sun god or any other gods. From a very early age, we were taught that religion is, according to Karl Marx, "opium for the masses." None of us knows what opium is, but we all understand that it must be something very bad, like rotten capitalism, wars, exploitation of the working class, or writing curse words on the wall. As for the sun god, that is the stuff of fairytales, like terrible *Baba Yaga* or young *Snegurochka*, daughter of Father Frost, who forgot about her frosty nature while playing with peasant girls and jumped over a flaming bonfire, then melted away and turned into a cirrus cloud.

We campers are not going to jump over the bonfire. We are here to see the birth of a new day. Quickly, we unroll our blankets, spread them around the wood pile, and watch our leaders ignite the fire. At first, a narrow red tongue appears in the middle of the twisted sticks and branches, licking everything within its reach. Then it breaks into several flickering lights that spread in all directions. Soon, a burning mass soars up, stretching its flaming hands toward the dark cosmos.

Sunrise is a night away. We spend the time singing "Soviet Pioneers Always Walk First" and other songs like that, and telling jokes. When the blaze crumbles into the winking embers, we bake potatoes and, tossing the burning-hot vegetables from one hand to the other, marvel at how much tastier they are than those we eat at home or at the camp.

After midnight, the other campers begin falling asleep, wrapped in their blankets like larvae in cocoons. The stars glimmer above us, the air smells of trees, mushrooms, and cooling ashes, and unfamiliar sounds of wildlife fill the woods. For a while, I peer through the dense darkness with a watchful eye, but not for long. The impressions of the day, the fresh air, and my sudden fatigue put me to sleep, too.

It seems that I have just closed my eyes, but when I open them to a loud "Wake up, wake up, look!"—everything around me is changed. The night is rolling up into the misty air, and a bleeding sliver appears on the horizon, pushing the darkness back into the shadows. The sliver grows larger and brighter, and also more rounded—until it rises like a floating bonfire.

We watch silently, engrossed by the grand performance unfolding before our eyes. This is a miracle! Not like the make-believe miracles we have seen in the theater. Here in the woods, we are witnessing a true everyday miracle, ordinary and amazing at the same time.

"Remember, children," Evgenia Vladimirovna's voice breaks the spell. "This is what your country and the Communist Party do for you! You must appreciate that!"

Confused, we look at her and then at each other. Is she talking about the sun or the camp? No matter. It is the time to go back. Suddenly everybody feels weary. Complaining about the cold morning and sleeping on the ground, we slowly pick up our blankets and trudge back.

When our disorderly column enters the camp, the sun is still low on the horizon, large and burning, but we no longer pay attention to it. We cross paths with other detachments walking to the *lineika*, and they greet us cheerfully. We do not pay attention to them, either. Our limbs are heavy, our emotions are spent, and we feel irritable and disheveled. Sleepy, too. At least I am. Everyone around seems to be moving too fast—the camp director is walking hurriedly to his office, both camp nurses are rushing toward the clinic, and the cook's assistant Lida, who's supposed to be in the kitchen, follows them with a large ladle in her hand.

Also, I have trouble focusing my gaze. Who is that man I see by the clinic talking to my mother and grandmother? From a distance, he resembles my father ... Wait! That *is* my father! A sudden burst of energy propels me away from our formation and toward my parents. Why is Dad here? Today is not a visitation day, not even a weekend.

Even before I get close to my parents, I sense that something is wrong. Mom's cheeks are flaming like last night's bonfire and Dad's are the shade of the ashes we left behind this morning.

I hear Grandma's voice, "Natán, calm down. Let's go inside and discuss things there."

"Don't tell me to calm down! She's having affairs and you're covering for her!"

I stop in my tracks. What are they talking about?

"Natán, be reasonable," Mom enters the conversation, her lips trembling. "I'm not having any affairs. Who would I have an affair with around here? With the children?"

"Stop pretending! With your camp director, of course!" Dad cries in a high falsetto, simultaneously pulling a piece of rumpled paper out of his pocket and thrusting it into the women's faces. "I have a letter. I know everything!"

Now Mom's cheeks turn the color of Dad's. "What letter? Who wrote it? Let me see ..."

With her hands shaking, she grabs the rumpled paper and brings it to her eyes, but at that moment Tanya's cry comes from the house, loud and desperate. Mom throws her hands up and the letter drifts to the ground like a giant snowflake.

"Natán, whatever this letter says, it is not true," she says, biting her lips, "Besides, I cannot discuss it right now. I'm working here, and Mother needs to attend to Tanya. Can you understand that?! And people are watching ..."

Mom looks around at the crowd of spectators: her nurses, Lida, and several more people attracted by the unexpected entertainment. Her gaze stops on me.

"Sveta, go back to your detachment, immediately!" she cries—which is the only phrase from this whole scene I fully understand. Then she turns to my father, "Do you see what you're doing to me? What authority can I have in the eyes of my own children? Or the staff? The nurses, the cook ..."

Here, Mom interrupts her tirade and the expression on her face changes—as if she just discovered a cure for cancer or another life-threatening disease. She slowly bends over and picks up the rumpled piece of paper from the ground,

"Let me see that letter again ..."

Despite my attempts to defend my mother, the cook did stab her—not with a butcher's knife, but with a pen—the way Shakespeare's Iago caused Desdemona's death with an ordinary handkerchief. It all started the day I found my mother writing in her clinic. It was not, as I assumed, a report about the sanitary state of the camp, but a letter to my Dad. The cook's wife, a local postal worker, took notice of the address on the envelope, and the rest, as they say, is history.

I never see the end of my parents' confrontation. Someone grabs me by the hand and delivers me back to my barracks, where I join other, already sleeping, sun-gazers. For a short while, I try to I concentrate on what I have just witnessed, but exhaustion and a vague recognition that whatever it is, I can do nothing about it, come over me and I fall into a deep dreamless sleep. When I wake up, the sun is high in the sky and we are getting ready for lunch. I ask Evgenia Vladimirovna if I can visit the clinic, but she gives me a funny look and tells me that I'd better not.

Next time I see my mother, she does not talk about the events of the previous day, nor does she—or Grandma—mention my father's sudden arrival and equally sudden departure. A couple of days later, Olga Fedorova, the girl with a large repertoire of ghost stories, reports to us in the dark that the cook has been reprimanded by the camp leadership for stealing. How does she know that? She eavesdropped on a conversation among detachment leaders—"Let me be struck by lightning if I'm lying!" Are they going to fire the cook and sue him? She does not think so.

Olga Fedorova proves to be right. The cook never gets fired, much less sued. In fact, he gets to keep his job (and more likely continues to steal from children) for another year, until vodka—or divine justice—drowns him in the lake nearby.

As for my mother, she, unlike Desdemona, survives the ordeal, and even adds another responsibility to her already numerous duties—inspecting the kitchen staff's bags before they leave work. She does so until the end of the summer, after which she returns to her regular job and her Moscow Othello—my father.

Soon afterward, I overhear her talking to my Aunt Raya.

"Am I glad to be back! Mother was afraid something would happen to me," Mom says, leaving me guessing whether she refers to the thievery of the camp's staff or to my father.

Next year, I go to the camp again, but Mom does not.

"Too much work," she tells me, when I ask her why.

Summer camp: I am fourth from the right in the third row

CHAPTER EIGHTEEN

THE ELEPHANT

We are visiting Father's older sister on her birthday. The scratched wooden door of her apartment flies open and Aunt Masha herself appears on the threshold.

"Come in, come in. I'm almost done," she says and turns back to the kitchen while my family heads toward the room with a table set for a typical Muscovite feast. I walk at the end of our short column. Another boring gathering with my father's family. Well, at least this does not happen often. For one thing, Father does not get along with his two sisters very well. For another, Father's parents do not pay much attention to Tanya and me, directing all their love toward our three boy cousins.

I have nothing against the cousins, though. It is not their fault. It is just that two of them are much younger than me, and the older one is as dull as his parents. And how could he not be? Nobody among Father's relatives plays a musical instrument or tells jokes, or does anything fun. I do not think they even read books. As for this apartment, there is nothing interesting here either. In fact, if not for its lack of a bookcase, Aunt Masha's apartment would be an exact replica of our own, and also of every other apartment I have ever stepped into—one gloomy room per family with a shared kitchen and bathroom out in the hall.

Wearily, I look around the space stuffed with bulky furniture and papered with faded floral patterns, and my gaze stops on a dark wooden dresser in the corner. The dresser is covered with a white crocheted doily, on top of which I spot something new—seven white elephant figurines, a current Moscow fad. I step closer and look carefully at the figurines crowded in the center of the dresser as though ship-wrecked. The largest elephant is about three inches tall and the smallest is so tiny that only a child with her attention to small details can make out his ears and trunk.

I cannot take my eyes off the elephants. Pale and shiny, they radiate the allure of a faraway country where women wear bright-colored saris, paint red dots on their foreheads, and sing love songs in high tremulous voices; and where men ride elephants, swallow fire, and charm snakes. I know this from a book of Indian tales I read recently. That book was so interesting that I could not put it down. I finished it in bed under my blanket with a flashlight, perspiring from the thrill of the stories and the lack of ventilation.

Behind me, a birthday party goes through its usual stages. The adults—my parents, grandparents, and other relatives—are gathered around the table in the middle of the room, toasting loudly to my aunt's health. Their enthusiasm, fueled by a disarray of bottles, steadily increases, and they pay no attention to anything around them. My sister and cousins are assembled in the opposite corner, where I hear them shout:

"Give it to me!"

"Yeah? Just come and get it!"

"You'd better give it to me *now*!"

I stand by the dresser alone, holding the smallest ivory elephant in my hand. The figurine appears so snug in my palm and so foreign to this room filled with rowdy voices and smells of food and alcohol, that I cannot bring myself to put it back. Instead, I cautiously look around. Nobody is watching me. All are immersed in the excitement of the moment. I slowly close my hand and, almost without thinking, quickly shove the elephant into the pocket of my skirt. Then, with my cheeks burning, I casually walk toward the other children, thinking to myself, "They won't even notice. They don't need it anyway."

At home, I take the elephant to bed and hold it in my sweaty hand while reading under the blanket. When I finally fall asleep, my dreams are inhabited by exotic animals, enticing smells of the jungle, and people speaking strange languages.

The next morning starts with a problem. How can I hide the elephant in a room where nothing is my own and everything is shared by all of us? After a quick appraisal, I put the figurine into my briefcase and go to school.

It is early, and the night's shadows still linger over our neighborhood of identical four-story concrete-block houses, where piles of coal guard the front entrances like giant watchdogs. It is also drizzling, and the wind spits wet needles and leaves into the faces of pedestrians who, with their heads lowered and torsos bent forward, look like a procession of hunchbacks. I walk tall, oblivious to the weather. With me, I carry the best toy I have ever had, a fragment of life as beautiful as pictures in my books and as tempting as the songs of Greek sirens.

The school day drags on: math problems appear on the blackboard, questions and answers hang in the air, and my classmates get up and sit down around me. I am not following any of that—my mind wanders, the dissonant classroom sounds seem muted, and the best I can do is stare at my teacher's heavily painted red lips and hope that she will not ask me a question.

During the breaks, I do not talk to my classmates. I do not even go to the hall but sit in the classroom with my hand reaching inside the briefcase, dreamily caressing the elephant with the tips of my fingers, imagining what I will do with it after school.

When the last bell finally sounds, I spring from my place and dash to the door. As I reach the doorway, a sudden blow on my back from a briefcase interrupts my flight. Instinctively, I strike back, but I miss and drop my case on the floor. On landing, it pops open, and a jumble of papers and text books flies out—along with a little white figurine.

"What's that?" The girl who hit me says, picking up the elephant from the floor.

"Nothing!" I scream and yank it from her before she has a chance to take a good look at the figurine.

At home, I lock myself in the bathroom and try to assess the situation. Clearly, taking the elephant to school was a mistake, but where am I going to keep it? I cannot leave it at home, and I cannot ask anybody to hide it for me. What would I say? I bought it? None of us kids has any money. My parents gave it to me? Then why didn't I leave it in our apartment?

Not knowing what to do, I no longer fantasize about playing with the elephant. I just keep hiding it again and again, several times a day, and every time my parents address me, I gasp for breath.

In the meantime, my aunt notices the loss.

"Did you see the little elephants at your aunt's?" my father asks me one day, looking at me attentively.

"Yes, I did. So what?" I exhale, leaning against the wall, suddenly fatigued.

"She says one of them is missing. You didn't take it, did you?" Father continues.

"Of course not."

The answer comes too quickly, and now it is too late to change anything. If found out, I will be in big trouble. What my punishment might be, I am not sure. Will my parents exile me from the family? Will they send me to prison or reformatory? I am a thief, after all, and that's what happens to thieves in books.

I dread going to bed now. Reading no longer comforts me, and I wake up weeping from nightmares in the middle of the night. At meals, I hardly touch my food, and my mother begins to wonder whether I need to see a doctor. I cannot concentrate in school, and my grades suffer. I cannot even return the elephant without first admitting to stealing it and then lying about it.

Finally, the day comes when I decide to get rid of the figurine. At dusk, I go out, clenching the elephant in one hand and a flashlight in the other. I pass old women gossiping on a bench by the front door, turn the corner, and walk slowly through a narrow alley of cottonwood trees, stopping where the trees border a construction site, empty at this hour. There is no moon, and the narrow rectangles of lighted windows behind the trees are my only beacons.

I peer intensely through the cool darkness, but see nothing except the dark silhouettes of the trees disapprovingly whispering in the light wind. I put the elephant on the ground, turn on the flashlight, and start to dig a hole with a tablespoon that I brought from home. When that is done, I line the hole with a handkerchief, place the innocently glimmering figurine in the middle, fold the ends of the handkerchief over it, and fill the hole with dirt. Then, with tears streaming down my cheeks, I turn off the flashlight, smooth out the ground with both hands, mark the place with a stick, and run home to the lighted windows.

The next day, after school, I hurry back to my secret burial site. Once again, I pass a group of gossiping women and dash around the house and through the tall cottonwood trees. In the daylight the place looks different and, somehow, wrong. Gasping, I look around, trying to spot the stick I left there the night before, and my heart sinks.

By the tree's edge, just where the stick should have been, a huge gaping hole in the ground opens up to my wondering gaze—a motionless bulldozer next to it. For a time, I stand there, unable to move, refusing to accept the obvious—my little treasure has been swallowed by the heartless machine, and all I have left now is ghostly memories and bitter regrets.

When tears begin drying on my face, I turn around and shuffle back home—the briefcase in my hand as heavy as ever. I climb to the fourth floor, unlock the door of our apartment, and … come face to face with Aunt Masha. My aunt's hair is disheveled, her cheeks are wet, and the look on her face is the one of utter confusion and anger. I step back, as scared as I am surprised—does she know what's happened to the elephant?

"Did you notify *militsia* (police)?" my mother says as she comes into view. I shudder. They must be talking about me! They know I stole the elephant and want to put me in prison! The briefcase drops out of my hand with a loud "clunk," drowning my aunt's answer.

"I'm so sorry …" I begin in a trembling voice, but Mother interrupts me, "You stay with Tanya. Somebody broke into Masha's apartment. We need to call *militsia*." After that, they both head down the stairs, and I hear Mother ask my aunt if she has two kopeks to make a phone call.

In an hour or so, Mother comes back alone—Aunt Masha went home accompanied by my father. When he comes home, tired and hungry, I finally find out what has happened. Apparently, Aunt Masha came home early. As she approached her apartment, two men rushed out of it, knocked her over, and ran down the stairs, leaving my aunt lying on the landing. When she finally got up and went in, she found her room in disarray, and the money, which she kept in the upper drawer of the dresser with the elephants, was gone.

What about the elephants?" I wonder aloud, but Father just raises his eyebrows and continues talking to my mother—something about my aunt's neighbors, children, and husband who is still at work and, therefore, has not yet learned the bad news.

The next several days pass in discussion of Masha's bad luck, the advantages of keeping money in the bank, and other stuff I do not care about. Soon, though, these discussions lose their urgency and my parents turn to their own problems.

As for me, with all that commotion, I recover from my loss faster. I even begin to wonder if I should have kept the elephant a little longer—long enough that it would have been safe to return it and say that I had found it somewhere on the street. After all, the other six were stolen, too, and, chances are, somebody will find them someday. I hope it will be me.

CHAPTER NINETEEN

WHITE ROSE

Changes come when you least expect them. For the longest time, I have been asking Mom to get me a kitten, and her answer has always been, "No. We don't have enough space for people, let alone pets. If you want to play, play with Tanya."

It is true that space is at a premium in our small apartment. Still, every summer that we spend outside Moscow I am allowed to keep a pet. Once, we even have a little hedgehog, prickly like a pin-cushion, with short legs, a foxlike muzzle, and two black beads of eyes. Dad and I find the hedgehog while picking mushrooms. He is hiding under the fallen leaves, and, when we approach him, he bristles up and tries to scare us by jumping and sticking out his dark needles with a touch of gray on the ends. After a couple of minutes of that, he curls up into a thorny ball and plays dead. Dad gives me his mushrooms and rolls the hedgehog into his backpack with a stick.

On our way home, the hedgehog shows no signs of life, and I begin to worry that he is truly dead. But when Dad dumps him onto our floor, scratched by the proprietress' cats and generations of summer renters, the hedgehog revives, uncurls, smoothes his sharp needles, and immediately hides under my bed. Despite all my tricks and a little bowl of fresh milk, which Mom places for him in the middle of the floor, he does not leave his new shelter until the room grows dark. Hedgehogs—my father later tells me—are nocturnal animals.

It is fun to have him, anyway. At night, lying in bed, I can hear his muffled footsteps and the rustle of the newspapers that I have pushed under my bed so he can make himself a paper nest. When my eyes get used to the darkness, I can make out his fuzzy shape busily rolling around the floor or lapping milk from a bowl, just like a cat. The hedgehog never lets me hold him in my arms or pat him on his back. Yet I feel disappointed when, one day, he slips out through a half-open door and runs back to the woods and the freedom of the animal world.

Today is a Sunday, which I mark by luxuriating in bed until 9 o'clock and Mom by cooking us a special weekend breakfast. It starts with a large glossy *seledka* (herring) swimming in vinegar and sunflower oil and covered with sliced onions—mashed potatoes on the side. Then comes freshly brewed hot tea and a pile of *blinis* (small pancakes), accompanied by sour cream. The breakfast is almost over when the doorbell rings.

Dad goes to the front door, and I hear two hoarse voices:

"Where do you want it, *khozyain* (boss)?"

"Just give us a minute," Dad says and quickly returns to the room where my mother, sister, and I are sitting around the table—bony remains of herring and smudges of sour cream on our plates.

"Fira, let's clear this corner," Dad says hurriedly to Mom. Then he turns to us: "Sveta, pull your chair to the right. Tanya, step aside and ne *meshaisya pod nogami* (don't get in the way)."

As if performing a battlefield maneuver, we all start moving, while Dad, our commander-in-chief, directs our progress.

"Fira, don't move the bedside table to the left, move it to the right … Sveta, what are you waiting for? Keep moving! Tanya, did you hear what I just said? Step aside!"

I look at my parents, puzzled. What's the matter?

"We got you a present," Mom says, smiling.

"A present? What is it?" I say, and a premonition starts sprouting its tentacles in my stomach, which is filled with herring and sour cream. Surely, this cannot be a kitten. Also, what kind of present needs so much space?

"We bought you a piano!" Dad says. The triumph in his voice is overflowing, and he is looking at me as if he just delivered the very thing I had been begging for every day of my life.

"A piano?! Why? I don't know how to play the piano!"

"We know that. But now you will!"

Oh, no! Once again, I realize that my parents and I live on two different planets, and, to make matters worse, these planets revolve in different solar systems. I have never asked them for a piano. I have asked them for a kitten! *Nobody* in my class plays piano. In fact, nobody in my class plays *anything*, and as far as I'm concerned, I can live without a piano, while a kitten, or at least a bike, would really make me very happy and grateful.

"I hope you appreciate what we're doing for you," I already hear Dad's refrain.

I want to say, "Of course, you never ask me what I want, but I have to be grateful for what you want," but I keep it to myself.

The corner of the room is cleared now, and two men in worn-out padded jackets and cloth caps tilted to the back of their heads appear in the doorway. Wide belts are girdled over the men's shoulders and under the belly of a huge object, which is wrapped in rough brown paper—the inquisitive faces of our neighbors looming behind it. With much grunting and panting, the men drag the object into the room and put it down in the corner. Then they pull out the belts, collect their tip and retreat, leaving behind their burden and the rough smell of *papirosi* (cheap cigarettes) mixed with a tinge of vodka.

Dad tears off the wrapping paper, and my new present reveals itself to my wistful gaze.

"This was the best looking piano in the store, and the sales guy told me it sounds great!" Dad declares, shifting his eyes from Mom to me, to Tanya, and then back to Mom, proudly resting them on her face for at least a minute.

Mom, Tanya, and I stare at the instrument. It does not look like the piano in my school—a black homely contraption with peeling varnish and worn-out keys, yellow like the fingernails of an inveterate smoker. This piano is glowing oak, with a white blossoming rose inlaid on its front panel. The rose looks so real that I find myself inhaling in an attempt to catch its delicate scent, and its petals appear both fragile and damp, as if covered by dew. For once, I have to agree with my father—this is a beauty. In fact, it is so exquisite that the rest of our room, including us, its residents, looks shabby and shrunken.

For some time, everybody is quiet. Then Mom says, to nobody in particular, "I always wanted to play the piano, but … we never had money," and when she lowers her gaze, the ends of her eyelashes sparkle, like grass after a summer rain.

Two weeks later, having passed an exam certifying my sense of rhythm and ability to carry a tune, I find myself enrolled at a music school. I am not enthusiastic about this. For one thing, unlike regular schools, which are numerous and located within walking distance, music schools are rare. My music school is about twenty blocks away from our home, and I have to walk there at least four times a week: twice for my piano lessons, once for lessons in music theory and solfeggio (sight-singing), and once more for choir. Never mind that all of this takes place after my regular classes and leaves me little time for the things I deem important: reading, daydreaming, or hanging around our *dvor*.

While my classmates and neighbors romp in the street, I—a bulky leather folder with music scores in my hand and bitter resentment of the adult world in my chest—walk for forty-five minutes (one way!) to a three-story brick building that radiates the dissonant sounds of various musical instruments from a block away. And, as if this is not bad enough, there are two places on my way there that I dread to go through.

The first is a long, sparsely traveled passage, so narrow and curvy that when I am in it, I do not see people coming from the opposite direction until they stumble into me and scare me to death. And the second place, which comes just after I get through the passage, is a wide and busy road with no pedestrian crossing anywhere in sight. The first couple of times, Mom crosses the road with me, teaching me to be careful and look left and right. Now, I'm on my own—zigzagging through the traffic like a hare chased by a pack of hunting dogs and cursing the day when the piano appeared in our apartment.

This is not to say that I do not like music. I like listening to my grandfather's guitar and even big orchestras on the radio. Yet *playing* music is a different matter. Every time I slide onto the piano bench and raise the keyboard lid—which, to me, looks like the full-toothed mouth of a smiling crocodile—a million things I could be doing instead rush through my mind—like playing with a cat, for one thing!

According to my music teacher Elena Abramovna, a small pudgy woman with dark ringlets of hair jumping about her head in time with her energetic gestures, I need to practice at least one hour a day: twenty minutes of pounding the keyboard with boring gammas, arpeggios, and accords, and forty minutes of studying the little pieces she shows me in school.

To make sure that I do not slack off, Mom winds up a large metallic alarm clock and places it on top of the piano.

"Watch the clock and don't leave before the hour is up," she says.

With a sigh, I strike my fingers on the woefully crying keys in an attempt to imitate Elena Abramovna, but I never get close. My fingers are slow and awkward, and the sounds I elicit from my beautiful piano are choppy and rigid. In fact, the only thing I do well is watching the clock. The strange thing is that, as soon as I approach my instrument, time slows down, seemingly from the sheer act of lifting the piano lid. And no matter how often I raise my impatient eyes to the clock, it remains indifferent to my plight, the way the stars are indifferent to the plight of sailors lost at sea.

After ten minutes of intense clock watching, I furtively look over my shoulder. (The good thing is that most of the time I spend at the piano, I am alone. Even Tanya, who constantly tails me around, leaves the room as soon as I start practicing.) Then I stand up and quickly move the clock's hand five minutes forward, and, feeling guilty excitement, continue practicing for a little longer, until time gets stuck again and I have to push it forward once more. After doing this three or four times, I finally arrive at the end of the hour and leave my prison bench until my next practice.

The catch is that later in the evening I have to move the clock back—otherwise I would have to go to bed earlier, too! That is tricky, because as soon as I finish playing, my whole family pours back into the room, and I have a hard time restoring the universal rhythm of time discretely.

That said, there are two things about my music school that help me tolerate it. First of all, unlike my regular school, most of the kids there are friendly—even the boys! (My only explanation for this is that suffering through hours of boring music exercises suppresses the boys' natural belligerence.) Secondly, being a music student gets me into a movie theater two blocks away from the music school, and I do not have to pay for my ticket at all!

This is how it works. Every Sunday afternoon, several of us perform in the movie theater's lobby before a matinee show. To tell the truth, playing in front of talking and ice-cream-eating strangers is embarrassing and unnerving. Every time I glance at my audience, I get a funny feeling in my stomach, similar to one which the Roman gladiators must have felt when lions poured into the Coliseum. Also, I sometimes spot my "regular" classmates, and they tease me in school the next day. Still, despite fears and embarrassment, my reward is instant—after the performance is over, I just stay on and watch the movie.

Today's music theory class starts with an announcement—next Sunday, we are going to a concert in a big hall named after the famous Russian composer Pyotr Ilyich Tchaikovsky. On a drizzly November day, some twelve of us meet at the music school entrance and, led by our music theory teacher Olga Ivanovna, set off for the concert. I toil along behind our group, grieving about the lost Sunday.

Why do we need to go? Music is all around us as it is! It splashes from the radio and TV, we play it at home, and we listen to *plastinki* (long playing vinyl records) during our music theory classes. Yet none of that, Olga Ivanonva claims, can replace a live concert.

Live? How so? Most of the music we hear or play was written a long time ago by people who have been dead for ages! Yet, if I do not go, I will get a low grade from Olga Ivanovna and a lecture from my parents. Also, I like Olga Ivanovna. She is young and pretty, with light flyaway hair, cute dimples on her resilient cheeks, and hazel eyes that seem to smile even when their owner gives us a good scolding.

The trip is long. First we ride a streetcar. Then we descend into the deep well of a metro station that is lavishly decorated with mosaics depicting male and female *kolhozniki* happily harvesting wheat. We squeeze ourselves into a metro car, and in an hour or so we emerge at the large city square *Mayakovskaya Ploshchad.* We cross the square and finally walk under the monumental columns of the Tchaikovsky Concert Hall.

It is a children's concert, and, despite the dismal fall weather, the large building is overflowing with excitement and voices of kids, all looking their best. We check in our wet coats and street shoes (we brought our best shoes with us in cloth bags) and climb the grand staircase, all the while admiring the light and airy feel of the building, its stately interior columns, and the scintillating chandeliers high above our heads.

Our seats are up in the balcony. From there, I look around. A large, deep auditorium looks like a volcano crater, ringed with seats down to the stage, behind which the tiers of organ pipes spread their silvery wings on the back wall. The lights grow dim, and the audience quiets down. Musicians in black suits walk ceremoniously onto the brightly-lit stage and take their seats. A conductor appears, eliciting a polite wave of applause, and the concert begins.

I recognize most of the music. These are pieces written by well-known Soviet composers: Kabalevsky, Khachaturian, and Prokofiev, all of whom we have studied with Olga Ivanovna in our music theory class. I like most of them, especially Khachaturian's

"Sabre Dance" with its pulsating rhythm and fiery sounds of clinking swords, which, to my surprise, sounds more intense in this hall. Is this because the music is "live"?

I look at Olga Ivanovna sitting next to me, but she is engrossed in the performance and aloof from my gaze. I turn away and glance at the program. The first part of the concert is coming to an end. Soon, there will be an intermission, during which I can dash to the buffet and buy one of those delicious deserts that are only sold in concert halls and theaters. I swallow hard, close the program, and wait for the lights to come on.

I spend the intermission standing in line with other fidgeting dessert lovers. By the time a grumpy waitress, wearing a starched white *kokoshnik* (head-dress) in her permanent-waved hair and a white apron around her immense waistline, hands me a napoleon (a French cream-filled pastry), a loud bell announces the end of the intermission. So, instead of savoring every ounce of the long-awaited treat, I stuff the whole piece into my mouth and rush back, trying to swallow the pastry at one go.

When I get back to my seat—a sweet residue still lingering in my mouth—the lights are already out. I look down. A gleaming black grand piano sits at the center of the stage. In contrast with the big orchestra that was there a short time ago, the grand piano seems lonely, and its open top makes it look like a fantastic black bird with a broken wing. How can this instrument alone fill an auditorium so large? That would be hard even if the concert hall were quiet. As it is, the room is bursting with noises: people are talking, laughing, turning pages of their concert programs, and rustling candy wrappers.

A sense of pity for the strange piano player fills my heart. I know firsthand what it feels like to play before a rowdy crowd that is waiting for the next, more exciting event. I hope that he, like me, will get his reward after the concert.

Uncoordinated clapping cuts through my sympathetic soliloquy as a tall man in a tuxedo walks to the piano, bows to the audience, and takes a seat. He shakes his long dark hair and, for some time, holds his hands above the keyboard, as if not sure what he is there to do. I sigh—this is not a good start.

Finally, with a subtle movement of his wrists, the man drops his hands. His fingers plunge onto the keys, and the piano responds with a melancholy melody—first loudly, then softly. Next comes a high, lonely note and a tremolo, as doleful as the call of migrating birds, and then a waterfall of sorrows washes over the quiet audience.

Sounds fall down as inevitably as rain drops and as burning as tears, and as if an invisible hand were squeezing my throat, I am suddenly choking with grief and my hands are clasped together in a beseeching gesture. Yet simultaneously I feel something sweet spreading inside me—as if a flower is opening in my chest, a blossoming white rose, covered in dew.

My body goes limp and I bend forward toward the brightly lit stage, toward the piano, and toward the dark-headed wizard whose hands glide effortlessly over the keyboard, caressing it, teasing it, making it produce impossible sounds and feelings.

The last passage soars in the air, soft and fleeting, and the pianist raises his hands. Applause erupts like lava and I realize it's over. My breathing is still laborious and, to my embarrassment, my eyes are wet. Also, although the music has stopped, the blossoming flower is still in my chest, and that makes me feel fulfilled and happy. I straighten up in my seat, furtively wipe away the tears, and look up to Olga Ivanovna.

"What was it?"

"Chopin," she says, turning her face away from me. "Live."

By the time I get home, a short November day is gone. Mom and Dad are talking quietly in the kitchen.

"Do you want to eat?" Mom says.

"No, I'm not hungry," I say and tip-toe into the room. Tanya is already asleep, so I do not turn on any lamps but open the window curtain and let in the flickering lights of the city. I unfold my sleeper-chair and, since it is so tight in the room, its head brushes against my piano with a soft bump. I stop my preparations and turn to the piano.

I put my hands on the lid and feel its smooth surface. Then I lift the lid up and, with my hands parallel to each other, silently stroke the keys—first white, then black. My gaze falls on the white rose inlay, which fluoresces dimly in the moonlight. I raise my hands from the keyboard and cover it.

The wooden flower appears hard and cool to touch, not at all like the rose I felt blooming in my chest during the concert. This rose is inanimate and static, and no dew disturbs its light petals. In fact, nothing can ever disturb them or cause them to wilt, as nothing can rustle them or make them smell. And yet, I now know that a piano can do wonders. It can play melodies that will echo in one's head even after it is silent. It can pull a person off her seat and make her feel as if a flower is blooming inside her. It can choke her throat and force her to cry for no reason at all. And it can bewitch her with its magical sounds for the rest of her life.

I look at the clock on top of the piano. Maybe if I don't cheat by moving the clock forward, and I practice for an hour every day, I can play like that, too. I take my hands off the rose and hold them in midair, letting my fingers move through the darkness in time with Chopin's music in my head. Then I slowly close my piano, knowing that I will never look at it the same way again.

I study the piano for several more years—sometimes for an hour a day, sometimes not—and I learn to play better. For my last exam, I play Rachmaninov's "Rhapsody on a Theme by Paganini," and my mother, proud of my achievement, hangs my straight-A music diploma on the wall above my piano.

My graduation night finds me by the piano, too. My gaze is turned to the rose on its front panel, my hands silently caress the keyboard, and my heart aches with the understanding that I will never play any better and the resignation that I will never become a piano wizard. Yet, it suddenly passes through my mind, when I have a family of my own, my daughter might.

I smile and step away from my piano. After all, what does it matter *who* the wizard is? As long as there is one.

CHAPTER TWENTY

THE LESS YOU KNOW, THE BETTER YOU SLEEP

This summer finds my family in a village near the City of Novgorod. The village is a speck in the midst of deep woods, splashed with small clear lakes that reflect the cold-blue northern sky. Not far from the village there is an oil rig where my father works. Many villagers work there, too. They are looking for petroleum, Father tells me. When they find it, the dark liquid, which has been preserved in the depth of the earth for millions of years, will gush from the ground like a fountain, and happy workers will celebrate their victory by showering in its viscous substance.

Once, Father takes me to see the rig. We board a truck and drive through a forest with trees so tall and dense that the morning sunlight cannot penetrate them. The rig stands in the heart of the woods with old pines crowding around it in a circle. It looks nothing like a future fountain, but rather like a giant watch-tower entangled in a web of cables. Inside that tower, a steel pipe moves rhythmically up and down, plunging ruthlessly into the earth with a loud "whoosh" that reminds me of a dentist's drill plunging into the teeth of a defenseless patient. Several husky workers in dirty padded jackets bustle around, and the air smells of heavy labor and machine oil.

Despite my father's enthusiastic anticipation, I see nothing romantic about the rig. Its heavy odor pollutes the air of the forest. Its deafening noise frightens away the wildlife, and its mechanical rhythm seems as merciless and unstoppable as columns of marching soldiers.

"What do we need petroleum for, Dad?" I say when we drive away from the violated ground.

"For many things," Father says. "For cars and trucks. For keeping us warm during the winter. Also, for fighting wars."

Yes, of course. Things often come down to wars—bloody and devastating yet inevitable and, in the case of our country, sacred, like the Russian Revolution and World War II. For what other power could have raised the poor and oppressed citizens of Russia to the never-before-seen heights of prosperity they enjoy now? What other country could (according to our history books) single-handedly repel the Fascist aggressors and bring peace and justice to suffering Europe?

In fact, that is exactly how a well-known war-time song describes it: "A people's war is going on—a *sacred* war." Not to mention that if we had not won that war, I—a Jew—would not even have been born! And while it is true that today some of my countrymen call me a kike, this is a small price to pay for being alive.

My father was not even fifteen when the war started. Yet with all capable adult males drafted into the army, he became an assistant train engineer and delivered ammunition to the front line—sometimes during bombing raids. He learned only too well about danger, hunger, wounds, and shell-shock, and he never spoke about wars casually before. But this day in the woods, he does. He speaks coolly and unemotionally, as if the word "war" were not charged with loss and suffering but is just a word like any other. After all, it has been seventeen years since the war ended, and nothing today excites fear of another disaster.

The Cuban Missile Crisis is less than three months away, but my father does not know that. In fact, almost nobody in the country does—not then and not for many years after the crisis is resolved and filed by historians into the category of terrible things that could have been.

Why are we so oblivious? The reason is simple. We know little about the outside world. Our radio, television, and newspapers—with names like "*Izvestiya*" (The News) and "*Pravda*" (The Truth)—do not exist to deliver the news, but rather to measure it out in small doses or to suppress it altogether. Like a doctor deciding what—and how much—medicine to give to a patient, our government carefully measures and monitors what we should or should not know. The Cuban Missile Crisis, it decides, is not anything the Soviet citizens should be informed about. Which may be a good thing, since according to our proverbial expression: "The less you know, the better you sleep."

As usual in the summers, we huddle together in a rundown rural house, where Mom and Grandma take turns caring for Tanya and me. Dad spends his days—and occasional nights—at the rig, and when he comes home, he smells of lubrication and sweat. On the weekends, he takes me to pick mushrooms.

We get up at sunrise, put on warm jackets and rubber boots, and leave the quiet house—Dad first and I, still half-asleep, behind him. Immediately, the early morning coolness gets under my jacket and wakes me up; I quicken my pace and catch up with my father.

Mushroom hunting is serious business. We use mushrooms to supplement our diet, which is very limited here in the provinces. I have an additional interest in our success, too. I've been trying to persuade Mother to stop feeding us meat—chicken meat that is, since red meat is not available here.

This is my new fixation, which started the day I saw our proprietress walk out of the house with an ax in her hand. She approached a flock of busily feeding chickens, grabbed one of them, and despite its hysterical clucking and thrashing, placed the bird on a block, and brought the ax down on its neck.

The red-combed head fell on the ground, and blood began gushing from the chicken's neck, splashing its white feathers and the woman's hand. And what was *left* of the chicken, blood-stained all over, started running forward! I closed my eyes with my hands and screamed so loudly that Grandma leaped out of the house, grabbed me by the shoulders, and pulled me inside—all the while muttering under her breath about "these city children."

After that, I could not eat chicken for a long time. Even now, I examine every piece of it before I put it into my mouth, to make sure there is no blood on it. So, as I see it, we could replace chicken with mushrooms, which don't bleed. Besides, I like hunting for them.

The woods are a short walk away. We cross a dew-covered field behind the village and enter a dusky kingdom of pine trees covered with moss, fallen pine needles, and low-growing berries. Smells of mold, mushrooms, and wet leaves fill my lungs, and I deepen my breathing. Birds call the roll above our heads, and old trees groan in the morning wind. Best of all, not a soul follows us around—everything here is just for us, waiting to be found.

I am good at mushroom hunting. My eyes explore the ground in search of a round shape the way a pearl-diver explores the bottom of the ocean. The smells of the woods excite me, and the sixth sense of an experienced mushroom hunter keeps me upright even when I miss a step, stumble over an obstacle, or slip in the mud.

I know where they grow, too: bright-orange patches of *lisichki* ("little foxes") cling to pine trees, tall umbrellas of *podberyozoviki* appear under birches, slimy saffron-colored *maslyata* ("buttery mushrooms") are driven to pines and spruces, and the ultimate thrill for any Russian mushroom picker, *belyi* ("white mushrooms"), with their thickset, white stalk, and dark brownish-red caps, favor places where beeches and oaks mingle with pines.

When I spot a fleshy mushroom cap, a low-voltage current seems to flow through my body and happiness fills my pounding heart, as if mushrooms are not inanimate fungi but priceless treasures. Of course, like every treasure hunter, I have my share of disappointments. Some mushrooms are old and crumbly, some are worm-eaten, and some, despite their appealing appearance, are poisonous, and I have to be careful not to bring them home.

Soon, the morning is gone, and before I know it, my basket is full. By the time Dad and I turn home, we have been through the dimness of pines, airy coppices, patches of trembling birches and shivering aspens, and islands of grass speckled with colorful wild flowers. The sun is high, the morning dew has dried out, and the birds are taking an afternoon nap. The pungent smells of warm earth and dried grass replace astringent fragrances of the morning, and grasshoppers jump from under my feet, chirring bitterly about human invasion.

I take off my jacket and tie it around my waist. My hair is covered with pine needles and cobwebs, my hands and arms are scratched by thick brush and stung by nettles, and the heavy basket drags my arm down. Dad carries a backpack.

"Is your basket too heavy for you?" He asks, and I say, "No, I'm fine." Which is not true—I am hot and tired, and the closer we get to the house, the heavier my basket feels. Yet I carry it myself through the open fields, thick woods, and over a wooden bridge behind our house. I carry it because I want everybody at home to gasp and say, "Look! Isn't she an amazing mushroom picker?" Or, better yet, "Isn't she amazing?" After all, I brought them all my treasures, everything I could find, and I wish I could find even more.

Dad opens the gate and lets me in. Mom is in the yard, beating clothes against a washboard.

"Look at you!" She exclaims as her hands fly high in the air splashing me with iridescent soap-bubbles. Then she says, "Now, eat quickly. We need to clean the mushrooms."

As usual, my moment of glory is short-lived, and I now have an afternoon of work ahead of me. The mushrooms need to be carefully examined, sorted, and cleaned of soil and pine needles. Some of them will go into tonight's soup, some will be fried tomorrow, and the best will be marinated or dried.

Weariness penetrates every cell of my body, but, as if reading my mind, Mom gives me a broad smile and says, cheerfully, "You're such an amazing mushroom picker!" And I walk to the house with my head held high.

At the end of October, when Moscow's skies turn heavy and gray, and green cabbage, potatoes, and carrots in our grocery stores begin to mold, Mom opens a jar with marinated *maslyata*. I come home from school, open the door, and walk into a room filled with the tangy smells of spices and wet woods.

The radio is on, babbling away about achievements of Soviet agriculture, a women's volleyball world championship, and, very briefly, about Americans navigating unlawfully somewhere on the high seas. The latter does not sound alarming, nor does it sound any different from what we are used to hearing about capitalist America or any other Western country.

After the bit on America ends, a woman begins talking about a new science-fiction movie *Chelovek-Amfibiya* (*The Amphibian Man*). Nobody is listening. Dad is still at work, and Tanya and Mom are at the dinner table. Tanya lazily picks food from her plate and Mom bends over a large mushroom jar, trying to stab slippery caps with a fork.

"This is a good one," Mom says and pulls out her first catch.

"It's mine, it's mine!" Tanya jumps to her feet.

"No, it's mine. *I* found it!" I exclaim.

"There's enough for everybody," Mom says, placing the mushroom on Tanya's plate.

"That's exactly why she could've waited," I say bitterly and plop onto the chair next to Mom.

Across the table, Tanya grabs the mushroom with her hand and stuffs it into her mouth—delighted to have beaten me to it. I turn away in disgust, but a gasping "Aaah!" sounds behind me and I swivel back—just in time to see Mom diving backwards and landing heavily on the floor. For a moment, I feel paralyzed. Mom looks ridiculous—her mouth is open, her eyes bug out, and she clenches her fork, the way a fisherman clenches a spear with a fish.

Why is she on the floor? Suddenly, it hits me. Because I have pulled her chair from under her! I burst into peals of laughter and jump to my feet. Mom drops her fork with the mushroom and scrambles to her feet, too.

"I didn't mean to pull your chair," I mouth through the convulsions of laughter, but Mom is not listening. Her nostrils are dilated like those of a race horse, her eyes are two balls of fire, and her hair is disheveled like a crazy woman's.

I move backwards toward the door, but Mom cuts me off and reaches for a *venik* (straw-made broom) in the corner of the room. With no way out, I spring around our dinner table, doubling over with laughter, while behind me, Mom stomps her feet, brandishes the broom, and screams, "I'll show you!" At the peak of this turmoil, Tanya, who thinks that we are playing a game, gets up in her chair and shouts—the way sports fans shout in the heat of a contest—"Catch her, Mom, catch her!"

The radio is still on, and between Tanya's excited shouts and Mom's panting and stomping, I hear the theme-song from *The Amphibian Man*—"In my heart, there's only the Sea-Devil, he's the one for me-e-e!"—and I laugh even harder.

The Caribbean crisis is at its peak, and the world hangs on the verge of a nuclear war. Somewhere on the other side of the globe, the American president is contemplating calling Khrushchev, and American children practice hiding under their school desks—"duck and cover" style—while their parents keep their cars filled with gas, in case the whole family has to go into hiding. Yet we, the Soviet people, know nothing about this and casually go about our business, which for my mother and me means running around our dinner table to the melancholy sounds of "The Sea Devil."

As they say, "The less you know, the better you sleep."

CHAPTER TWENTY ONE

CANNED APPLES

Our lesson in World History ends with a description of another horrible event from the past. This time it is the burning of the astronomer Giordano Bruno by the Inquisition. If you ask me, history is one of the most depressing subjects on earth: torture, wars, natural disasters, terrible rulers—not to mention deadly diseases like the plague, cholera, and consumption. Sometimes I wonder if anything good ever happened in the world before the Great Soviet Revolution. After the revolution, according to our teachers and textbooks, things have been getting steadily better—in our country that is—although, unfortunately, not in my class.

I hear "Hey, you!" behind me as I get up from my desk, trying to erase from my mind the image of Giordano Bruno writhing at the stake. "Yes, you! Dintcha hear me?" A push in my back accompanies the words. I stumble and turn around to face a stocky thirteen-year-old girl with straw hair, blue eyes, pale skin, and colorless lips twisted with disdain.

"Who do ya think you are?" She says, her eyes piercing me with the force of a drill. "My mother says there're too many of your kind around. No place to spit without hitting one!"

I glance at her. If there are too many of "us" anywhere on earth, that place surely is not our classroom. Here, I am the only Jew. In fact, outside my extended family, a couple of mother's friends, our neighbors from the third floor and their daughter Mila, who is two years older than me, I do not know anybody else who is Jewish. My classmate, on the other hand, is surrounded by a large group of "them," all thoroughly enjoying the unexpected spectacle that breaks the monotony of the school day.

This is not the first time Lena Popova has singled me out. She hates me. But why? I never speak to her first and never talk about her with anybody but Mila. Still, every time Lena Popova finds herself near me, she "accidentally" pushes me into the wall or kicks my briefcase so hard that it flies open, spitting out my books and notes, or she says something hateful, like now.

"You, kike!" Lena Popova gives me another look of disdain, turns around, and leaves the classroom—a string of supporters slithering behind her. I stay still. My cheeks burn with humiliation. Is she mad at me because I got an A in the class? She could've studied the lesson, too. And I wasn't the only one who knew the answers. Why didn't she lash out at the others? Well, I know why. They are not "kikes."

I take several deep breaths, but tears begin to fill my eyes. Why do I have to go to this horrible school at all? I'm already twelve. I can study at home. In fact, the only thing I would miss here is our drawing class. I like drawing, and I like our teacher Vladimir Alekseevich, who brings wooden pyramids and papier-mâché fruit and vases to class and lets us draw them. When I first started, I drew triangles for the pyramids and circles for the apples and vases, and they appeared abstract and lifeless. But then Vladimir Alekseevich showed me how to draw light and shadow, so my drawings would no longer look weightless and flat but three-dimensional and life-like.

I rub my eyes with my fists. There is nobody to complain to, neither in school nor at home. Father is always out of town. As for Mother, she would give me her usual, "Don't pay attention. Look at Mila, she never does."

Easy for Mother to say. Mila is very pretty: tall, with a waterfall of dark wavy hair, huge hazel eyes, and legs so long that when she walks, she looks like a ballerina fluttering on the points of her dancing shoes. Even Mila's nose, which appears a little large in profile, does not spoil her, but makes her look distinctive—just like the famous Soviet poet Anna Achmatova. The boys in Mila's class adore her, so nobody dares to call her names. As for me, I'm ugly.

The worst thing about me is my nose. It is long and protruding—a typical Jewish nose that I inherited from my father. Mother's nose, on the other hand, looks normal. In fact, her nose is so normal that she does not look Jewish at all, and her factory patients tell her anti-Semitic jokes and complain about the global domination of Jews: "Those kikes took over all the good places, so true Russians don't have anywhere to go!" Mother, whose miserable salary is often smaller than the salaries of her "true" Russian patients, only nods and says, "Take these pills twice a day and get a lot of rest."

The bell must have sounded, for my classmates begin pouring back into the classroom, laughing and talking as if nothing has happened. The last to enter is our Russian Literature teacher Marina Petrovna.

"Why are you standing here? Didn't you hear the bell?" she says on finding me standing in front of the teacher's table.

"I'm sorry," I say, sniffling and rubbing my eyes with both hands. Marina Petrovna eyes me suspiciously, "Are you sick? If not, you're interrupting the class. Go and sit down. I'll talk to you later."

She puts her things on the teacher's desk and her briefcase on the chair next to it, and slowly turns her gaunt face right and left, making sure that all eyes are turned to her and all minds are emptied of anything that is not related to Russian literature.

"Today, we'll talk about poetry," she announces in a stern voice, apparently satisfied with the state of the class. Then she picks up a piece of chalk and writes on the blackboard, "Great Russian poet Alexander Sergeevich Pushkin."

We open our textbooks and start discordant chanting:

> "I like May's thunderstorm the most,
> It flies in quickly from up high,
> And rumbles frolicking and gaily,
> And playful in the cobalt sky …"

"What's the matter with you?" Marina Petrovna says, her eyebrows taking on the shape of checkmarks. The lesson has ended and Marina Petrovna and I are alone in the classroom. She sits at the teacher's table, and I stand in front of her.

"Nothing," I mumble, looking at Marina Petrovna's brown shoes, hidden underneath the teacher's chair—worn but perfectly polished.

"Then you disregard class discipline," Marina Petrovna says—her eyes directed at me like two rapiers. "I won't allow that in my class!"

I blink. "I didn't mean to disregard discipline. It's just ... because ... because of Lena Popova ... She called me names," I mumble, still studying the teacher's brown shoes.

"What names?"

"She called me a kike," I whisper.

Marina Petrovna winces and lowers her gaze. She does not like it, I can tell. After all, she is our head teacher. She tells us about the poor workers of the world, how they need to act together and demonstrate their united front to the vultures of capitalism, and how our country is always ready to help suffering and oppressed people everywhere.

But am I not suffering? Don't *I* need help and support? Of course, Marina Petrovna will help me! How come it never occurred to me to confide in her?! The tightness in my chest begins receding, and I straighten up and look at my teacher.

Marina Petrovna bites her narrow lower lip, and a pen in her hand begins drawing circles, one inside the other, until she ends with a tiny dot. Then she puts the pen down and says, looking above my head, "You must've misunderstood."

"No, no!" I protest. "Everybody heard it. You can ask them!"

"I'm telling you, you misunderstood!" Sharp notes punctuate Marina Petrovna's voice, and her eyes are fixed on the ceiling. "I'll talk to her tomorrow and you'll make friends. Is that clear?" Then, with one swift motion, Marina Petrovna picks up her briefcase and hurries to the door.

"Yes, Marina Petrovna," I exhale into her broad back.

"Mom, I'm sick," I announce as soon as I open my eyes next morning and see Mother waking up my little sister.

"What's the matter? Do you have a fever?"

Fever is not easy to fake. I have tried many times, but it has never worked. Mom does not even look at the thermometer, which I rub and shake on the sly until the column of mercury creeps above normal. Instead, she puts her hand on my forehead and, in a split second, concludes: "You're fine. Go to school."

I clear my throat and cough, loudly. Then, for a good measure, I pound myself on the chest.

"Have some water," Mom says.

"Sveta, have some wa-a-ter!" Tanya echoes, happily.

"I have a headache," I say.

"Everybody has a headache sometimes," Mom says, putting a dress over my sister's head.

"Every-body-has-a-head-ache-some-times!" my sister sing-songs in delight.

"I have a headache *now*!"

We have repeated this same scene too many times. True or false, Mom never wants to hear that I am sick. Probably because of Tanya—who is sick a lot!—and also because Mom, a doctor, is "sick" of sick people at work. Which cannot be helped, since seeing sick people is, after all, her profession.

Mom does not even look at me. "It means that you're alive. The only people who don't have aches and pains are the dead."

"Dead-dead-dead, Sveta-is-dead!" my sister carries on.

"Tanya, put on your shoes. Hurry!" Mom says and turns to me, "I don't have time for this. Stop pretending and go to school!"

"I'm not pre…" But Mom is already out the door—my singing sister behind her.

I sigh. Being dead would not be so bad today. In fact, if I were dead, I would not have to go to school, and I would not have to see Lena Popova ever again. Yet since I am alive, I get up and start putting on my school uniform.

The day is uneventful. The teachers do not ask me any questions, and Lena Popova does not seem to pay attention to me either. Yet after class, I run into her at the school entrance. She is standing there alone, as if waiting for someone. I keep on walking.

"Hey, you, stop!" I hear behind me. Reluctantly, I turn and look. Lena Popova's face is blank, and her eyes are screwed up so tightly that I can hardly see her pupils, as if she is trying to take in as little of me as possible.

"Marina Petrovna said I shouldn't call ya a kike in school. She said Jews can be good people, too," Lena Popova says.

I inhale deeply, but say nothing.

"She said we must make friends, but … if you don't wanna," Lena Popova pauses and opens her eyes a little wider, "It's fine with me."

I clasp my briefcase to my stomach. My adversary obviously has no regrets, nor does she sound apologetic.

"I need to go home now. Maybe we'll talk tomorrow," I say, moving sideways from Lena Popova and her "friendship" until my back rests against the school wall.

"Who's home?" Lena Popova says, watching me the way a butterfly collector watches a new specimen while planning to pin it onto her mounting board.

"Nobody."

"Really?" Lena Popova's eyes flicker with sudden interest. "I'll go with ya then."

I clench my teeth. What can I say? I give in to my fate and trudge home with Lena Popova by my side.

"What's here to eat?" Lena Popova looks around our communal kitchen and walks straight to our neighbors' refrigerator.

She has already examined our room: a sleeper-chair for me, a small bed for Tanya, a sofa for my parents, a wardrobe, a large bookcase, a dining table, and my piano—a cheap reproduction of a famous Russian landscape painting hanging above it. Lena Popova is not amused by any of this, as if everything in our room is exactly as she imagined it to be. She quickly closes the door and heads to the kitchen.

"*This* is our refrigerator," I say, pulling the heavy refrigerator door open and getting out my dinner: a bowl of *shchi* (green cabbage soup) with a piece of meat peeking from under its yellowish greasy surface. "I don't like *shchi.* You can have it. I'll flush it down the toilet anyway."

"You'll flush it down the toilet??? Why? Are ya stupid or somethin'?" Lena Popova says. I bite my lower lip and swallow, hard, "I just told you. I don't like it."

"That's why yer so skinny," Lena Popova says, twisting her mouth and reaching for the bowl. "Where're the matches?"

She finishes the soup standing by the stove, wipes her mouth with both hands, and looks at me.

"What else?"

"There're canned apples up there, but the jar is heavy," I say and point to a wooden shelf above our kitchen table, which holds the preserves Mom made to last us through the winter and into the spring: jars with wrinkled tomatoes, burgundy-colored jams, and a large jar with pale-green apples sunk in colorless liquid.

"Good," Lena Popova says and, without taking off her shoes, climbs onto a chair and comes face to face with one of my drawings—a vase with red and yellow tulips that my Father brought back from a business trip to Turkmenistan, a land where snow is rare and spring is a month or two ahead of ours.

Lena Popova turns to me, "Yours? I hate drawing. Bo-o-ring." Then she reaches for the jar with the apples. "What are ya starin' at? Hold it!" she orders, and together—Lena Popova gripping the jar by the neck and I holding the bottom—we lower the jar onto the kitchen table.

Lena Popova pries the jar open and reaches for an apple. "Hm, tasty," she says biting into it. "My mother don't cook much. Just drinks."

What about your father?—I open my mouth to ask, but I do not. Chances are Lena Popova's father is an alcoholic. I may have even seen him passed out on the streets of our neighborhood.

Drunks are common around here. People just walk around them the way they walk around puddles on the sidewalk. My mother often stops and says to my father, "Wait, Natán. What if he's having a heart attack?" To which Father invariably replies, "What are you talking about? He's drunk, that's all. Let's go."

One by one, apples disappear inside Lena Popova's mouth, and she reaches deeper and deeper inside the jar. Finally, she pulls out the last four apples, looks at them, and puts one back.

"I need to go now. I'll take several with me. See you tomorrow."

After she leaves, I take the last apple and bite into it, too. It *is* tasty—I think to myself.

Next day, in school, Marina Petrovna talks more about poetry, and we recite more of Pushkin's verse. The teacher never looks at me and, to my relief, Lena Popova ignores me, too. When the last bell sounds, I grab my briefcase and rush to the door, but a familiar voice stops me: "Hey, do you wanna walk together?"

No!—I feel like shouting into Lena Popova's face. Instead, I lower my gaze and mumble, "Whatever."

It is early May. Snow is long gone, but the streets are wet from a thunderstorm that is still rumbling in the distance. The sun illuminates patches of fresh grass, which sprout here and there. The wind carries sweet after-rain smells, and the birds chirrup in the cottonwood trees. We walk silently—not bitter enemies and not friends, but prisoners chained together by misfortune and chance.

At home, Lena Popova hurriedly eats my *shchi*, slurping like my little sister. Then she looks at me,

"Do ya have more apples?"

"No, that was the last jar."

This is true, but Lena Popova does not believe me. "Don't be a greedy kike," she says.

A hot lump rises in my throat. "I said, the apples are gone!"

Lena Popova screws up her eyes, "You'd better find where they've gone to or I'll tell yer mama that ya flush your *shchi* down the toilet."

Her statement takes me aback, but I quickly recover, "You won't! You don't even know my mother!"

"I don't hafta. I'll just sit here and wait for her to come home," Lena Popova says, positioning herself firmly on the kitchen chair and crossing her arms on her chest.

My heart skips a beat. Throwing away food is an enormous offense. First of all, food is hard to come by, even simple things like milk and eggs, not to mention meat. And the money—we never have much—and the time Mother spent cooking. She will never forgive me. As for my father …

"Please, go," I say, my throat sandpaper dry.

"Why should I? I like it here," Lena Popova says, and wicked exultation illuminates her colorless face. "You Jews have it good! Soups, tulips, pianos, pictures."

Here, she uncrosses her arms, stretches her right hand, and pulls down my drawing of Turkmenistan tulips. The top of the drawing tears in the middle.

"Oops," Lena Popova says and, looking straight into my eyes, tears the damaged page in half—the yellow flowers in a half-vase on one side and the red ones on the other. She drops the piece with the yellow tulips to the floor and brings the other piece to my face.

I stop breathing. The red flowers seem paler without their yellow counterparts, and they look vulnerable in the half-torn vase. Lena Popova twists her mouth into a satisfied smile and, holding the paper above the kitchen table, tears the piece into halves, then the halves into quarters, and so on—until the tulips turn into tiny pieces of paper. Lena Popova gathers the pieces with both hands, emits another "Oops," and lets them all drop.

Tiny bits flutter to the floor like fall leaves. Lena Popova looks around—How can I do more damage?—but the sound of the opening front door spooks her.

"Who's that? Your mother?" She says, suddenly shrinking, her expression lusterless.

"No," I begin, my throat still parched, "It's too early for her. Probably our neighbors …"

There I stop. How could I have been so stupid? She was just bluffing! She would never say anything to my mother. For one thing, she would have to explain how she happened to be in our apartment and what she said to me in class—which, it suddenly occurs to me, she would be afraid to repeat to an adult. As for my destroyed picture, she is just jealous! Of course she is. She never gets decent grades for her drawings, and Vladimir Alekseevich, our teacher, never smiles at her and never stops at her desk, the way he stops at mine.

And—as if an invisible wizard is whispering into my ear—I realize that Lena Petrova does not hate *me*. Or rather, she does not hate me for who I am, but for the *life* I have: the dinners waiting for me at home, the books in our bookcase, and the piano with the picture above it. She hates me for my obligatory "how I spent my summer" essays, in which I write about swimming in a lake or about the hedgehog my father and I brought home from the woods. Lena Popova has nothing like that, nothing but alcoholic parents and habitual abuse.

I look at Lena Popova without fear, almost without anger. She is mean, for sure, but even more so, she is miserable.

"Stay. If you want to."

She stares at me, "Ain't ya afraid what your mama will do to ya?"

"You won't tell her," I say. "And even if you do … Well, I shouldn't have done it. As for the drawing …"

I look at the kitchen floor, covered with the torn fragments of a Turkmenistani spring, and something stubborn begins growing in my chest: a power I never knew was there—an innate strength similar to that which makes grass grow through pavement and birds migrate to the other side of the world.

"I can always draw another one," I say, enjoying the ease with which my words roll off my tongue. "I can draw lots of them. Flowers or whatever."

Lena Popova clenches her fists until her knuckles turn white; but, gazing straight into her eyes, I say, "I know why you hate me, but it's not *my* fault."

Lena Popova grabs her briefcase. "You, kike," she spits out in a quavering voice and springs to the door, almost knocking down our neighbor Klavdia Petrovna. In a moment, I hear the sounds of her feet clattering down the stone staircase. I feel calm, very calm—calmer than I have ever been. And sad, too.

When Mother and Tanya come home, I summon all my courage and say, in one breath, "Mom, there's something I have to tell you. I know you'll be angry, but I don't eat your *shchi*. I flush it down the toilet."

My punishment is severe. I stay at home after school for two weeks: "No playing outside and absolutely no books!" I spend more time with my little sister than I ever thought possible, although Tanya's only response to it is an utter lack of appreciation and—once—open hostility, which she expresses by throwing her heavy toy iron at me. The iron scratches my left arm deeply, and for the rest of my "sentence," I wear a bandage.

On top of that, I have to endure Father's lectures about children who do not understand that money—and food, for that matter—do not grow on trees. I also have to listen to Mom's numerous laments: "How could you do that? How could you throw away food that I spend hours getting and cooking? How could you be so ungrateful?!"

Gradually, though, my parents calm down and—with some exceptions—life settles into its usual channel. The exceptions are good, though. Lena Popova ignores me, and Mother no longer leaves me dinners in the refrigerator. When I come home from school, I am allowed to make myself a jam sandwich.

Other things do not change: I still have to babysit my sister, I still have to eat food I dislike, and, of course, I am still Jewish. But I do not complain too much. There are worse lives.

CHAPTER TWENTY TWO

ICE PATCH

Clumsy and fat, Naúm must have resigned himself to being mocked. He never shouts to his tormentors, "*Sam duràck!*" (You're stupid yourself!), the way I often do. He never tries to fight back (nor would he be able to) and never calls his parents for help. All he does when things get bad for him is lower his head with his oily black curls, hide his squinting gaze, purse his pudgy lips, and retreat to the front door of his apartment house, the way a wounded animal retreats to its burrow. And, of course, there is always a kid who comes after him with taunts like, "Look at that sniveler! Is he crying or is it his fat dripping?"

Naúm and I live in different sections of the same concrete building, which is adorned with a tall column of smoke in the winter and red Soviet flags during government holidays. We are the same age, and we go to the same school, but since I went a year early, we are in different grades. I only glance at him during intervals between classes, and sometimes on my way home, I see his stooped figure in front of me—in which case I stop and wait until the distance between us insures no possibility of contact. And if our eyes meet, I hurriedly avert my gaze because Naúm seems to look at me with the grieved expression of a sick old man asking for help, although it is hard to read the expression of someone whose eyes point in different directions.

Naúm's parents never do anything to help him either, and I suspect they do not even know about the abuse he endures in our neighborhood. Of course, his parents, especially his mother, are partly responsible for his trouble. For one thing, Naúm's mother stands out too much. Her dark eyes bulge, her lips are pudgy and brightly painted, and her dresses cling too tightly to her cello-shaped body. Also, according to local gossip, Naúm's mother has been seen at night leaning bare-bosomed out of her third floor window.

Ira, the girl who lives on the floor above us, told me this in a giggling whisper, her pupils dilating to the size of buttons. Ira is the only girl in our house I consider my friend. She is everything I myself yearn to be. She has a small straight nose and flawless pale skin. Her strawberry-blond hair is braided into a thick tress, long enough to be thrown over her shoulder and reach to her waist. She is well developed, and in the locker room where we change before our PE lessons, Ira is one of three girls who already wears a white cotton bra—of a size I can only dream about. (The rest of us wear a *lifchik*, a short cotton vest whose purpose is to hold up our misshapen cotton stockings.) Most importantly, Ira already has her periods, which she discusses with me in great detail every time they take place. In short, next to Ira, I look like a spindly, shivering aspen growing alongside a stately fir tree.

The only thing that prevents Ira from being popular is her parents. In our neighborhood, where everyone knows everything about everybody else, her parents remain an enigma. For one thing, they are foreigners, which is a rare thing in Moscow during the 1960s. Her mother is Finnish and her father is Polish. Both of them ended up in the Soviet Union after the last war, yet nobody knows how this happened. Different explanations have been suggested. One of them is that Ira's father was a Polish POW who got caught on the wrong side and spent several years in a Siberian labor camp. As for her mother, gossip has it that she was taken hostage during a secret military operation somewhere on the Soviet-Finnish border.

Whatever the case, both of Ira's parents speak with an accent, and they rarely talk to the house residents. This frustrates everyone beyond measure, since inquisitive neighbors have no chance to ask an "innocent" question or catch Ira's parents contradicting themselves. The common opinion is that Ira's parents must be hiding a skeleton in their closet, so their daughter has no chance of being popular around here. Still, in our local hierarchy, Ira's status is much higher than mine, and I am lucky to have her as a friend.

When Ira told me about Naúm's mother leaning out the window bare-chested, I did not believe her. Nobody walks around the house naked, especially in a northern city like Moscow. Besides, what was Naúm's mother looking at? There is nothing to see from her window but piles of coal, noisy children, and gossiping women.

I did not argue with Ira, though. Why would I? She was not gossiping about *my* mother. Besides, I do not really know this woman. Once in a while, Mother talks to her in front of our house. Yet our families have never gotten together, and there are only two things about her I am sure of: one—she is Jewish, and two—she is married for the second time, to an Armenian.

I know nothing about her first husband, Naúm's father. As for Naúm's stepfather—a smallish, scrawny, balding man—he works as a manager in a grocery store, and, according to Ira, he has been seen coming home with full bags, the contents of which are anybody's guess. (And there have been many people guessing!) In a city of shortages and suspicion, that fact alone would be enough for the neighbors to hate Naúm and his family.

But even without his parents, Naúm would be a lost cause. Every time I see his stout body propped against the front door—his cheeks trembling like gelatin and his squinting eyes clouded with tears—I cannot help but feel angry with him. "Do something!" I want to shout into Naúm's unfocused face. Be a *mensch*! Kick them! Fight back! Don't let them spit on you!

Of course, I never say anything. Why should I? He is not my brother or my friend, not even my close neighbor. So I just shrug and turn around, as disgusted with Naúm as with his tormentors.

It is Sunday afternoon. I sit in a chair, reading a story about the Italian pilot and engineer Umberto Nobile and his expedition to the North Pole on the dirigible Italia. Due to a storm, the dirigible crashed. Nobile and eight of his crew survived, but they were stranded on the ice.

Outside, the sky is obscured by milky clouds, and a strong wind is wailing its ominous song. Snow, which has been falling almost every day, surrounds our house the way icebergs must have surrounded the desperate group of people stranded at the North Pole in 1928. I have never been to a place colder than Moscow, and even though it is my home, I never like it when days become short and long winter nights set in, when no matter how many layers of clothes I put on before going outside, I am soon freezing and my nose turns red. Yet it is a different matter to *read* about the frigid vastness of the North Pole while curled up next to the warm ribs of a gurgling radiator.

The story is so engrossing that I feel as if I am part of it. In my mind's eye, I see the injured Nobile and his men set up their red tent, and I watch the weary radio operator send hopeless messages into the frozen nothingness. I despair that the search is going in the wrong direction, and I follow the treacherous journey of the Swedish meteorologist Malmgren and his Italian companions Mariano and Zappi, who dare to walk to the mainland over ice. Most of all, I worry about Roald Amundsen, a famous polar explorer himself, who decides to come to Nobile's rescue and takes off in a French seaplane.

At this heart-wrenching moment, Mother enters the room. "Ira's here," she says, picking up her black vinyl purse and snapping its metal catch with a sound as loud and sinister as the sound of ice cracking under the North Pole castaways' feet. I jump in my chair, while Mom continues, "She's going for a walk. Go with her. Tanya and I have shopping to do."

With my heart pounding, I slowly withdraw from the unforgiving North Pole, put my book on the windowsill above the radiator, and look out the double glass window, insulated from the cold with strips of cotton tucked into the cracks between the window panes.

The world that stretches outside our window is as white as the one I have just left. But unlike the imaginary world, the real one offers nothing worth exploring, nothing that can match the drama unraveling on the pages of my book, and therefore, nothing worth interrupting my reading for.

"No," I say, "I want to stay at home."

"Enough reading," Mom says, not listening to me but counting the money in a small wallet she has fished out of her purse. "Go, go. Look at yourself—pale like death. You need fresh air. Hurry. Ira's waiting."

By the time Ira and I step outside, the snow has stopped and the whiteout that has shrouded the city for weeks begins to recede, uncovering a washed-out blue sky. Immediately, frigid air fills my lungs, and I burst into coughing. Clearly, it is too cold for a leisurely walk.

"What are we going to do?" I say, annoyed with my friend for dragging me out of the warm house and away from my book.

Ira, who is methodically kicking the base of a tall snowdrift with the toe of her gray boot, does not seem to notice. "We could skate," she says, and her eyes light up with eager anticipation that makes her pupils appear darker and her irises lighter.

I sigh. Last year, for Ira's birthday, her parents bought her a pair of fancy figure skates, snow-white and sturdy, with shiny blades and notched toes. Since then, Ira is ready to go skating any time the temperature falls below freezing. She was a good skater even before, but on her new skates, tightly wrapped around her strong ankles, she is really great. She glides across the ice with the speed of a jet plane, spins around, folding and unfolding her arms like a whirling dervish, and jumps almost like a professional figure skater. She can even do *pistolet* (a Shoot-the-Duck move), for which she squats down, bends her skating knee, and extends her free leg in front of her body—a position I would not be able to sustain even without skates.

"Too cold," I say defiantly. "Too far, too."

Ira looks in the direction of a skating rink, as if evaluating the validity of my statement, and a shadow of disappointment dims her eyes. A couple of minutes pass quietly, until the snowdrift that Ira has been kicking with her boot collapses and a small blizzard splashes our faces. This, apparently, gives Ira another idea. "There's an ice patch behind the house," she says, wiping her eyes and starting on another snowdrift. "We can slide there."

I sigh again. What can I do? I cannot go back home. Besides, invisible frosty needles have already begun to pierce my toes and bite my cheeks, prompting me to get moving.

"Okay," I say, and we start walking.

The ice patch—about fifteen feet long and two feet wide—was built the day before. This is easy to do: bring several buckets of water from the house, pour them onto the snow, and smooth the surface. With the temperatures nearing minus 20° Celsius (minus 4°F), wet snow soon turns into ice and—*voila*!—a perfect strip of ice is ready for sliding.

Even before Ira and I turn around the corner, we hear shouting and laughter.

"I can do better than that!" A high girlish voice soars in the freezing air.

"You wish!" A breaking teenage tenor responds. "Not a chance!"

A "who-can-slide-farthest" competition is at its zenith. A group of neighborhood children forms a line on one side of the icy stretch, from where they take turns gliding down the path while balancing with their mittened hands.

Igor Shubnikov, a stocky fifteen-year-old keeps order and calls out results. He sounds authoritative, the way a professional referee or a Communist Party leader would. In fact, Igor *is* our self-appointed leader. Being older and stronger than most of us, he not only passes judgment, but he also sets the rules by which judgment is dispensed, and no neighborhood kid has ever had the nerve to question him.

At Igor's silent nod, Ira and I take our places at the end of the line. Ira slides first. She does very well, covering most of the sparkling ribbon and stopping about two feet short of Igor's own record, which is marked by a piece of coal brought from the pile in front of our house. I take a run next, throwing myself forward as hard as I can, stretching my hands out—longing to reach the opposite side.

My flight ends just past the middle of the slippery path. Somebody cheers, somebody laughs, but I pay no attention to either one. It feels good to glide through the frigid air, inhaling its prickly freshness and basking in the weak winter sun. Let's do it again! And Ira and I get back in line, jumping with impatience, cheering successes, and good-naturedly laughing at failures.

After a while, low clouds raid the sky, robbing us of our enthusiasm. Everybody suddenly feels tired, and the mood of the crowd starts changing. Peals of laughter subside, and shouting becomes more competitive and insulting.

"You pushed me!"

"No, I didn't!"

"Yes, you did!"

"You, asshole, go home and complain to your Mama!"

"Coming from another asshole …"

Having tried a dozen times, I stop, catching my breath. I have reached my limit, and sliding has ceased to be fun. Other children begin quitting, too. Now the contest dwindles down to just three participants: Igor, Ira, and Lida, a pale skinny girl with a face whose every feature is disproportionate to the rest—her forehead is too narrow, her mouth too large, and her nose too wide.

At first, we continue to cheer them on, but soon the expressions of the remaining competitors harden and they begin to throw hateful looks at each other.

"Don't cheat, you *zarazi*!" Igor suddenly explodes at the girls who are slowly approaching his marks. "I see whatcher doin'. Start from the edge!"

"Don't cheat, yourself!" Ira hollers back. "You didn't slide that far either. Bring your mark closer!"

"What did you say, bitch? Did you say I cheat?!" Igor moves toward Ira. His blue eyes turn purple with rage, and a black woolen mitten flies off his right hand like a rock launched from a slingshot. "You wanna taste this?" He raises his clenched fist to Ira's face.

Goose-flesh creeps down my spine. "Ira, let's go," I shout. "Your mother just called you. We need to go home!"

Whether Ira hears me or not, she does not budge. "Just try!" she screams at the boy in front of her and stretches her neck like Joan of Arc challenging her inquisitors.

"Ira …" I try again, but my voice hangs in the freezing silence, too hoarse to calm the adversaries and too soft to bring help.

Now Igor's fist is just inches away from Ira's head, but instead of dodging, she tosses her head even higher. Her red woolen hat falls off, exposing strawberry blonde untwined hair, which, freed from the confinement, falls down and frames Ira's small face with her flaming cheeks and eyes the color of a tempest sky.

"She's so pretty," suddenly goes through my head. I shift my gaze to Igor, who is rising above Ira with his fist poised in midair, and, with rare certainty, I know that he sees it, too: she is beautiful, and he cannot bring his fist down on her.

For a long moment, everything stands still. Then, as if waking up from a spell, Igor makes a slow and awkward backward movement and, still glaring at Ira, spits on the snow—his saliva burning a narrow hole at her feet. Then, he turns around and heads toward our building.

Nobody speaks, just a vague sound tumbles away, as if everybody exhales at the same time or a sudden gust of wind blows over.

When the silent crowd of children starts scattering, I pull Ira by the sleeve, "Let's go."

She does not move, but the dark clouds in her eyes disappear, replaced with tears. I pull again. "Are you crazy?" I say, also sniffling. "He could've killed you!"

"I know," she says blowing her nose, "I …

"Hey, you!" Igor's husky voice slices through our conversation.

"Yeah, you, fat ass! Come here, slide with us!"

I strain my eyes in the direction of our building and see Naúm.

"Oh no, not him!" goes through my head. He can't slide, just as he can't run or jump, or do a thousand other things that boys enjoy doing. Everybody knows that.

Once again, tension heats up the freezing air. Only this time, Igor's rage is directed not at pretty Ira but at the fat and ridiculous boy, who, to my dismay, starts shuffling through the deep snow towards us.

"Don't come here, you idiot! Go home!" I want to shout. But I keep quiet, as does Ira and several more kids who have not yet left the icy battlefield.

In a minute or so, Naúm appears in front of us in a new, good quality coat with a dyed rabbit collar and matching fur hat with dangling ear-flaps. Also new are his sparkling eyeglasses, which make his eyes look large and vulnerable. Had Naúm not been a neighborhood scapegoat already, these glasses alone—a mark of "wimpy intelligentsia"—would make him a target. But coupled with the perfect outfit that none of the other neighborhood parents can afford—least of all Igor's alcoholic father and hospital-janitor mother—Naúm's appearance is an open invitation to bullying.

"You, *ochkarick* (four eyes)," Igor begins, "Go ahead, try!"

"He can't," I whisper to Ira, careful not to attract Igor's attention. She glances at me, "I know."

Once again, it becomes very quiet.

"So? Are ya goin' to try or should I kick your fat ass?" Igor growls.

Naúm makes several small steps back and then clumsily runs forward, attempting to gain speed. Yet just before he reaches the slippery edge, he slows himself down and instead of gliding, he skids for hardly a yard and stops, puffing.

"Try again," Igor says.

"I don't want to," Naúm mumbles under his breath and hunches his shoulders, so the top of his collar and the flaps of his hat blend together.

"Sure you do. It's fun. Try again," Igor bellows.

Naúm moves backwards. "I'd better go home."

"The hell you'll go home. Try again!" Igor shouts, shoving him.

Naúm jerks and his pressed lips start to shake, while his new glasses grow misty. He turns his head toward a small crowd of spectators and looks at me with the expression of a homeless dog asking to be taken in.

I tug at Ira's sleeve, "Say something." She does not respond. I turn to her, "Ira ..."

But the Ira standing next to me is not the Ira I admired a short time ago. Her courage and her newly awakening female power seem to have left her, exhausted possibly by the cold or recent excitement, or by the recognition that this is no longer her fight. Whatever the reason, the pendulum swings the other way, and instead of Joan of Arc I see a scared teenage girl.

As if on cue, Igor grabs Naúm by the shoulders and starts shaking him—Naúm's thick body swaying in Igor's hands the way a jelly fish sways in the waves. Not meeting any resistance, Igor swings his right arm and clips his victim on the back of the head, sending Naúm's fur hat into the air.

"Leave him alone ..." My voice is as soft as a sigh, and I am not sure that anybody hears it.

"Be quiet," Ira's mitten covers my mouth, its rough threads prickling my lips.

Something begins screaming inside me, and I inhale deeply, preparing to let it out. Yet somehow, it is already out, loud and demanding:

"Leave him alone!"

I expect Ira to pull me away, but she does not. In fact, with her mitten still raised to my face, she is staring past me at something to my left. I look, too, and realize that it was not *me* screaming at the top of my lungs. It was small, scrawny Lida.

"Leave him alone!!"

Too late. With all his strength, Igor pushes Naúm onto the ice. At first, Naúm slides a little, but his feet stumble and he falls down. His bare head hits the ice with the sound of a crackling bottle, and his glasses jump off his nose and land by Igor's feet.

"Oh, look. Whose glasses are these? Does anybody know?" Igor says mockingly, while pressing the glasses into the snow with his right foot. Then he turns towards Naúm: "Hey, ya. Get up. We'll try again."

Naúm does not move.

"Get up an' pick up your fucking glasses!"

No response. Naúm lies on the ice with his face up—his eyes are as immobile as the buttons of his coat, and his arms are spread out on the ice.

"You must've killed him!" Lida screams and snatches Igor's sleeve like a watch dog attacking a thief. And as if she were a dog,

Igor pulls his sleeve from her grip and throws her back onto a pile of snow so deep that she almost disappears from our view.

"Ira …" I stammer, my eyes focused on the dark parody of the crucifix in front of me. "We should do something …"

"What? What can we do?" she whispers.

I take my eyes from the ice and fix them on Ira. Her hair is tousled, her lips have lost their bright color, her shoulders have sagged, and she no longer appears foolhardy or even pretty.

"He needs a doctor …"

Did I say that or did somebody else? No matter, for these words pull me from my stupor and give me something to do. Finding a doctor is a concrete task. It is also my only way of redeeming myself for not helping but just standing there *watching*. Naúm needs a doctor, and my mother is one.

The next hour of so is a series of fragments, like a book I read in a hurry, skipping pages and whole chapters just to get to the end. I run through the deep snow, stumbling and gasping. My mother, home from shopping, opens the door and grabs her bag with medical instruments. Two paramedics carry Naúm on a stretcher while somebody picks up his lifeless hand and lays it across his body. And finally, the ambulance speeds away leaving behind a line of idle spectators and silent snowdrifts.

The days that follow are also vague in my mind—some memories have been buried under the weight of passing years and some have been purged, for we tend to discard shameful memories the way we discard spoiled food. I do remember, though, that, one day, Naúm's mother comes to our apartment, and my mother pulls me out of the bathroom where I have been hiding and orders me to tell the woman what happened. When Naúm's mother finally leaves—her large eyes are red, her lips colorless, and her usually tight clothes hang loose—she no longer looks like a walking cello but a shapeless, old woman.

For some time, I avoid everybody who has witnessed the incident, including my best friend Ira and especially that girl Lida, who also lives in our building. After school, I mostly stay at home, which is why I miss the news that Naúm has moved out of our neighborhood.

I do a lot of reading. I finish the book about the Nobile expedition and learn that the North Pole claimed even more lives. The Meteorologist Malmgren perished in its sparkling vastness, killed by indifferent nature or by his companions Mariano and Zappi. Amundsen, who rushed to save Nobile and his men, disappeared, too—only the wreckage of his seaplane was spotted from the air some time later.

Yet Umberto Nobile, the cause of all these deaths and suffering, survived—the Swedish pilot Lundborg airlifted him from the tiny red speck of his tent. Lundborg did not take anybody else, though, and it would take Nobile many years to restore his reputation, damaged by the abandonment of his men in their ice prison. He would live under a cloud of suspicion, ashamed and disgraced, just like me.

By the time I reach the end of the story, spring begins its annual assault on winter. At first, tiny streams trickle from the caked snowdrifts. Then, their sagging piles crumble into pieces and slide down the streets like miniature ice-floes. And finally, one day, there is nothing left on the ground but shallow puddles, where sparrows take quick baths and kids stomp with renewed energy.

Once again, Ira and I spend time together: doing homework, talking about our changing bodies, classmates, new teachers, and other things important to girls of our age. But we never talk about

Naúm. And why should we? He is not our brother or our friend. He is no longer even our neighbor.

As for what happened, would it be better if Igor had thrown Ira or me on the ice, and Ira had had a concussion, or my head had been fractured? Would that have helped Naúm? Surely not, just as it did not help Umberto Nobile and his crew that Amundsen died somewhere in the unfathomable vastness of the North. And yet, pitiful Naúm still separates Ira and me, for because of him we have explored our own limitations and have learned things about ourselves that we would prefer not to know.

When, several years later, my family moves to another neighborhood and we say our "good-byes," I do not expect to see Ira again. But I do. We are both college students by then—she studying to be a chemist and I an engineer. We run into each other in a little café, popular with the budget-conscious student crowd since the only things on the menu are cheap coffee and ice-cream. We both come with friends, smoking cigarettes and laughing with the boldness of the young who believe that nothing will ever hurt them.

"How are you?" Ira says.

"Good, and you?"

"Great!" she answers, while a young man next to her looks at her attentively and admiringly, as if trying to memorize every feature of her beautiful face.

"Are you still living in our old house?" I say.

"No, but we didn't move far. Sometimes, I see our former neighbors. Those who are still there."

"Do you ever see Lida?" I say, immediately regretting my question.

"Lida? Who's that?" Ira raises her eyebrows—her sparkling gray eyes are clear and thoughtful.

"That girl from the first floor. You must remember her." I say, now desperate to hear the answer.

"Should I? Well, I don't. One cannot remember everybody. Right, Vovik?" She turns to her male companion, who, to my surprise, suddenly breaks into laugher, as if Ira has said something funny that only the two of them can appreciate.

For a moment, I study her, animated, confident, at peace with herself and the world. She must be right. Life goes on. People come and go. We cannot remember them all. Perhaps I still recall pitiful Naúm and skinny unattractive Lida because of the book I was reading at the time—about Nobile and Amundsen, and a Russian ice-breaker that saved the rest of the Nobile crew. That story was so sad and courageous, and romantic—people risking their lives to save others. *As long as I was only reading about it.* But in life … well, life has its own rules. Forgetting is one of them, and Ira has just taught me that.

I smile at her, "Good seeing you."

"Call me!" she says.

"I sure will," I say. But I never do.

CHAPTER TWENTY THREE

THE GAME OF CHESS

Eight years have passed since we left my grandparents' apartment. By now, the birch seedlings that my parents planted in front of my grandparents' building when I was born have turned into tall bushy trees. The stone staircase of their house, so challenging for my toddler's legs, no longer seem steep, and a family of four has replaced the old invalid who used to live across the landing—she died several years ago. Yet, as far as I am concerned, the biggest change of all is that Grandpa has retired and spends most of his time at home.

"I'm too old to work every day," he laughs when I come to visit—his eyes sparkling like sunrays on rippling water. "I can only work when the weather is nice. The rest of the year is for the young, like you."

"I cannot work yet, Grandpa," I say, peering into his screwed up eyes, not sure whether he is joking, as he often is.

"Well, I'll have to do it for you then," he says. "Your grandma doesn't want me to sit around the house all day long, so I'll sit in Sokolniki and collect tickets at the Exhibition Center."

"You'll work at the Exhibition Center?!" I say, impressed. "I wish I could work there with you!"

The International Exhibition and Convention Center is still a new thing—for me anyway. It is located in my favorite park, Sokolniki, and it is open only in the summer. The first time I go there, I feel as if I am transported into the future. The building itself—a large dome structure with a multifaceted aluminum roof that scintillates in the sunlight—looks like a space station from a science-fiction book. Inside, the building is divided into multiple areas—the way, I imagine, a space station would be—and every area represents a different foreign country and its products.

And what products they are! Sleek Western furniture fires our Muscovite imagination. Novel kitchen appliances tease our senses. A multitude of awe-inspiring objects leave us guessing about their origin and purpose, and glossy brochures describing the places where all these treasures come from (and where Soviet visitors are not allowed to go) leave us dizzy and exhausted.

People walk around the Exposition Center with big eyes, while keeping vigilant watch for the time when the foreign staff—all dressed like Western movie stars or, at least, high-ranking Soviet officials—give away chewing gum (known to us only from American movies), colorful plastic bags (no comparison to our string sacks!), and other small souvenirs that seem to be made on another planet, if not in another solar system.

And now my grandfather is going to work there as a ticket taker! This means I can go to the Exposition Center any time I want to, and I won't have to wait in line for two hours.

"Well, I'll work there only twice a week," Grandpa says, winking at me. "I have to leave enough time for playing chess, you know."

This time, even without examining Grandpa's eyes, I know that he is joking. Grandpa does not play chess. Sometimes, he and I play cards, and I have to admit that he is a much better player than I am. Ten or so minutes into the game, he begins fidgeting in his chair, tapping with his heels, and singing to himself in Yiddish, "*Bub-litchki bagelach bub-litchki*…" (Bagels, hot bagels), which is a sure sign that, for me, the game is over.

More often, though, Grandpa plays dominos with other men in the park. They sit on benches around a long, weathered wooden table—usually not far from a beer joint—slapping the boards with their dominos and with their raucous voices frightening away begging pigeons, promenading babushkas, and young mothers pushing baby buggies.

Yet today when Grandpa and I enter the park, Grandpa stops by two men playing chess. The men sit at a table across from each other. Their faces are fixed in deep concentration, and their demeanor suggests a total rejection of bodily pleasures in favor of those of the mind. Unlike the domino players, who bang their dominos against the table as hard as they can and then break into triumphant laughs, the chess players take turns tapping a timer and falling into a state of temporary paralysis. They must be good players, though, because several other spectators have gathered around to watch their game.

Chess is very popular in our country, and it is common to see people—mostly men and boys—play chess in city parks and alleys, or study chess matches in magazines and newspapers. In fact, the current world chess champion is a Soviet citizen, Tigran Petrosian, or "Iron Tigran," as he is known in chess circles. He is so famous that even children recognize his pictures. Yet I get quickly bored with the game.

"Let's go, Grandpa."

With a warm late summer wind propelling us forward, we walk across the lawn, which is dotted with wooden tables and benches occupied by people engrossed in chess—their bodies bent forward, their eyes locked on the board, and their hands clutching their temples.

"Everything matters in chess: castles, kings, queens, even pawns." I hear Grandpa mumble under his breath. "Not like in life ..."

"What are you talking about, Grandpa?"

"Nothing. Just an old man talking to himself." Grandpa's lips move into a show of a smile, but his eyes lack their usual spark, and his lips are crooked, more like a grimace than a smile.

"Grandpa, do you want to learn how to play chess? I can play with you," I say, not sure what Grandfather is upset about but trying to make him feel better. "I know the moves. Father taught me."

"Too late for me to start," he says, examining the grass under his feet.

"Father says that nothing is too late, you just have to work on it," I say.

"Sure. Nothing is too late. *For you.* But, some things are too late *for me*. I'm old, you know."

I stop and stare at my grandfather. His face is crisscrossed with cracks and crevices, his eyes are like wilted autumn grass, and the hair on his head is so thin that I can almost count the individual strands. Why have I never noticed this before? Something sad begins creeping into my chest. Grandpa is standing next to me, but his eyes are distant. This is not the Grandpa I know—the one who tells jokes, drinks *Pertsovka*, plays the guitar, and sings Yiddish and Ukrainian songs.

I grab his hand and squeeze it as hard as I can. "Grandpa, you won't leave me, will you?"

"Of course not," he says. "Not now. We have to get you to the exhibit first!" His usual sly smile flickers over his soft features but quickly melts away. "But, you know, everybody leaves ... eventually."

Several months go by. The weather turns cold, the bright colors of summer fade, and people put on warm coats.

Once again, we are visiting my grandparents. Dinner is over. My older cousin Sima and I collect dirty plates and take them to the kitchen, where Mother washes them and Aunt Raya and Grandma dry them. Little Tanya runs in circles around the apartment, and my cousin Roma reads *The Last of the Mohicans* on the small couch that used to be my bed. The plates tinkle in our hands, water gurgles in the sink, and the women quietly talk about domestic affairs. Only the men are still sitting around the table, red-faced and agitated.

"And now Khrushchev's retired! Just a couple of days ago the newspapers wrote that he was on vacation, and today they say he's retired. Why so suddenly? What happened?" I hear my father's voice.

"It's always the same. They feed us lies. We'll never know what happened," Abraham, Aunt Raya's husband, replies.

"What difference does it make? Khrushchev, Smushchev. They're all the same. For us, anyway." That is my Grandfather.

"You don't know that. Remember Stalin? Things can always get worse," Father gives his usual pessimistic line.

"Well, there's nothing we can do about it," Grandfather says.

"They play their own game, and in that game, we don't matter. Never did. Pawns matter only in chess."

I look at Mother. "They say Khrushchev's retired. Why?"

Mother—an apron around her waist and a wash cloth in her hand—busies herself with the wet plates and says nothing.

"What do you think he'll do now?" I ask again.

"It's not our business," Mother says, still not looking at me.

"I'm just wondering ..."

"Don't. It's not for children to talk about things like that," my aunt says.

"And don't you say anything in school," Mother echoes her sister—her hands fiercely polishing the dinner plates, as if trying to turn the faded ceramic into fine China.

"Why? What can happen?" I say.

"I don't know, and I don't want to know."

"In Stalin's times, people got arrested for saying small things. Jokes even. And this is not a small thing, Sveta. This is the government," Grandma says, taking off her apron and wiping her hands with it. Then she hangs the apron on a hook by the sink and continues, lowering her voice,

"There was this man on the first floor, who …"

I have heard this story before. The man she is talking about — a pilot with several medals for bravery during the last war—lived in my grandparents' building just before I was born. One day, he got drunk and started shouting that nobody cares about those who "*prolivat krov za nashu rodinu*" (shed blood for our country).

The man's drinking buddies heard this, and one of them even egged him on. Later, some people claimed that this provocateur was an informer, although it is entirely possible that the other drinkers, as soon as they sobered up, rushed to inform on their "friend" for fear of being accused of being his collaborators. One way or another, the former hero was arrested and, two days later, people in black came for his wife. Their teenage son also disappeared—nobody knew where or why.

As if the men in the room have overheard Grandma's story, their conversation turns to Stalin's day, too, although instead of the ill-fated pilot, they talk about someone called Ekhil Ulitsky.

"Let him rot in hell!" My father hits the table with his fist, and the wine glasses protest with melodic tinkling. "So many people reported that scoundrel!"

"Yeah … You can never be too careful," my uncle says and knocks back another shot.

"Always cunning!" Father continues. "Starts with a joke, offers a drink, and then flings out something political. And some drunken dummy nods, 'Yeah, life is not fair.' Or tells a joke himself. And in a day or two, that dummy is gone. Vanished into thin air."

This is no news for me either. In the eleven years after Stalin's death and Khrushchev's denunciation of Stalin's Great Purges, cases like this have been surfacing one after another. People were arrested for talking politics or telling political jokes, for complaining about the injustice of life or for being late for work, for being talented or successful—too talented and too successful in the opinion of those who envied them. And that is not counting thousands of military commanders, writers, scientists, artists, and other prominent people who were arrested for no discernible reason at all.

In all cases, the story was always the same. In the wee hours of the morning, a loud knock on the door let the victims know that their life as they knew it was over. Disheveled and vulnerable, they opened the door to secret policemen dressed in black leather who marched into their apartments and conducted thorough searches: pulled out drawers, knocked books off shelves, and turned mattresses upside down—looking for compromising materials. In the end, no matter what the result of the search, the accused, still trying to button their shirts and adjust their clothes with shaking hands, were taken away in a van called a black crow.

As they were leaving their apartments, they would mumble to their loved ones that this must be a mistake and they would be released as soon as it was cleared up. Their spouses or parents would start writing to the authorities, even Stalin himself, about the innocence of the accused—only to be arrested themselves. And more often than not, all of them would disappear for good—first tortured and branded *vragi naroda* (enemies of the state), and later shot in prison or buried in Siberian gulags.

They vanished as if they never existed. New people replaced them at work and moved into their apartments—often the same people who informed on them in the first place—and life continued as if nothing had happened. As for the children of the accused, they were put into orphanages, where their caregivers taught them to love their Motherland (and especially their Father Stalin) and hate the *vragi naroda*, the parents they had lost.

"Did you hear what happens to those who talk too much?" Grandma says. "You should ..."

Grandma is always the same. Stalin died when I was a baby, and it has been years since Khrushchev denounced his cult of personality and the terror Stalin inflicted on our country. Everybody knows that!

"Stalin is dead," I interrupt my grandmother. "Things like that will never happen again. That was all Stalin's fault. Khrushchev said so."

"Exactly. And where is he now?" my cousin Sima chimes in.

"Girls, I don't want you to talk about this," Mother says, and her bow-shaped lips turn into a narrow line. "*Berezhennogo bog berezhet.*" (God saves those who are careful, a Russian proverb.)

The next day in school, as soon as I plop down onto my student bench and look in front of me, I notice an empty space on the wall behind the teacher's table where Khrushchev's portrait used to hang. I turn to my neighbor on the right, Polina Grusheva, a busybody and well-known class gossip, and see that her gaze is also fixed on the empty space on the wall. I expect her to say something about the sudden change, but she lowers her eyes and says nothing. In fact, none of the students or teachers comments on the glaring spot, and neither do I, as if we experience a mysterious case of mass blindness and do not notice the exposed patch of peeling plaster that is a shade or two lighter than the rest of the wall.

Several weeks later, during a school break, my parents send me to stay with my grandparents. As soon as Grandpa and I find ourselves alone, I say: "That man you were talking about with my father and Uncle Abraham, Ekhil Ulitsky, does he still live around here?"

"Did you girls eavesdrop on us?" Grandfather raises his eyebrows. "I guess we have to be careful around you!" He smiles, but a shadow falls over his brow. "No, he doesn't. Somebody informed on him, too, so he got deported to Birobidzhan" (a remote area on the border with China where Stalin planned to exile all Soviet Jews).

"Who did?"

"Other informers, I guess."

"Why did they deport *him* to Birobidzhan? Dad says that they only sent Jews there."

"That's right. But he *was* a Jew."

I stare at my grandfather. A Jew informer?!

"Rats are everywhere, *bubala*," he says, answering my unspoken question. "Saving their skin at the expense of others. He didn't save his skin, though. People said that he got sick there and needed medicine. Well, Stalin sent many Jewish doctors to Birobidzhan, but not the medicine."

"Did he die?"

"Yes, he did, that dog," Grandpa says, and the hostility in his voice takes me aback. Should I stop asking? But when will I get another chance?

"Grandpa, Mother said that when Stalin died, people cried as though he were their true father. Why?"

"With all that propaganda, they believed that he was. The newspapers, the radio, all of them called him the Father of the Nation, Coryphaeus of Science, and whatnot," Grandfather says, his voice oozing with sarcasm. "He was our Generalissimus, too (the highest Soviet military rank awarded only to Stalin). He won the war!" Here Grandfather pauses.

"Stupid people. He couldn't care less whether they lived or died, but they charged the Germans shouting 'For Motherland, for Stalin!' *Tjfu*!" He spits with disgust.

"Did you cry, Grandpa?"

"Me?! Surely not! He tried to starve us in the Ukraine, you know. And then that camp in Siberia… Three years out of my life!"

"You were in a prison camp? When?!" What else do I not know about my grandfather?

"Shortly after the war," he says. "I worked on the railroad weighing freight cars. Somebody stole equipment from one car, and my boss blamed me."

"Why you?"

"I was the only Jew in his team, and he was a real anti-Semite. Besides, he may have stolen the stuff himself and needed an easy scapegoat," Grandfather says.

"Did you tell them that you didn't steal anything?"

"Yes, I did. But who'd believe a Jew in those days?"

"Was it terrible in the camp, Grandpa?" I say, picturing my grandfather in the striped clothes of a German concentration camp inmate, and a chill runs up my spine.

"Let's not talk about that now, *bubala.* It was a long time ago and … Hell, I made it! Had only one arm broken and several teeth."

I peek at Grandfather's silver-plated front teeth, dimly glimmering between his narrow lips.

"No, I was happy when that devil Stalin died," he says, catching my glance. Then a sly smile lightens his face, "Well, *net gorya bez dobra.*" (Even bad luck can bring something good, Russian proverb.) One good thing came out of that camp. I met your Uncle Abraham there and brought him to Moscow."

This is how my aunt met her husband! I had no idea!

"Why was *he* there?" I ask.

"Well, he's from Poland, you know," Grandfather says. "When the Germans occupied the country, some Poles retreated to our territory. They thought they'd be welcomed here, but far from it. Stalin didn't trust even his own people, let alone foreigners. Who cared that the Germans had killed everybody in Abraham's family? As far as our authorities were concerned, he couldn't be trusted. So they sent him to Siberia."

"You never told me this before, Grandpa," I say. "Why?"

"You were too young. Still are," Grandfather smiles and his face ripples with wrinkles. "But, I think I'd better tell you these things now, before it's too late. Right?"

"Right," I say, uncertain of his meaning.

"Listen *bubala,*" Grandfather says, putting his heavy hands on my shoulders and pulling me closer. "Our life's been hard. Wars, pogroms, not much education. Your life must be better. You just need to study and make good grades." Then he winks at me, "Who knows, you may be a famous musician one day!"

"I don't think so," I sigh.

"A doctor, like your mother?"

"I'm afraid of blood, Grandpa."

"Well, then … then you should go to America and make a success of yourself!"

To America? Nobody I know has gone even to socialist Bulgaria, and it is less than 2,000 kilometers away. America is on the other side of the world! Going there is like flying to the moon. Besides, America is a rotten capitalist country, while *our* country is the best country in the world.

I try to shrug off my grandfathers' hands. "Only traitors leave their Motherland!"

"Who told you that?" he says, not letting me go.

"Everybody! My teachers, for one."

He pulls me so close that I can see the tiny red veins in his eyes. "Don't believe them, *bubala*. They don't know anything."

I twitch harder. What does he mean? Of course they know! They are teachers!

"How do *you* know?" I say. "You didn't go to America!"

"No, I didn't … didn't have the guts," Grandfather says. "I should have, though …" Abruptly, he takes his hands off my shoulders, and I stumble backwards, almost falling. He does not seem to notice but turns away from me and, as if pleading with somebody, whispers, "Let them go ..."

Who are you talking to? I want to ask, staring at his stooped back. But my grandfather keeps whispering and bowing toward the empty wall, and I do not dare to interrupt him.

At home, I say to my mother, "You don't think that America is better than our country, do you?"

"Why are you asking?"

"Grandfather said that he wants me to go there. Can you imagine? Like I'm a traitor or something!"

Mother gives me a long look—her gaze impenetrable, like a pond covered with duckweed.

"Your grandfather is a wise man."

"He's not educated. He said that himself!" I say, feeling bad for criticizing my grandfather, yet still upset with his words.

"Education is one thing. Wisdom is another. Some people have education, but not wisdom," Mother sighs. "Believe me, that's not good either."

What is *she* talking about? And what does it have to do with my question?

"Mom," I say, attempting to direct the conversation my way, "you wouldn't go to America, would you?" But Mother busies herself with never-ending domestic chores, and my question hangs in the air unanswered.

In the end, Grandfather's prediction that not much would change after Khrushchev's hasty retirement proves to be true. As before, our country heads toward a "wonderful" communist future at the expense of our not-so-wonderful present. As before, the state media sing the praises of our never-successful five-year economic plans, and as before, our "wise" Communist Party presides over all aspects of our lives.

The only discernible change takes place in school. One day, when I enter my classroom and look at the spot where Khrushchev's portrait used to hang, I see a portrait of a man with coal-black bushy eyebrows, flabby features, and a triumphantly important expression. This is Khrushchev's replacement, Leonid Ilyich Brezhnev, our new leader.

Neither the teachers nor the students comment on Brezhnev's arrival in our classroom. We are used to seeing images of government leaders everywhere, and it is only natural to us that our new head of government has claimed his rightful place next to the portrait of Lenin, so both of them can follow our educational progress from the wall. Also, as Stalin himself liked to say, "*Les rubyat, shchepki letyat*" (chips fly when you cut down trees, Russian proverb) or, in other words, we must dispose of those who divert us away from our extraordinary goals.

A true change—for me anyway—occurs next summer. It has nothing to do with our government but with my grandfather's death. I am in a summer camp when he dies, and my relatives bury him without me. When I come back to Moscow, he is gone, and all I have left of him are faded black-and-white pictures in the family photo album: my grandfather surrounded by people I never met. Grandma and he are side by side, looking into the camera with strained and alienated eyes, and another photo of Grandfather alone, with a sad smile, as if saying, "We are all disposable."

Grandfather

Yet unlike Khrushchev and other Soviet leaders whose portraits rotate through the empty spots on Moscow's walls, my grandfather will never be disposable to me, and his place in my heart will never be filled. In my mind's eye, I will always see him winking at me or hear him singing, and eventually I will follow his wish and immigrate to America.

On the chess board of history my grandfather may have been only a pawn, but for me he remains the greatest of chess grandmasters, greater than Tigran Petrosian or the American Bobby Fisher. Not only because I loved him, but also because, like them, he was never tricked by false maneuvers. He saw things clearly—as they were—and several moves ahead.

CHAPTER TWENTY FOUR

BABI YAR

"Isn't it beautiful?" Mother says, and a smile spreads across her face like ripples in water.

"It sure is," Dad echoes, also breaking into a wide grin and lovingly caressing our new *shkaf* (wardrobe)—a polished dark-oak affair with two doors and a large, top-to-bottom mirror.

My sister Tanya dashes to our new acquisition and pulls both doors wide open. One side of the wardrobe is divided into six horizontal sections; the other, with a cross-beam at the top, is for hanging clothes.

"I want my own shelf," Tanya announces loudly, like a prospector filing a mining claim.

"We'll see about that," Mother says, visibly pleased by the immense possibilities our new furniture gives her in organizing our meager possessions.

I take several steps forward and carefully close the doors—Tanya is so rough with everything, she can break this beauty even before we start using it. For a time, I, too, admire its shiny surface and the broad pattern of the wood. Our botany teacher says that it is possible to find out how old a tree is by its rings and layers, maybe even where it grew and what the weather was like while it stood in all its splendor somewhere in the woods before an ax brought it down.

Behind me, I hear Mother chat with our neighbor Klavdia Davidovna, who drops in attracted by the commotion "for just a second." Mom tells Klavdia Davidovna how long she had to wait in line for a chance to buy the wardrobe, and how much she wanted to buy a dining table to match it but could not afford it.

"Not even a bedside table," Mother sighs. "They are so expensive, you know." Klavdia Davidovna sighs, too, "Too bad, dear," although the only sentiment I detect in her voice is jealous satisfaction.

I turn my attention to the mirrored side of the wardrobe. I step back and look at my reflection in its silvery surface, and my heart sinks. The girl looking at me is gangly, with dark, slightly wavy hair, a swarthy complexion, and a very prominent nose. I stare at my reflection, grief-stricken—surely I must stand out among my light-haired, light-skinned, small-nosed peers. I look so-o-o Jewish. Being unattractive is bad enough, but being unattractive *and* so typically Jewish definitely quadruples my bad luck. Of course, with the exception of my mother and cousin Sima, all my relatives stand out.

"Mom, why doesn't Sima look like us?"

Both Mother and Klavdia Davidovna turn to me in surprise.

"Why should she?" Mother says. "She's not *our* daughter." And Klavdia Davidovna who has no interest in our family affairs quickly reports, "I have things to do," and retires to her room.

"But she's your sister's daughter," I insist. "Aunt Raya looks Jewish, Roma (Sima's half-brother) looks Jewish, but Sima doesn't. She's blond and her eyes are blue. Why?"

Grandmother, Sima, and Grandfather, 1951

"The mother is not all, you know. Roma's father Abraham is a Jew. Sima's father is Russian, so she takes after him."

I gawk at Mom. "Sima's father is *Russian*? I never knew that!" Mother winks but says nothing.

"Didn't you say that he was killed in the war?" I continue my investigation.

"Well," Mother stumbles. "Maybe he was, maybe he wasn't." Then she quickly recovers and reaches for her habitual magic wand, "Did you do your homework?"

"Mom, wait! Which one is it?"

"Don't tell anybody that you know," Mother says and glances in the direction of our new wardrobe, as if somebody might be hiding there. "Raya and Sima's father got divorced."

Divorced?! This is the first time I have heard about *anybody* in our family getting divorced. I had always thought that only bad people get divorced: incurable alcoholics, adulterers, people like that. What did Aunt Raya's first husband do?

"Well, our father would not allow Raya to marry a goy."

"Why?"

"Because people should stick to their own kind. Those who don't end up badly," Mother says in an instructive tone of voice. "It's not good for a Jewish woman to marry a Russian man. Even if things seem to be fine at first, his family hates her." (Obviously, our family did not love that Russian husband either!) "So, eventually, they turn him against her, and they all treat her badly." (As if Uncle Abraham always treats my aunt very well!) "Now, did you finish your homework?"

"So, Sima is Russian?" I say, disregarding Mother's question, fascinated with the fact that my own cousin Sima has a *live* Russian father and therefore may be Russian herself.

"Well, she could've been registered as Russian. When she turned sixteen and went to get her passport (the most important document in our country), they expected her to register as Russian, but she said no."

"She did not!" I choke.

"Yes, she did. The clerk in the passport office told her that she was making a big mistake and gave her a week to think it over. But she didn't change her mind!" Mother says, and her face takes on the proud expression of a TV announcer reporting about the great achievements of Soviet agriculture. Then she pauses and the pride on her face melts away, "Well, it wouldn't be good for her to displease Abraham. After all, he raised her." With that, Mother turns around and heads to the kitchen, leaving me to ponder the news.

Sima said no? She must be crazy! I always knew that she was *vibrazhala* (one who puts on airs)—all older girls are. But I never thought of her as stupid! What Jewish kid would pass up a once-in-a-life-time chance to be registered as Russian? Life would be so much easier. Nobody would scowl at you, nobody would call you names, not to mention that you would never hear "You Jew, go to your Israel!" thrown at your face.

Of course, having a passport that reads "Nationality—Russian" would never work for somebody like me. But if blond, fair-skinned Sima had registered as Russian, *nobody* in the world would guess that she was tainted by anything Jewish. In fact, people must be surprised to learn otherwise.

Time goes by, and, on May 9, our whole family gets together to celebrate Victory Day—the capitulation of Nazi Germany.

"If not for our victory, you children wouldn't have been born," Mother says to Tanya and me when our loud argument begins drowning the sounds of a TV broadcast of the military parade from Red Square. "Sit down and watch the parade."

Mother says this every year while watching huge rocket launchers, missiles and tanks clattering over Red Square's cobblestones and hundreds of troops goose-stepping in front of Lenin's red-granite mausoleum, where high government officials wave at them and smile to shouts of "*Slava*!" (glory) from the crowd.

I know Mother is right. If the Nazis had won the war, they would have killed all the Jews in our country and, possibly, everywhere in the world. Sometimes, I even try to imagine what life would be like with all of us gone. Who would live in our apartment, sit in my class, or play my piano? These thoughts make me feel invisible and also weightless, like a balloon torn from its thread and rising into the sky to its inevitable demise. Yet the parades are always the same, with deafening military machinery crawling through the Square, orchestras playing rousing marches, and solemn announcers reciting patriotic slogans over the loudspeakers.

I sit down, but instead of watching TV, I watch my older cousin. Sima no longer takes part in our "childish" games. Her light eyelashes are colored black, her blond hair is pulled back and arranged into an elegant bun on top of her head, and her blue eyes are turned to the ceiling, as if she is praying to an invisible deity to get her out of this boring place ASAP.

Ever since I learned about Sima's true identity, I cannot decide if she is a hero like Alexander Matrosov, who sacrificed his life by throwing himself onto a German pill-box, or a crazy woman like the wife of Mr. Rochester from *Jane Eyre*. Also, my old doubts about my own identity surface with renewed intensity.

If my family managed to hide the fact of Sima's parentage for all these years, who knows what else they might be hiding. What if I *am* adopted? While I do look like my father, I don't look at all like my mother. For all I know, I could be my father's daughter from a previous marriage! Of course, if that is true, my parents will never tell me. My only chance to find out the truth is by talking to Grandma.

The Victory Day parade is over and most of my family goes for a walk in the park. Under the pretense of helping to wash dishes, I stay behind with Grandma, who does not believe in walking for pleasure.

"Grandma, what did Mom look like when she was little?" I say, drying off a porcelain tea cup with a flowery pattern, from a set of china that my grandma uses for festive occasions.

"Oh, she was a tomboy. Short hair, very fast. Just like Tanya," Grandma says, handing me another thoroughly washed cup.

I carefully dry it off, put it on top of the first cup, and, trying to sound very casual, say, "Did she ever look like me?"

"No."

"And she was always pretty," I continue my line of questioning. "Right?"

"*Bubala*, don't get it into your head. You know what they say, '*Ne rodis crasivoi a rodis schastlivoi.*' (Do not be born pretty, be born lucky, Russian proverb.) You're good as you are," Grandma says and picks up another dirty cup. Then she suddenly turns to me and, still holding the cup in one hand and a washcloth in the other, says, "My brother Pinchas had a fiancée, Dorka. She was so beautiful—tall, slender, eyes like violets, lips like red roses. All young men in her *shtetl* were crazy about her."

I wait for Grandma to continue, but she just stands there, staring at something above my head, as if expecting beautiful Dorka to appear somewhere behind me.

"Did they get married?" I hurry Grandma.

Grandma puts down the cup and the washcloth, and lowers herself heavily on a chair next to the kitchen table. "Just before the wedding, they drafted Pinchas to the Tsar's Army. And while he was at the front (during the First World War), the Cossacks raided Dorka's shtetl—a pogrom, you know. Killed and looted, and whatnot."

Memories cloud Grandma's face and rain drops appear in her tired eyes, but she continues. "One Cossack chased after Dorka. She ran to the lake nearby, but he caught up with her and …" Here Grandma stops and gives me a strange look.

"Did he kill her, Grandma?" I say, goose bumps tickling my skin.

Grandma bites her lower lip, "No. But he … taunted her and left her there, unconscious." Then she takes a long breath and continues. "It was in the winter, and she lay on the ice all night long. In the morning, people found her and brought her home. But she never fully recovered. Got tuberculosis on that lake."

Grandma puts her hand with fingers distorted by arthritis and life-long work on my head and strokes my hair, "So you see what her beauty brought her? Nothing but *tsores* (misery, Yiddish)."

"Did she die?"

"Not then," Grandma sighs, getting up and picking up her washcloth. "Pinchas came back from the war and married her anyway. They moved to Kiev (capital of Ukraine). She was very sickly, though. He took her to doctors and sanatoriums, and she would be better for a while, and then worse again. Up and down all the time. They did have two daughters, though, Shura and Rosa … Well, *genug*, enough talking. Go read a book, *bubala*."

"Grandma, when did Dorka die?"

"Soon as the war started, in 1941. But let's not talk about that."

"Grandma, we studied that war in school. The battles, the generals, the war heroes—everything. You can tell me," I say, feeling confident and worldly.

The washcloth in my grandmother's hand flies up as if she is about to strike me, "Heroes, you say? They're only heroes if they're Russians. We, Jews, don't count. When *we* die, they don't even put up a tombstone!"

"What are you talking about, Grandma?" I say, shrinking back.

"When the war started, they never told us that the Germans were exterminating Jews—not in the newspapers, not on the radio. They knew about that, but we didn't. You see, in the first war (World War I) the Germans treated everybody the same, no matter Jews, Ukrainians, or Russians. So when they began advancing toward Ukraine, the Jews didn't leave immediately. But then it was too late."

"How did the Germans know who the Jews were?"

"They always knew. We're 'noticeable,'" Grandma says with a crooked smile. "And Ukrainian 'volunteers' helped them, too."

Here she stops, but not for long, "As the war started, Pinchas and Rosa's husband were drafted in the army, so Rosa moved in with her mother Dorka. When the Fritzes burst into their house, Dorka lay in bed, sick, and Rosa had just given birth to a baby boy. They pulled Dorka outside on her blanket and dragged Rosa out by the hair with her baby in her arms. Dorka couldn't walk, just lay on the ground and moaned. They shot her in the head."

Grandma's face looks like a ravaged *stetl*, but I cannot stop. "What happened then?"

"They rounded up all the Jews and marched them to a ravine," Grandma says. "Made them dig their own graves and then shot them with machine guns. They were very economical, you know. Put people in double rows, so they could kill two with one bullet. And those who did not die, the soldiers and the Ukrainian police buried alive."

"What about Rosa?" I say, squeezing my cold hands.

"Oh, Rosa was very patriotic. Shouted that the Soviet Army and Stalin would avenge their deaths. Sure they did!

Bitterness in Grandma's voice floods the apartment and splashes outside through a half-open window. "So many Jews were killed and buried in that ravine, just like stray dogs. But Stalin didn't allow a monument to their memory. Who cares about dead Jews."

"How do you know this, Grandma?"

"Several people survived and told others. We're all survivors, *bubala*, our ancestors before us, those who escaped death during the war, and even those who are being born now. We have to be. Nobody cares about us, nobody defends us."

At that, Grandma turns around and heads to the other room, leaving unwashed cups on the kitchen table.

Back row: Grandfather and Grandmother (far left); Dorka and Pinchas (far right). Front row: my uncle, my mom, and my aunt; Rosa (far right), 1929.

I stay behind, feeling small and lonely, the way I felt a long time ago, when I got lost in the wintery Sokolniki park. But there was a woman who helped me then, who took me to my grandfather. She *did* care.

There are some good Russian people! I want to tell Grandma. But the door is closed and, who knows, maybe I just got lucky. As they say, "Do not be born pretty, be born lucky." And I am not pretty.

The next day, Mother and I sit beside each other darning my cotton stockings. Mother's fingers quickly fly over a damaged heel, leaving behind neatly intersecting rows of threads. I try to mimic Mother's precise movements, but my fingers are awkward and my mind is wandering.

"Mom, is it true what Grandma told me about her Ukrainian relatives?"

"What did she tell you?"

"She said that the Fascists shot them and buried them in a ravine, together with other Jews and their babies."

Mother glances at me. "That's true, but don't talk about that in school, okay?"

"Why? They were victims of Fascism!" I say, studiously repeating the words from my history textbook.

Mother says nothing, but her fingers begin moving even more quickly, like bees buzzing around their hive.

"How many people did the Fascists kill there, Mom?"

"Tens of thousands. In just a few days."

In my mind, I try to envision how many people that is. Is it like the crowds at the Victory Day parade?

"Do we have any relatives left in the Ukraine?"

"They are all there. In Babi Yar."

"Where is that?"

"Babi Yar is the name of that ravine," Mother says and adds, "Let's talk about something else."

At night, I have a hard time falling asleep. I toss and turn in my bed, and listen to the wind howling outside the window as if mourning the terrible fate of the people I never knew.

"They are all there," sounds in my head, and when I close my eyes, I see skulls and bones—large and small—sticking out from the black earth like worm-eaten mushrooms in the deep woods, and I hear the muffled cries of invisible children.

A month later, we are invited to my Aunt Raya's birthday. When we appear on her threshold, the table is already set, but my aunt and her daughter are still in the kitchen. Aunt Raya, red in the face, is delivering a monologue about Sima's "impossible absent-mindedness," while Sima silently crawls around the floor, wiping up bits and pieces of multicolored vegetables—an expression on her face like that of St. Sebastian shot with arrows.

"Raya, let me help her," Mom says, quickly assessing the situation. The pride and joy of any Russian party, *olivje* salad, made of boiled potatoes, eggs, dill pickles, green peas, and finely chopped bologna—all liberally doused with mayonnaise—is scattered across the kitchen floor.

"No," Aunt Raya says, in the tone of a nun who won't give in to the temptations of the world. "She dropped it, she should clean it up! You just go in and enjoy yourselves." And as my aunt directs us to the dining table, she turns around and says to her daughter, "Don't you leave the kitchen until you fix the salad!"

I look at Sima. Her eyes are glistening suspiciously, her lips are quivering, and her usually meticulous hair-do has shifted off center and looks disheveled. Whatever her 'impossible' faults are—besides not paying attention to me, that is—she is a sorry sight.

I let my relatives get ahead and approach my cousin. "Sima," I say quietly. "Your hair is tousled. Do you want me to bring you a comb?"

"No." Sima says abruptly, but as I turn around to leave, she softens her voice and says, "Wait, bring me a couple of hair-pins. They're in our room, in the top drawer. Thanks."

Flattered to be of help, I dash to the room that nineteen-year-old Sima still shares with her sixteen-year-old brother. There is no mistake about which chest-of-drawers belongs to her and which to Roma. I approach the one with balls of wool and knitting needles on top and pull the top drawer open: a comb, mascara, lipstick, eye liners, and other items from a young woman's treasure box reveal themselves. I grab two hair-pins and close the drawer. Then curiosity gets the best of me, and, instead of turning back to the kitchen, I pull out the next drawer.

There I see a thin pile of official-looking papers and, next to them, a small red-colored leather book with the word "Passport" on it. Without hesitation, I reach for Sima's passport, open it, and read.

Name: Seraphima (Sima's full name); date of birth: November 19, 1945; Father: Nikolai Podberezov, Russian; Mother: Raisa (Aunt Raya's full name) Podberezova, Jewish. Then my eyes jump to the ubiquitous fifth line—Nationality: Jewish.

So, it is true that half-Russian Sima chose to be registered as Jewish. Mad, isn't she? I shake my head, put Sima's passport back, and keep looking. The third drawer reveals a stack of knitting patterns and a fashion magazine in a language I do not recognize. I open it up. Pretty, well-dressed coquettes stare seductively at me from every page, manifesting a life that my school teachers would never approve of.

I want to put the magazine back, but something falls out of it and lands on the floor. I pick it up. It is a hand-written paper. The words "Babi Yar" appear on the top of the page followed by a name—Yevgeny Yevtushenko. I have never heard of Yevtushenko, but he must be a poet, for underneath his name runs a column of short uneven lines:

"No monument stands over Babi Yar.
A drop sheer as a crude gravestone.
I am afraid.
Today I am as old in years
As all the Jewish people."

How strange! This is the second time I have heard about Babi Yar in a month, and in a poem, of all places!

"I seem to be Dreyfus ..."

I stumble over the unfamiliar name but keep reading.

"Beat the Yids (kikes). Save Russia!"

This, unfortunately, sounds too familiar.

"I seemed to be Anne Frank ..."

Another name I do not recognize, but I hurry forward. Finally, the conclusion:

"In my blood there is no Jewish blood.
In their callous rage, all anti-Semites
Must hate me now as a Jew.
For that reason
I am a true Russian!"

I finish the last verse and turn the page over, trying to find an explanation for what I just read. The back page is blank—no comments and no dates. Is this really poetry? The rhyme is different and the rhythm, too. Not at all like Pushkin or Lermontov or Esenin, not even like the famous Soviet-era poet Mayakovski, all of whom we study in school. As for the subject, I have never read poems about Jews. In fact, I have never read anything about Jews that does not portray them as conniving or greedy, or worse.

Yet these lines bleed with anguish and compassion, and although there is nothing in my school curriculum about Alfred Dreyfus and Ann Frank, and I do not understand some of the poem's allusions, I understand one thing. This poet, Yevgeni Yevtushenko, who, by his own admission, has no Jewish blood, mourns for Jewish victims, whether they were betrayed by their countrymen, killed during the pogroms, or executed by the Nazis. He mourns for people he never knew and was not related to, for those like Dorka, Rosa, and her little baby boy, and also for the fact that there is nothing at Babi Yar that marks the place of so many terrible deaths.

I wish I could read the poem one more time, but Sima's voice draws me out of my trance, "Did you find my hair-pins?"

I rush back to the kitchen.

"*Za smertju tebya posilat*!" (Finally! As if I sent you to fetch death!) Sima greets me, irritated. She stops cutting vegetables, and with both hands pulls back loose strands of her hair and secures them with hair-pins.

I quietly stare at her, unsure if I know her at all. Well, I know that she is a college student, that she likes movies, that she always seems to know about current fashion and supplements her dowdy store-bought clothes with her own knitting. Stuff like that. Yet I know nothing about important things. Like how did she learn about Evgeni Evtushenko and his poem? Why did she register as Jewish? Did she ever meet her father?

Mother said that Jewish women who marry into a Russian family are all miserable, but is that always true? Evtushenko must be Russian or Ukrainian, but surely Mother was not talking about him—if he were to marry a Jewish woman, that is. There must be some good Russian men, and in fact, my Aunt Raya might have been happier with her first husband, who was Russian, than with my Jewish Uncle Abraham, and Sima with her biological father.

"Sima, are you done?" I hear my aunt's voice.

Sima grabs the bowl of freshly made *olivje* salad and takes it into the room. The salad is passed around, voices get louder, and glasses are raised—wine for women and vodka for men: "Happy birthday!" My uncle leans toward his wife and kisses her on the lips, and she, flushed from the attention or the incident in the kitchen, gets up, makes a circular gesture with the glass in her hand—"Thank you, my dears!"—and drinks the contents of her glass.

I shift my eyes from one familiar face to another—everyone seems happy, even Sima's lips curl into a weak smile. Suddenly, deep hostility rises inside me like heartburn. How can they celebrate Aunt Raya's birthday or anything else, for that matter? With all those people killed and buried in a hole, with Grandpa gone, and Aunt Raya forced to marry a man she does not love? Or … does she? I look at my aunt again. She gives me a carefree smile and turns to her husband who is busy telling jokes.

Laughter and clanking of glasses intensify my gloom even more. I turn to Grandma. She's gone through so much. She must be feeling like me! But the look on Grandma's face is one of pleasure and contentment. She is still alive, and she presides at a table surrounded by her offspring. What else can an old woman desire?

I give up. I must be the only person here who recognizes the shame of this gathering and who resents the cruelties and unfairness of life. I get up and go to the kitchen. Immediately, Tanya appears behind me, "Let's play cards!"

I turn to her, ready to say, "Leave me alone!" but, once again, Grandma appears in my line of vision. Her thin wavy hair is smoothed out and her eyes are gleaming. What did she say the day she told me about Babi Yar? "We are all *survivors*." What did she mean? That our lives are forever shadowed by the terrible past? Or that we should go on living?

Another explosion of laughter bursts into the kitchen and into my thoughts. The people in the other room are having a good time. They have left their painful memories behind, and now they are making the best of it. Is that what survivors do? It must be.

I give my aunt and uncle another look. Uncle Abraham, too, lost his first wife, as well as his four children and his parents. Yet at this moment, he seems happy. In fact, they both do. Who knows? Mother might be right about people sticking to their own kind.

I turn to my sister. "Okay. Where are the cards?"

CHAPTER TWENTY FIVE

UNTIL NEXT SUMMER

"There is a *kvass* vendor on the corner," Mother's voice pulls me from the wondrous world of books into prosaic reality. "Take a *bidón* and go get us some *kvass*."

I look up from my book. My eyes are clouded with the image of a young Persian woman dressed in exotic flowing clothes, and my ears are still tuned to her melodic voice weaving an endless tapestry of stories, night after night, 1001 in all. The woman sits at the feet of a bearded man. Her arms stretch toward him in an unspoken plea, and her eyes follow his every movement, the way a sunflower follows the sun.

The woman's name is Scheherazade and the man's Shahryar. He is a Persian king. He is handsome and powerful, but he hates women. He killed his unfaithful first wife, and he has been killing innocent women ever since. Every night, he marries a young virgin, and every morning he orders her execution.

Scheherazade is his newest bride, and if she does not find a way to stop this vicious cycle, he will kill her, too, and who knows how many more young women like her. Alas, Scheherazade's resources are limited: she has nobody to defend her, no one to buy her freedom, and no weapon. All she can do to avoid death is tell tales, because she stays alive only as long as the King listens.

Scheherazade speaks of undaunted heroes and beautiful women, brave sailors and desert dwellers, thieves and traitors, and many other things. Her tales are long and intricate. They are nested inside each other like brightly-colored Russian *matryoshki*, with each tale adding surprising twists and turns and whimsical characters to the already fantastic scene.

"Hurry, before the *kvass* is gone," Mother says.

Mother has an uncanny ability to interrupt me at the worst possible moment, as if she has a device implanted in her head for measuring my mood. When I am bored, this device is idle, and Mother leaves me alone. Yet when I am engrossed in a book or a game—bam!—the device springs to life and sends Mother a signal, "Sveta's really excited now! Is there anything she could be doing instead?"

As much as I like *kvass* (a non-alcoholic beverage made of rye bread, a perennial favorite in Russia), I do not care about it when Scheherazade's life is at stake. Of course, telling this to my mother would be as useless as telling Shahryar that he ought to stop killing his innocent wives. So I curse *kvass* under my breath, put my book down, and drag myself to the kitchen. I reach inside our kitchen cabinet, yank out a jangling *bidon* (a small bucket), and rush outside. The sooner I satisfy Mother's request, the sooner I will be able to dive back into the world of the *Arabian Nights*, with its amazing stories and its spellbinding sensations.

These sensations took hold of me the first time I opened our well-worn tome of the *Arabian Nights* and saw a picture of the Persian king. It was a rather small picture, more like a sepia-colored sketch. I had seen much better pictures in catalogs of the famous Russian art museums—The Hermitage, Tretyakov State

Gallery, and others—which Father kept in our bookcase and, when he was in a good mood, showed to me with meticulous explanations.

Many of these pictures were in color, and some of them depicted naked men and women. Yet, not until the moment I glanced at the picture of the gloomy King sitting cross-legged on a large pillow did a painfully sweet ache pierce my heart and a tingling sensation shoot through my body, making me take a deep breath and squeeze my thighs.

Something must be wrong with me, was my first thought. I should tell my mother, was next. But how could I? Mother and I had never discussed anything intimate, and her only acknowledgment of my changing body was limited to telling me how to take care of menstrual blood.

"Here's some cotton. Put it inside your pants and change it as needed," she said, looking somewhat above my head. Then she lowered her gaze and added, "Wash your panties in cold water or the blood won't come out." After that nugget of women's wisdom, she never again expressed any desire to advance my knowledge of physical maturation.

I open the squeaking door of our building and inhale the tangy aroma of *kvass* wafting from a *kvass* cistern that sits on the street corner, encircled by women and children—men having better things to do. I take my place at the end of the long line and entertain myself by watching clouds shaped like sheep while staring enviously at those who have already filled their *bidons* and, weighed down by the foaming amber-colored liquid, carry their treasure home.

Meanwhile, the crowd around me goes through its usual evolution. At first, women quietly watch their feet and throw impatient glances toward the head of the line. Then they begin eyeing those next to them, and finally their habitual suspicion gives way to boredom, and they start chatting.

"Nice weather we're having. *Babiye leto* (a season known as Indian Summer in America) is my favorite ..."

"And what do ya think, next day he comes back as if nothing's happened! 'Where did you spend the night, *pyaniza* (drunkard)?' I says …"

"Can't tell ya how much I like *kvass*. What's warm weather without it? And *okroshka*, of course. I add turnips to mine …"

Okroshka is a cold soup made of boiled eggs, potatoes, beets, and fresh cucumbers, all drowned in *kvass* and flavored with sour cream. I like it, too, and the conversation makes me hungry. Yet before I have the time to add hunger to my list of today's grievances, I pick up a loud argument somewhere at the head of the line.

"Didja see her there? Did anybody? Scram!"

"Scram yourself! I've stood here. I just left for a little while. Let me back in!"

"Don't push me, you *hooliganka*, or you'll be sorry!"

"What did you say, *blyad*? I'll show you *hooliganka*!"

The calm September air suddenly reaches the temperature of a blast furnace, and heated threats and curses, one uglier than the next, transform the boring wait into a raging war. In a minute, *bidons* are raised for weapons, the orderly line is broken, and decades of misery and distrust erupt into a chaotic shouting match:

"Don' touch me, you *zaraza*!"

"Who's *zaraza*? You're *sterva* yourself!"

"Scratch her shameless eyes out!"

"It's because of thieves like her an honest person can't buy anything!"

One woman shoves another, who stumbles backwards— her arms flapping like wings—and collides with a woman bystander holding a large glass jar of *kvass*. The bystander, unprepared for an attack, loses her balance, and the jar slips from her grip and explodes on the asphalt with a loud "whoosh!"

"Ahh!" the bystander exhales, momentarily paralyzed, and then erupts, "You bitch!"

The *kvass* vendor, a large woman in a stained apron turns off the stream of *kvass*, and the cistern's faucet, still covered with froth, takes on the appearance of a large runny nose. The vendor reaches under her apron and pulls out a whistle.

The whistle is still ringing in our ears when another whistle answers. Help comes in the form of a young, broad-shouldered *militsioner* (policeman). He approaches the *kvass* scene, removing his uniform cap adorned with a hammer-and-sickle cockade and wiping sweat from his narrow forehead:

"What's the matter, *grazhdanochki* (female-citizens)?"

"That *hooliganka* tried to jump the line! Arrest her!"

"And she broke my jar, too!"

"Who?"

"That *nakhalka* … tall, in a brown dress … with bulging eyes …" The women look around, searching for the source of commotion. "She was just here …"

"Well," the *militsioner* says, turning condescendingly from one face to another, "Where is she?"

The women look at each other, perplexed. The help came too late. The instigator is gone, and the crowd has nothing left but anger and unsatisfied righteousness.

The *militsioner* exchanges meaningful glances with the *kvass* vendor, who purses her lips, crosses her arms on her abundant bosom, and announces, "*Kvass* is gone. You go home now, *grazhdanochki*."

"Whad'ya mean 'gone'? You said nothing before! *Davai, rabotai*—keep working!"

The crowd flares up again, fury foaming at the women's mouths like frothed *kvass*.

"Yeah, right! Who's going to believe ya?"

"Don't put noodles over our ears!"

"What the hell! Where's the law?"

Yet under the *militsioner*'s iron stare, the temporary alliances quickly break down, and streams of unhappy "*grazhdanochki*" scatter reluctantly up and down the street, leaving behind a smelly spot on the sidewalk and the *kvass* vendor talking quietly to the representative of the law.

As soon as I open our front door, Mother says, "You're back? Good. I got everything ready for *okroshka*."

"I didn't get any *kvass*. It's all gone," I say, shoving the *bidon* back into the kitchen cabinet.

"Gone?! What am I going to do with the cut vegetables? I didn't plan anything else for supper!"

I do not want to hear Mother's lamentations. I have wasted my time and gotten nothing for it. At the very least, I deserve peace and quiet. I turn around and head to our room.

The *Arabian Nights* is still on my sleeper-chair. I plop down, pick up the book, and look at the picture of Scheherazade stretched before Shahryar. Only this time, instead of admiring the King, I notice Scheherazade's clothes, silky and colorful, accentuating her curvy body.

I have never had anything so nice. Of course, I do not have Scheherazade's curves either. Mother does, but her clothes are dark and plain, and she wears them for years. As for my sister, Tanya, her stuff is passed down through many generations of our family. Well, Tanya doesn't count—she's only seven. I am almost fourteen, and next quarter I will join *Komsomol* (the All-Union Leninist Young Communist League), which will bring me one step closer to adulthood and the Communist Utopia long promised by our government.

All students at the age of fourteen become members of *Komsomol*, unless they are church-goers (a "sin" in our atheistic society) or *cruglie dvoeshniki* (failing students). I am not aware of any religious black sheep in my class. As for grades, our *dvoeshniki*, Vitka and Kolka have been given passing grades lately, so they will not spoil our class records and our school's reputation. After all, Vitka and Kolka's knowledge is their families' business, but, according to our principal, our school's reputation is important to all of us.

In any case, we will soon exchange our Young Pioneers' scarves for a *komsomolski* badge, a miniature red banner with a profile of Vladimir Ilyich Lenin in the middle and the letters BLKSM on the bottom. I am not excited about joining *Komsomol*, since I no longer believe everything I hear at school and read in our textbooks. The things I hear at home, spoken in an undertone behind closed doors or during our family gatherings, are very different. They are bitter, critical, pessimistic, and completely the opposite of everything that pours out of the state radio, television, newspapers, and speeches of our leaders.

Sometimes I feel as if my family is not even part of our country, but an alien faction within it. Everything is "we" versus "them," as if "we" are a tiny group of renegades who struggle to survive among "them," a large, self-satisfied Russian *matryoshka*. That said, being a member of The All-Union Leninist Young Communist League is a must if I want to go to college. Besides that, I need to behave in school and make good grades.

When my physics grades recently began to drop like a cannonball, my father immediately confronted me: "You don't plan to work on an assembly line, do you?"

"No, I don't," I said sincerely, since the only assembly line I had ever seen was the one in Charlie Chaplin's silent movie *Modern Times*, where poor Charlie was forced to screw nuts onto parts of machinery at such a fast rate that he suffered a nervous breakdown. That, of course, happened in America, a "rotten capitalist country soon to be destroyed by the oppressed masses," in the words of our history teacher. Still, I strongly suspected that assembly lines in our own country were not any better.

In truth, my parents have nothing to worry about. My failing grades have nothing to do with physics, but everything to do with its teacher, Anatoli Petrovich. He is young and athletic, with bright hazel eyes, a wide smile that makes my heart race, and wavy blond hair, just like the late famous Russian poet Sergei Esenin. Anatoli Petrovich is also witty, and he uses a lot of big words, which makes him sound both learned and important.

In short, my physics teacher is completely different from my male classmates, who never say anything worthwhile and whose pimply faces look like miniature mine fields. All of Anatoli Petrovich's female students—and possibly all the single female teachers—are in love with him, and when he conducts experiments, the quiet of the physics lab is charged with our high-voltage unspoken desire.

The only person who does not appreciate Anatoli Petrovich is our class clown Grisha, a narrow-shouldered, scrawny boy with crow-like dark eyes and large, mushroom-shaped ears. Most of my male classmates keep to themselves during physics class, but not Grisha. Instead of being quiet in the presence of a true deity, he constantly shouts stupid jokes and then looks around the class with the victorious expression of an opera tenor who has just hit high "C" and waits for applause. On top of that, Grisha often strikes me on the back with his briefcase, and when I turn around, he makes stupid faces or wiggles his ears—he is the only person I know who can do this—which I find neither funny nor amusing.

Anatoli Petrovich, on the other hand, does not notice me at all. Had I been pretty, I would have given him meaningful glances or sighed deeply when he looked at me, the way some of my classmates do. But I am not pretty: I am too short, too skinny, too flat-chested, and, worst of all, my nose is too big.

Actually, my nose used to be average. But, by the age of nine, it began growing much faster than the rest of my face—or my body for that matter. Even Mother was unnerved: "Don't look down," she would say. "It makes your nose appear longer." When my nose reached its ultimate size, my lips and mouth began catching up, and my distraught mother added another cadence to her old song. "Purse your lips," she would say, looking at me with such pity that I knew I had no future whatsoever, even if I were the only Eve in a garden inhabited by thousands of Adams.

The only way I can attract Anatoli Petrovich's attention, I figure, is by failing in physics. This causes him to keep me after class together with our d*voeshniki* Vitka and Kolka. Anatoli Petrovich talks about physics, Vitka and Kolka stare out the window, and I stare at Anatoli Petrovich with the kind of adoration that my Western counterparts reserve for the Beatles, minus the screaming.

"Electric current is the flow of electrically charged particles. It's measured in amperes …" I hear Anatoli Petrovich's voice, and a flow of charged feelings sweeps along my body at a rate no ammeter can measure.

"Do you understand?"

"More than you think," I feel like saying, drunk on the sound of his velvety voice and the bitter-sweet taste of my first love. I have no illusions about my situation. My feelings are unrequited. I am like the poor young clerk in Anatoli Kuprin's famous love story "The Garnet Bracelet," who fell in love with a beautiful married woman from a wealthy family and killed himself after a confrontation with her brother. Or, maybe, I am more like the dreamer Tatyana Larina from Alexander Pushkin's masterpiece *Eugene Onegin*, enamored with the selfish and vain Onegin.

The setting sun is already burning on the horizon, but I am still in my chair, looking at the picture of Scheherazade prostrated at the Persian king's feet. Did she love him as much as I love Anatoli Petrovich or did she just want to save her life? And if she did love him, did she experience the same sensations I do when I look at this picture or at my physics teacher?

I put down the *Arabian Nights* and take two steps to the bookcase in the corner. I raise my hand and pensively stroke the dark-colored spines with lettering that announces the names of famous Russian writers: Pushkin, Lermontov, Kuprin, Turgenev, Chekov, Dostoevsky. The volume of heart-ache and sadness that flows from these tomes would be enough to fill many *kvass* cisterns, and yet, none of them mentions anything about physical feelings. Is there something about love that these books do not reveal?

My fingers slide from one spine to another, as if the answer to my question is written in Braille, and I have to read it by touch. After several rows of novels and poetry, I reach a thick catalog of the Hermitage Museum, mindlessly pull it out, and open it at random.

There is a painting of a woman lying in bed. Her blankets are thrown off, her gaze is intense, and her ample naked body is turned toward an opening in the dark curtain at the foot of the bed, where a lustrous milky light is pouring into the dark room–Rembrandt's Danae is waiting for her lover Zeus, who comes to her in the form of golden rain.

I have seen this picture before, and it has never impressed me—just an overweight woman in bed. And yet, this time, something in Danae's pose, the atmosphere of waiting, and the darkly peering figure in the background strike me like a lightning bolt. Everything around me suddenly changes, even the air, which now smells fresh and intoxicating, as it does after a thunderstorm.

With my hands trembling, I flip through the pages. I skip landscapes, still life, portraits of numerous Madonnas and self-important aristocrats, and devour shamelessly beautiful Aphrodite and Eros, Cupid and Psyche tangled in a sensuous embrace, and the marble statues of nude satyrs. As if scales have fallen from my eyes, I suddenly see details that I have never noticed before—heaving chests and swollen nipples of women, men's hands groping women's breasts and resting between their legs, and males' private parts depicted in all their anatomical glory.

My heart is pounding, and I lean against the bookcase to catch my breath. Surely, I observed baby boys before, but these still images suddenly seem more real than anything I have seen in life. They are disturbing and gross, and yet, I cannot take my eyes off them, and, to make matters worse, I cannot control my own body either—its rhythmical tensing is as frightening as it is pleasurable.

What's happening to me? I am trying to catch my breath, but another image comes suddenly to my mind's eye—that girl, Dasha, from my summer camp. Her bed was next to mine, and sometimes I heard her thrashing and stirring in bed and making muffled moaning noises, which I attributed to bad dreams. But then, one day, I saw Dasha leaving the office of our Chief Camp

Leader. Dasha's eyes and nose were red, and the Camp Leader looked at her with an expression like the one that must have been worn by members of NKVD court troikas when they sentenced prisoners to firing squads during Stalin's purges.

The Chief Camp Leader's office, a large room decorated with portraits of Lenin, Brezhnev, and a painting of happy collective farm workers, was adjacent to the camp library, where I was gulping down Leo Tolstoy's *War and Peace*. The chapter I was reading described Natasha Rostova's love triangle with the honorable Prince Andrei Bolkonsky and the dissolute Anatole Kuragin. I was so engrossed in the story that it took me some time to notice loud voices in the room next door.

I could not hear everything that was said–only separate words and phrases: something about Dasha's dirty and antisocial behavior, the stain she put on our detachment and the camp, and her inevitable bad end. None of that made any sense to me, since as far as I knew, Dasha was a quiet and aloof girl. Yet very soon, Dasha's mother arrived and took her back to Moscow. Is this what that was all about?

At night, after my little sister falls asleep and Mother turns on a bedside lamp and opens her book, I get out of my bed and tiptoe over the bare wooden floor to my parents' half of the room.

"Mom, do you remember that girl from our summer camp, Dasha?"

"What about her?" Mother says, half of her face glowing in the golden light of the lamp and the other half hidden in deep shadow.

"Why did they expel her from camp?"

Mom puts her book down and turns away from the lamp—the illuminated side of her face sinks into the shadows, the way the sun sinks into a dark cloud. "I don't know."

"Mom, please, tell me!"

"It's too late to talk about it now. Go to bed."

"What did she do?"

"You're too young to talk about such things."

"But she was my age!"

"Listen, Sveta. I'm not your friend. I'm your *mother*. Some things cannot be discussed between children and parents." And with this, my mother brings her face back to the light and to her book, "Go to bed."

Who should I discuss these things with, Mom?—I want to shout. But I bite my lower lip and retreat to the even breathing of my sleeping sister and the disturbing questions that adults do not want to answer.

Next morning, I pack the Hermitage catalog into my briefcase and head to school. The first class is math, and our teacher Evgenia Sergeevna gives us a test. She writes math problems on the blackboard, and we diligently bend over our notebooks to solve them.

In twenty minutes or so, heads begin popping up like fishing floats, and relaxed whispering indicates that the exercise is winding down. I am done, too, and while the class waits for Evgenia Sergeevna to collect our papers, I carefully pull the Hermitage catalog out of my briefcase and open it under the desk at a bookmarked place—a full-frontal statue of a handsome, curly-haired young man, clothed with nothing but his seductive smile.

"What's that?" My neighbor Zoia peers under the desk and, before I have the time to close the book, goes into a breathless "Ahh, …"

For a while, we both gawk at the naked man, careful not to look at each other.

"Did you solve the second problem?" Big-eared Grisha turns to us from his desk. Recognizing that our attention is elsewhere, he quickly changes his question. "What are you looking at?"

"Nothing," Zoia whispers, quickly straightening up and adjusting her hair. I slam the catalog and, trying to distract Grisha with math, turn my notebook upside down.

"What's going on?" Evgenia Sergeevna thunders, suddenly behind us.

"They're reading something under the desk." Grisha reports, winking and moving his ears like a spooked deer.

"Idiot," I hiss.

"And she called me an 'idiot,'" Grisha adds, smiling happily from ear to ear.

You *are* an idiot!—I feel like saying, but I keep quiet and make an attempt to shove the Hermitage catalog back into my briefcase inconspicuously.

"Give me that," Evgenia Sergeevna orders. There is enough steel in her voice to forge a sword.

Evgenia Sergeevna is a seasoned teacher with twenty years of experience, and she knows how to handle misbehaving students. She grabs the catalog from my shaking hand and her eyes shift to the title.

"The Hermitage Museum," she reads aloud and looks at me—her pale blue eyes piercing through me from behind her thick-rimmed glasses. Then Evgenia Sergeevna notices my bookmark and opens the book to it.

"What is this?" she exhales, holding the book at arm's length as if it is some slimy creature she stumbled across in the woods. "Get up and answer me!"

The poor clerk in "The Garnet Bracelet" could not have been more mortified by the confrontation with the brother of his love interest than I am now by the confrontation with my math teacher. He had to kill himself to get out of his predicament, and I momentarily consider doing the same to get out of mine.

"I'm going to pass this on to your head teacher," Evgenia Sergeenva says, and her distorted face lets me know that committing suicide may not be the worst thing that can happen to me.

When I come home, my mother is in the kitchen, grinding meat. For a minute, I watch red fleshy worms come out of her *myasorubka* (cast-iron meat grinder) and coil into a large aluminum bowl.

"*Kotleti* (small hamburger patties made of meat, onions, and bread) will be ready in half-an-hour." Mom says without looking at me.

"My head teacher wants to talk to you," I respond.

"Why? What did you do?" Mom looks up.

"Nothing. I just took the Hermitage Museum catalog to school, and my math teacher found some naked pictures there."

"Naked pictures? Of whom?"

"Nymphs, satyrs, and other men, too ..." I suddenly feel tired and my voice trails off.

"Wait, wait, I don't understand. Why in the world did you take the catalog to school?!"

"You didn't want to talk to me about … you know … Dasha and … the feelings. So, I thought I'd show the catalog to somebody in school, and we'd talk."

My mother's hand slips from the handle of her meat-grinder and hits the bowl. The bowl tilts to one side and, after hesitating a moment, slides off the kitchen counter and lands on the floor with a loud "bam!" Its meaty contents fly out every which way and, in a moment, our kitchen is transformed into a bloody battlefield, where I feverishly perform the duties of a medic, while my speechless Mother watches me like a general who has just lost the battle of her life.

Mother is still frozen, when the front door opens and my father comes in with a newspaper in hand. "What's going on?"

"Why did you show her the Hermitage catalog?" Mother blurts out.

"What are you talking about? What's wrong with the catalog?"

"Nothing! If you have a smart daughter. But we don't!" Here both of them fix their eyes on me the way gamblers fix their eyes on their disappearing riches, and I shrink on the kitchen floor, calling fire and brimstone down on my head.

The next several days are filled with rhetorical questions and bickering: "Do you understand that they won't let you into *Komsomol.* Do you? And you'll never go to college?" This is to me, after Mom's meeting with my head teacher.

"Why do *I* have to disentangle everything?" This is to my father.

And at night, muffled sounds of arguments reach my ears from my parents' half of the room: "What are you blaming me for? It's art!"

"Art? Tell that to her teachers! They say it's perversion when a 14-year-old enjoys pictures of naked men!"

"They are unintelligent retrogrades! If they had had their way, all paintings would've been painted over and statues draped in blankets! It's bad enough that every word in this damn country is censored. Now I have to worry about museum catalogs, too?!"

"All I'm saying is that we have to be careful. If she doesn't understand what can or can't be taken out of the house, then we shouldn't have anything around here that can get her in trouble."

"I can't believe you said that! So now I can't enjoy my art books when I have a free minute? I work like a horse! I rely on *you* to oversee her reading!"

"And I don't? I do, too! And I buy food, I cook, I clean. You're always out of town!"

"I see. You're just like your mother! I am not good enough for you and your family ..."

In the end, there is one thing my parents can agree on. Only a "complete fool" takes delicate issues—or any important issues, for that matter—outside the family. Since I have proved to be just that—a complete fool—and my parents cannot rely on my discretion, I am not allowed to see any art books or read anything ambiguous. As a result, a complete collection of Guy de Maupassant moves to my aunt's apartment (fine with me, I've already read it), and all museum catalogs, as well as a thick tome of Greek mythology with color pictures of naked gods and goddesses, disappear into thin air.

I am in trouble in school, too. I have soiled my class's reputation and, therefore, I will not be admitted to *Komsomol* with the rest of my classmates. Yet not everything is lost. If I do not slip up again—and my parents will make sure of that!—I may achieve the honor of joining The All-Union Leninist Young Communist League next semester. That is my last chance, as it is for the school's worst students and for one girl who got caught with her mother at church services, and, pressed by school authorities, repented afterwards.

For now, though, my teachers treat me as if I am a leper who ought to be exiled from healthy Soviet society and made to wear a bell announcing my whereabouts to the chaste student body. Every time the teachers see me, they lower their eyes, and they raise their voices addressing me. The only exception is Vladimir Alekseevich, my art teacher from two years ago. When I run into him in the school halls or staircases, his eyes sparkle, and a couple of times—I swear!—he even winks at me.

The good thing is that my reputation as a fallen woman has considerably improved my standing among my peers. Even those who never acknowledged my existence before, now treat me as if I had won the state lottery or had gotten official permission to register as a true ethnic Russian. I thoroughly enjoy it, since I know that it is not going to last long. Already several of my classmates have had "soul-to-soul" conversations with me, and since there is only so much I can fake, it is a matter of time before my aura of sexual experience disappears forever. Luckily, I recently discovered Mother's old gynecology textbook, which may get me through this quarter.

Another unexpected change is in my feelings for Anatoli Petrovich. Like Pushkin's heroine Tatyana, who finally realizes that Eugene Onegin is not the hero she imagined him to be, I am disillusioned with my physics teacher. For weeks, he hardly acknowledged my existence, but now his gaze, heavy and oily, slithers around me the way a snake slithers around a meekly squeaking rabbit, making me feel small and dirty.

Also, he is not *really* handsome—not with that square jaw of his, squat figure, and cold, screwed-up eyes. I no longer believe that he is even smart. He knows physics, of course, but his vocabulary is pretentious and his jokes are flat, and even Grisha, once in a while, tells better jokes.

With love stories and art books gone from our bookcase, I read a lot of poetry: Lermontov, Tyutchev, Nekrasov, and other famous Russian poets. My favorite is Puskin's "I Have Outlived My Aspirations," and I read it often. I open the book with Pushkin's black-and-white profile on the title page, drawn with an old-fashion quill pen by the poet himself, and admire his receding forehead, long nose (Pushkin had a long nose, too!), and copious curls. Then I flip to the bookmarked page and read:

Ja perezhil svoji zhelanja,
Ja razljubil svoji mechti;
Ostalis mne odni stradanja,
Plody serdechnoj pustoti.

I have outlived my aspirations
I have outloved my every dream
Suffering is my sole persuasion,
My heart feels only what has been ...

I soak up Pushkin's words like a sponge. Their grieving message penetrates my skin and sinks inside my own empty heart. If love disappointed the greatest Russian poet, how can an ordinary girl like me expect happiness? And what about my own parents? Are they happy? Do they love each other? They sure argue a lot, and Dad makes scenes every time Mom talks to another man and, afterwards, grabs at his heart and proclaims that he is dying. Is that love?

What is love, anyway? A feeling that burns you from inside? A physical sensation that takes over your entire body? A mirage that makes a thirsty traveler walk for miles to an elusive goal somewhere in the deserts of Persia, a country where people still tell Scheherazade's stories?

Yes, despite my parent's strict surveillance, I have finished the *Arabian Nights*. I hid it underneath my sleeper-chair and read it under the blanket after the lights were out. During 1001 nights with the king, Scheherazade bore him three children, and the king–finally!—pardoned her.

The children come as a surprise to me, since the book never mentions Scheherazade's pregnancies, just vaguely states that every night the king "had his will of her," and I still do not know how to find out what that means. In any case, at the end, the king fell in love with Scheherazade, and they lived happily ever after. Well, the book did not actually mention that, but the magical *Arabian Nights* world, unlike the stringent world around me, must have been happy.

Time goes by, first slowly, like a panting freight train, then faster and faster, like a high-speed express. *Babiye Leto* passes its colorful torch to the late fall, which extinguishes it with winds, leaden clouds, and drizzle. With the onset of winter, my life returns to its usual order. My teachers, overwhelmed by bad students, miserable salaries, long lines for simple necessities, and the difficult duties of promoting healthy Soviet morals and principles, begin to forget my sins. My peers recognize my utter sexual ignorance and treat me the way they used to. My overworked parents slowly fill up our bookcase.

The question of who should oversee my reading is still unresolved. And gradually, my troubles become another memory, firmly pressed under the layers of time and the piles of early snow. Even my tingling sensations, the reason for all this turmoil, suddenly vanish, like grass and flowers, chirruping birds, and frothy dark amber liquid *kvass*. Until next summer.

CHAPTER TWENTY SIX

TRAITOR

This year I have a new best friend, Ulya. She is very short—shorter than I am! Puffy clouds of unruly light hair surround her sunny face with big dark eyes. A slightly large nose curves gently above her full lips, and her arms and legs are as plump as a baby's. Ulya and I attended the same music school for years, but since she plays the violin and I the piano, we barely knew each other—until one day, our respective teachers decided that the two of us should play together at an annual end-of-the-year concert. That concert marked the beginning our friendship.

We were the last students to perform that day. When we finally appeared on stage, we were so worn out from nerves and the long wait that we failed to start our piece together. During rehearsals, Ulya always waited for my nod, but at the concert, when I lifted my chin from the piano and looked at her, I realized that she was already playing, and if I wanted to be a part of our number at all, I had to catch up with her.

Unfortunately, I could not figure out how far along in the piece Ulya already was, so I started from the beginning—several bars behind her. Had this been an athletic event, a judge would have declared a false start and we would have been given another go. As it was, nobody told us to stop, and we played on until the end of the piece—with Ulya crossing the finish line first and me second.

Later, our teachers told us that they had never been so ashamed in their "entire lives" and that it was the worst number at that concert and, quite possibly, "in the entire history of our music school!" After our teachers left us alone and we had exchanged several rounds of "It was all your fault, you dummy!" we looked at each other and began laughing—mostly from relief and embarrassment, but also from the recognition that we would never be good musicians; therefore, there was nothing to fight about.

We laughed and laughed, until Ulya said, "Let's go get some ice cream." That turned out to be an excellent idea, because it gave us a chance to discover that we had lots in common. We both liked the same kind of ice cream—*eskimo-na-palochke* (Eskimo pie). We were both poor athletes who hated PE. We liked reading books far beyond our age level, and we were both Jewish.

To be precise, Ulya was half-Jewish—her mother was Jewish and her father Russian. In a country like Israel, where ethnicity is defined by one's mother, that would have made her one hundred percent Jewish. Yet in Russia, where paternal relations are more important and where being "Russian" is imperative for success, she was registered as Russian. However, all of Ulya's Russian relatives—including her father—died before Ulya was born, while all of her mother's relations were alive and actively present in Ulya's life. So we both decided that for all practical purposes, Ulya was as Jewish as I was.

After we had successfully dealt with the Jewish question, we revealed to each other that we were not popular in our regular schools, we had very few friends, and we worried about being unattractive. Of course, when we got to that topic, we both said, "Oh, you're much prettier than me," but neither one of us believed the other.

When the ice cream had become a sweet memory, I told Ulya about my past infatuation with my physics teacher, and she confessed to me that she was hopelessly in love with a boy in her school. Together, we reached the grievous conclusion that true love is always unrequited and life in general is not fair. After that, our friendship was cemented forever.

Ulya and I live about an hour away from each other, so we don't spend much time together. We don't talk on the phone either, since our families, like all the families we know, have no telephones. We usually see each other on weekends or at the music school—we linger after classes until it occurs to one of us that she has been expected at home a long time ago.

Most of our conversations are about books, movies, and love. Other topics include our families and our future. The latter is a special favorite with Ulya who, unlike me, is practical and focused, rather than a daydreamer. Perhaps this is due to the early deaths of her relatives, which taught her at a young age that time is limited, or perhaps her present does not inspire her, whereas the future promises an escape that she yearns for.

It is a cool weekday, lit by an anemic early-spring sun and fanned by a damp breeze. Ulya and I are taking a stroll in a small city park not far from our music school. We have already discussed burning questions of the heart in general and Turgenev's story "First Love" in particular, and we have sworn never to get involved with the opposite sex but to dedicate our lives to our careers instead.

There are few others in the park. A couple of dry-faced babushkas watch little children launch ships made of newspaper down the stream of melting snow, a hunched old man on a bench pokes the thawing ground with his cane, and a young couple walks furtively holding hands.

"Have you noticed that pretty girls are all dumb?" Ulya says.

This thought has never occurred to me before, but as it comes out of Ulya's mouth, I immediately recognize its wisdom, and I can hardly believe that I never figured this out on my own.

"Sure," I say, fixing my eyes on the couple: a young pimply-faced soldier in a gray wool uniform and his companion, an attractive blue-eyed woman with unnaturally long eyelashes and perfectly drawn eyebrows.

"If I had to choose between being smart and being pretty, I'd choose being smart," Ulya declares, and I nod in not-very-sincere agreement.

For a moment, we enjoy our newly-achieved sense of superiority and we almost feel sorry for the blue-eyed woman in front of us and others like her who are pretty but dumb. *We* do not want to be dumb, and if being ugly is the price we must pay for being smart, we are happy to pay it—not that we have a choice anyway!

Also, none of those gorgeous creatures who bathe in the glow of male attention will be attractive forever. By the time they are old—twenty-five or thirty—their charm will disappear, and everybody will see how shallow and self-centered they are. As for us, even twenty years from now, our intellect and wisdom will continue to shine.

We look at each other satisfied with ourselves. "What school are you going to next year?" Ulya says, picking up a stick and throwing it at a crow cawing behind us.

"The same one I've been going to since we moved to our apartment. Why?"

"If you want to go to a good college, you need to transfer to a better school," Ulya says, stopping in her tracks and bringing her face close to mine, as if revealing an important government secret. "Mother says that if you don't have *svyazi* (connections), you need to start preparing now. I've decided to go to the University (Lomonosov Moscow State University, the best school in the country). Where do you want to go?"

"I don't know," I say, my sense of self-worth shrinking. Maybe I am not as smart as I thought I was a couple of minutes ago; surely not as smart as Ulya!

"The University has more than twenty applicants for every place," Ulya says, and her dark eyes become as round as the buttons of her coat. "Mother says that to get in I'd have to study with tutors or transfer to a good school, like that one by Minaevskij Marketplace."

"Will your mother hire you tutors, then?" I say.

"No, we have no money for tutors. I'll transfer to that school. What about you?" Ulya says. "Wouldn't it be cool if we both went there?"

The school Ulya is talking about opened a year ago, and it is one of those rare "special" schools that are sprinkled unevenly throughout the city. In addition to the regular curriculum, these schools give their students advanced training in certain subjects, usually foreign languages or hard sciences. The foreign language schools rarely admit students with no connections, no matter what the students' abilities. Hard sciences, however, are less popular among the "connected" families, so admission to them is based mostly on merit. The school by Minaevskij Marketplace is one of these.

"I don't know," I say, surprised by Ulya's purposefulness—after all, college is still two years away! "Everybody says that school is tough. And you have to pass an entrance exam."

"You make good grades. Surely you'll pass the exam," Ulya says brightly, as if she is a government official delivering a speech about the unlimited possibilities of our great country.

I say nothing. True, I am one of the best students in my regular district school, but will I be good enough for *that* school?

"You do want to go to college, don't you?" Ulya says, sensing my reluctance.

I do not answer. I have never doubted that I would go to college. Both of my parents are professionals and both of my older cousins are already college students. I would be the black sheep of the family if I did not go. Yet do I have to change my life *now*? It is still early, isn't it? Besides, unlike Ulya who has already decided that she wants to be a geologist, I am not clear what I want to do with the rest of my life, besides writing romance novels based on my own and Ulya's experiences and traveling to the North Pole, that is.

"You'll need it even more than me," Ulya says averting her eyes, and I immediately understand her hidden message.

Wherever Ulya's true sympathies may lie, she is registered as "Russian" and I as "Jewish." This means that my admission to college will be affected by a Jewish quota. Depending on the prestige of the college and the number of candidates, that quota varies, but invariably, more Jewish students must compete for fewer spaces. I have heard my relatives talk about this many times; I just never realized that one day this would apply to *me*.

"Do you think I could pass an entrance exam for the University?" I ask my father at night.

"Probably not," Father says, not lifting his head from his book. "Of course, you need to go to college, but it doesn't have to be the University," and he turns the page.

"Do we have *svyaz*i, Dad?"

Father puts down his book and looks at me.

"No, we don't," he says, stressing every word. "That's exactly why you need to make good grades. Any more questions?"

I turn to the dark window and away from Father. This really sucks. More times than I care to remember, I have heard people say that Jews have connections "everywhere." How come my family doesn't? What's wrong with us? Like everybody else, we stand in long lines at grocery stores, and Mother and I freeze our butts off to buy Tanya and me a pair of winter boots, or anything else for that matter. We don't have much money, we don't own a dacha, and we live in a small communal apartment.

Yet, apparently, admission to a college will be tougher for me than for my Russian peers, while going to the University is out of the question altogether. Why? And where are those sly, well-connected Jews who have everything on a "silver platter"? I don't know any of them! Do they really exist? And if they do, why don't *we* belong to that exclusive group? Nobody likes us anyway, so shouldn't we, at least, possess something that will give people *reasons* to dislike us? Yes, Ulya is right. I need to go to a better school. I turn to my father again.

"Dad, I want to transfer to the special school by Minaevskij Marketplace. Ulya wants to go there, too."

Father closes his book. "Um. That's an interesting idea," he says and looks at Mother, who is ironing linen on the dinner table. Mother puts down her iron, neatly folds a freshly ironed bed-sheet and returns his glance.

"We'll think about that," Father says. "You know they have an entrance exam, right?"

The exam takes place at the beginning of June. By that time, the school year is over and so is my music career. On May 15, after months of rehearsing, Ulya and I, and fifteen more music school students perform our final exams. We play our numbers with hands cold from nerves and hearts heavy with the fear of failing. A panel of teachers evaluates our accomplishments, while famous musicians look upon us mournfully from their framed portraits. In a week or so, we receive our music diplomas and our parents frame and hang them on the walls of our respective apartments.

When I leave the freshly painted classroom where one unsmiling male and two unsmiling female teachers interrogate me with a variety of math and physics questions for what seems like forever, I feel weak and lightheaded. The school hall is packed with potential students: those who are waiting to be tested and those who have already gotten through the purgatory of the exam and now lean against the walls, exhausted. Some kids wear glasses and have an intellectual air about them and some look ordinary. Also, contrary to Ulya's statement about the stupidity of pretty girls, several girls in the hall are rather good-looking.

Ulya rushes toward me from the other side of the hall—her cheeks flushed and her eyes sparkling with the enthusiasm of a sure winner, "How did you do?"

"I don't know. The questions were real hard," I say, trying to keep my voice even. "I think I flunked."

"I'm sure you did just fine," Ulya says, containing her excitement and lowering her voice. I say nothing. Ulya looks at me with concern, "Do you want to grab some ice cream?" And we turn and head silently to the exit.

The results come three days later. I have passed! Both of us have passed! I stare at the students' roster in utter disbelief. There it is—my name, in black and white. Next to me Ulya is jumping up and down, "I told you! Didn't I tell you?! You're such a pessimist!"

The smile on my face must be as wide as the great Russian river Volga, and my body feels so light that it would not surprise me if my feet separated from the ground and I found myself floating in air. It's over! Well, actually, it is just the beginning of what must be my bright and wonderful future. Just one thing, a little footnote at the bottom of the roster states that all students should deliver their previous schools' records within a week.

"Mom, could you ask our school principal for my records?" I say to Mother as she leaves for work next morning.

"I can't get off work until late. You have to do it yourself," she says.

"What about Father?"

"He's leaving for a business trip. He has no time," Mother says, and the front door slams behind her.

"I can go with you," my sister Tanya chimes in. "You'll talk to your principal and I'll wait for you in the hall. And then we'll go and get fizzy water with …"

"No, you can't," I say. Taking Tanya with me is the last thing I want to do. She will ask how hard the new school will be and what I will do if I do not like it. But I cannot answer these questions even for myself. Besides, doubts about my abilities still churn in my stomach.

"You wait for me here. I'll come back and take you out for fizzy water," I say and rush outside, rehearsing what I am going to tell the school principal.

"What? What did you just say? You want to leave our school?" The principal Elizaveta Vasilievna, a small woman with unnaturally black permanent waves, dark piercing eyes, and a shadow of mustache above her upper lip, bends her head to one side, as if looking at me from that angle allows her to see something inside me that she would not spot otherwise. "Why do you want to leave?"

"I want to go to college, and I need to be better prepared," I mutter, carefully avoiding the principal's stare.

Elizaveta Vasilievna rises from her desk—her face red and her bosom heaving. "Are you saying that our school is not good?!" I step backwards and stumble on a chair behind me, while she continues, "That we don't prepare our students for college?"

My hands go cold. Not that I expected the conversation to be pleasant exactly, but I am not prepared for such animosity either.

"I just need my records," I say in a small trembling voice. "That's all."

The principle puts her hands on her hips, the way a Soviet saleswoman does when she prepares to reprimand a demanding customer, and steps even closer. "Look at her! Our school is not good enough for her!" she sneers. "Who do you think you are?" Then she brings her face next to mine, and her pale twisted lips and gold-crowned front teeth appear at my eye level. "You can forget about college! I won't give you your records!"

The floor begins waltzing under me. This *cannot* be happening. After all, I did not do anything wrong. I just asked for my papers. This must be one of my nightmares. I need to wake up. I shut my eyes tight, hoping that when I open them again, I will find myself in my bed—sweaty, scared, but safe. Then I open my eyes. Nothing is changed. Right before me stands an adult, a teacher, with undisguised hatred on her face, eager to destroy me.

I clench my fists. What should I do? Retreat? Forget about Ulya's plan and the roster with my name, and go home? Or should I fight? But how? We children are taught never to argue with adults, even with strangers, not to mention the head teacher. I cannot do it, can I?

"You have no right!" My voice is breaking and my fingernails are piercing my skin, and I gather all my will power to keep from shaking and crying.

"Rights? I'll show you rights!" Elizaveta Vasilievna sputters—her breath heavy and vile, like the breath of a hydra-headed monster from a fairytale. "You're a traitor, and traitors have no rights in our country! I'll report you to the authorities!" And she raises her hand as if for a blow. I recoil.

"You're crazy!" Is it me screaming or is it the sound of blood rushing inside my head? "I'm not a traitor! There's no crime in wanting to transfer to another school and … and …" The words stick in my throat like fish bones and I struggle for air. If I do not leave now, I will break down crying.

I push the door wide open and flee the office, almost knocking down our janitor who is eavesdropping by the door, attracted by the commotion. Behind me, the raving dragon is spouting mencingly: "I'll show you records! I'll spoil your career! I'll ..."

"What happened?" Mother's hand lands on my quivering shoulders.

"She won't let me go to college!" I sob. "She said that I'm a traitor, and she'll spoil my career."

"Who?"

"The principal!"

Mother takes her hands off me and lowers herself on a chair by the dinner table. Her eyes take on a darker, tired expression. "I thought there might be trouble."

"But why? What did I do?"

"It's not only about you. She reports to the school district, so she doesn't want to lose a good student. Besides, who are you to tell her that her school is no good?" Mother says and adds under her breath, "*S nami plocho e bez nus nechorosho*." (They don't like it with us, but they don't like it without us, either.)

"What do you mean, Mom?"

"Nothing. I'll see what we can do."

As I lie in bed at night, my eyelids feel heavy and my mind is exhausted, but as soon as I close my eyes, Elizaveta Vasilievna's wide-open mouth with gold-plated teeth appears in my imagination, threatening to swallow me up. When I finally doze off, I have another of my war nightmares.

It is a cold November morning in 1941 in the small Russian village of Petrischevo, which is occupied by Germans. The village is preparing for the execution of a young Soviet partisan, Zoya Kosmodemyanskaya, who was caught by the Germans a day before. Beaten up, burned by cigarette lighters, and barefoot, Zoya walks in the snow to her gallows. A dozen soldiers surround her, and a silent crowd of locals, driven by order of the Nazi commander, gloomily shift from one foot to another in front of the scaffold. I am among them.

The fatal moment draws near. One soldier pushes Zoya forward and another places a noose around her neck. Yet just before the trap door opens under her feet, Zoya straightens up, looks directly at me with her blood-shot eyes, and spits into my face,

"Traitor! People will find out that you left your school, and they will never forgive you! They will spoil your career!"

When I open my eyes, Mother is already at work, and only my little sister stands by my bed tugging on my shoulder, "Why are you moaning?"

Most of the next day I spend moping around the apartment. What will I do if the principal does not give me my records? Will I have to go back to my old school then? And what if the principal does not give me my records and does not take me back either? Is that how she will spoil my career?

When I hear the sound of a key turning in the keyhole, I rush to the front door to meet Mother. "Did you see the principal?"

Mother walks past me and straight into our room. There she puts down her purse and turns to me, "Did you feed Tanya dinner?"

"Yes, I did," I say, "What about the principal?"

"I did talk to her," Mother says, her voice emotionless. "She told me to come back in two weeks."

"Two weeks?! But I need my records now!" I cry. "The new school won't admit me if I don't bring them this week!"

Mother gives me a long look, "Why did you decide to transfer? *Kakaya tebya mukha ukusila*? (What fly bit you?) This is nothing but grief."

"Ulya got her records. Why can't I?"

"What does that have to do with anything? You're not Ulya, understand?" Mother says, exasperated. Then she adds, "Okay, I'll talk to your father."

Father comes home late, a cardboard suitcase in his hand.

"We have a problem," Mother says as soon as he puts the suitcase down. "The principal won't give out Sveta's records."

"Can this wait until after I eat my dinner?" Father says. "I haven't had a *kroshki* (crumb) since this morning. Besides, what can *I* do? I'm leaving the day after tomorrow."

"You're always leaving and I have to deal with everything on my own!" Mother says—frustration oozing from her every word. "Maybe before you leave, you can talk to her principal for a change!"

"What's that 'for a change' about?" Father's raises his voice. "I don't travel for pleasure. I travel so we can make ends meet!" Here he pauses and looks at me. "And who said that she has to transfer? She can stay where she is."

"I'm not going back there!" I scream. "Mom, tell him!"

"You know she can't go back to that school," Mother says, biting her lip. "*Oni eye so sveta szhivut.*" (They'll hound her to death.)

"She needed to consider that earlier. She's not a child. *Ona zavorila ety kashy, pust ona ee sama e raschlebivaet*!" (She cooked this kasha, now she should eat it!) Then he turns to me, "I don't know what they teach you in school, but you surely could use a lesson in how to get along with people. Why are you always in trouble?"

"I'm not *always* in trouble …" I start but quickly stop. That is not what Father means. He means that I should be quiet and obedient, should please everybody and conform to everything, whether I like it or not. That is what he does. The couple of times Father took me to his office, I could hardly recognize him. He wasn't the nervous and sickly man I knew at home, but an easygoing person with a broad smile, who looked at his coworkers like a puppy that admires everybody who pets him.

But it was all a sham! At home, I heard him tell Mother that his boss was a dull functionary whose work status was based on his position in the Communist Party, and many of his colleagues were anti-Semites. Yet while he was among them, he pretended to be a nice guy who was happy to be there. Who'd believe that the same man made jealous scenes at home and claimed to have a heart attack every time things did not go his way? I wouldn't believe it myself—that is if I were not the one who brought him water when he grabbed at his heart or called the ambulance when he fell to the floor as white as the ceiling. And he wants me to be like him?

"Not everybody can be as two-faced as you are!" I say, tossing my braid over my shoulder and feeling righteous and free-spirited.

I do not immediately register what has happened, just that my right cheek is suddenly on fire. Did he slap me? Not that I am new to corporal punishment—it is wide-spread and acceptable in our society. In fact, for a long time Father had a belt that he used on us when we didn't "behave." If not for little Tanya, who hid that belt one day in her doll's blanket, took it outside, and threw it into the garbage, it would still have reddened our rears. But I am fifteen now! How dare he slap me in the face!

"I hate you!" I cry and rush out of our apartment, choking with tears and helplessness.

"Did anything happen?" Ulya asks when I appear at her door.

"I've left home, and I'll never go back!" I say, short of breath from the long walk and from my emotions. "Can I stay with you for now?"

"Let me ask Mom," Ulya says, her eyes as round as ever. "What did you do?"

"Nothing. It's all my father's fault!"

Ulya, who has no father and therefore no knowledge of men's behavior, cranes her neck, "What did he do?!"

"He slapped me in the face! I'll never forgive him!" I say.

"He did?" Ulya says, clasping her hands and disappearing inside the apartment.

"You can stay with us tonight," Ulya's mother tells me after a short negotiation with her daughter. "But I think you should make up with your father. I'm sure he wants what's best for you."

She puts her hand on her forehead—her eyes half-closed—and sighs, "You, children, don't understand. Life is not simple." Then she turns to Ulya, "You can put a cot in the kitchen for your friend, but please be quiet. I have a migraine."

The next day goes quickly. At first, Ulya and I discuss how I can get my school records. Can they be stolen from the principal's office? Is there somebody else who can give them to me? Then we talk about our families: how the adults never understand us, and how we—in the unlikely case of our having children—will be much better parents than our parents are.

When Ulya's mother comes back from work, she asks me if I have decided to return home, and I say no.

She gives me a funny look and goes to the kitchen. During supper, which we eat together, she asks me about my parents, what they do, and where they work. Then Ulya and I wash dishes, and Ulya's mother announces that she still has a migraine and goes to bed.

The next day is slow. We have already exhausted our main topics, and our conversation switches to where I am going to live now.

"Maybe Mother will let you stay with us," Ulya says irresolutely, and I look at her not knowing how to respond. I would love to live with Ulya, but her mother … I don't really know her. She seems okay, but she is sickly. My own mother is rarely ill, and when she is in a good mood, she is fun to be around. Also, Ulya's mother does not make much money, so they cannot afford having me here. But where will I go? The fear that has been nesting in my chest since yesterday begins swelling like a sponge soaked with water, while my mind circles endlessly around the same question—what's next?

In the end, I do not have to make a decision. When Ulya's mother comes home the next day, I hear a familiar voice at the front door. I peek from the room and see my mother.

"Sveta, let's go home," she says warily. "We've been worried sick about you."

"No, I won't!" I want to say, but a sense of relief empties me of my anger, like air escaping from a balloon, and instead of resisting, I answer with tears.

"It's okay," Mother says, starting to tear up herself and pulling me closer. "It's okay."

"What about Father?" I say when we find ourselves on the street. "He hit me!"

"He won't do it again," Mother says. "He's not a bad man. He's just nervous and … weak. Life is hard for him, so he tries to get along with everybody."

"Not with everybody!" I interrupt. "And definitely not at home. He always shouts at me, and if I respond, he grabs at his heart and you rush to help him!"

"Everybody has to get things off his chest sometimes. Where else can he do it if not at home?" Mother says. "He is the same way with me. Gets agitated, says something terrible, but then comes back and begs me to forgive him."

"That's *exactly* what I'm talking about! He offends you, and you let it go. Where is your integrity?" I say, feeling that my words come across as stilted and bombastic.

"Integrity is the stuff of literature," Mother sighs. "In real life, I have two children, a difficult job, and a sick husband."

"He's not sick, he just pretends. You should leave him!" I cry.

"No, no, you're wrong. He doesn't pretend. He'll die without me. Or kill himself. He's said that many times."

"And you believe him?" I do not want to give up. "You just said that he's weak. He'll never kill himself. I'm sure of it!"

"Well, I don't want to find out," Mother says quietly, fixing her eyes on the asphalt path under her feet. "Besides, he's your father, and he wants what's best for you. Even if he did something wrong, you should forgive him. After all, he went to see your principal, and he got your records."

I stop in my tracks, "He did?!"

Mother keeps walking. I catch up with her and open my mouth, wanting to ask, "How did he do that?" But after everything I have just said, I suddenly feel embarrassed. Instead, I, too, lower my gaze, and we silently walk home through the mild, breezy summer evening.

Everything is quiet in our apartment. Father has left for a business trip and my sister is asleep.

"I hope you won't regret it," Mother says, reaching for a slim folder sitting on our dinner table. She opens the folder and shows me its contents: my grades for the past two years, medical records, and an unasked-for "Conduct Report." She pulls out the report, as if it is a splinter stuck under her fingernail, and shoves it aside, "I don't think you want to read this."

I shake my head, "No." Then I look at Mother, "Can the principal really hurt me?"

"Probably not. In any case, it's too late to worry about that now. *Snyavshi golovy po volosam ne plachut.*" (When you've lost your head, there's no use crying about your hair.) And she sighs deeply.

CHAPTER TWENTY SEVEN

THE END OF CHILDHOOD

Grandma is sick, and because of that we are spending the rest of the summer in Moscow. That is just as well, since the summer is cool and drizzly, and when I look at the sky in the morning, all I can see is a murky amorphous mass that stretches over the city, sucking out its sounds and energy. Time seems to stretch, too, the way it does during boring school lessons or in the paintings of Salvador Dali. Even the neighborhood boys appear sluggish and subdued, and I rarely hear their war-game shouting in the courtyard.

I get used to this muffled world, as I get used to the monochromatic sky, to Ulya's absence (she is staying with her out-of-town relatives), and to Mother's frequent visits to the hospital. I even get used to taking care of Tanya, which is easier than it used to be. The bad weather confines my sister to our apartment, whose small size limits her ability to get into trouble. Besides, she has finally learned to read, and she spends time with my old fairytale books.

Once in a while, Mother takes me to visit Grandma. The hospital is on the other side of the city, and we have to ride a street car, the metro, and a bus to get there. During that time, Mother, who is tired after work, mostly keeps quiet, so I occupy myself with watching the people around us and imagining what their lives are like.

That is a new game Ulya and I play. We spot a middle-aged man walking along the street with a bouquet of roses, and Ulya says, "What do you think his life is like?" I pause for a minute and then respond with something like, "Well, his wife died of cancer last year and left him with two little children. Recently, he fell in love with a young neighbor, and now he's trying to persuade her to leave her boyfriend and marry him."

The after-work crowd is tough to read, though. Most of the people appeared weary, almost comatose. Their faces, lit by the mercilessly bright florescent light, are gray, their eyes expressionless, and no matter how much I try to ignite my imagination, all my guesses are hopelessly dull.

The hospital is a three-story cement block building, saturated with the strong smells of medicine, disease, and a whiff of urine. Doctors and nurses hurry along its long halls wearing white smocks and starched caps. Tiredly-important expressions on their faces protect them from unwanted questions. Visitors tiptoe hesitantly, keeping close to the walls.

By the time we get to the hospital, visitors' hours are often over, so Mother puts on her white smock and cap, assumes an authoritative expression, and pulls me towards the room at the end of the first floor. Grandma lies there with nine other patients—different ones every time I come. She seems small and thin, and her face is sickly yellow.

"*Mechaieh*!" (a Yiddish expression of great pleasure), she exclaims when she sees us in the doorway, and the patients who are not yet asleep regard us with unfriendly glances. Mother sits on the edge of Grandma's bed and unloads her favorite food. I stand by and watch Grandma eat. She never eats much, but complains about the hospital food, which is all *chazzerei* (awful), "Worse than in that summer camp you took me to with the children." Mother, in her turn, talks about Grandma's treatment and what the doctors have said.

Grandma never seems to pay attention to "doctor's talk." Instead, she turns to me and asks how I am, how Tanya is, and how we are getting along. Before we leave, she looks at me, teary-eyed, and says, "Svetochka, I hope you won't end up like this—all alone among strangers."

I look at Mother, not knowing what to say, feeling sorry for my grandmother but also uncomfortable. Mother says, "Mama, please. Here there're doctors to monitor your treatment and nurses to take care of you. We can't take you home now, not till you're better. Just be patient."

"You *are* a doctor," Grandma responds. "You don't want me. Nobody wants me," and she turns her face to the wall.

The last time I see Grandma, she mostly keeps quiet, just looks at us the way a wounded soldier must look at his retreating battalion. As we leave, she says—to nobody in particular—"*Oy vey is mir*. What's going to happen to me?"

"Will she get better?" I ask Mother on our way home.

"I don't know," she says, looking out the bus window at the bleak streets and dark silhouettes of people walking in the rain—their troubles and worries hidden under their black umbrellas. Three days later, Grandma is gone.

"Hold one side," my aunt Raya meets me at the door of a funeral home and hands me a black fabric belt.

"Why?"

"I'll cut it and you'll tie it over your dress."

For a moment, I stare at my aunt blankly—Has she gone mad? Then it dawns on me. It's an old tradition. In mourning, Jews are supposed to tear their clothes. We, of course, have no extra clothes to tear—for mourning or for anything else. We cannot afford to follow the tradition, except symbolically. I tie the torn belt around my waist, cover my head with a dark headscarf, and walk into a small white stucco building.

The first person I hear is Mother. She is talking to a small crowd of relatives who have gathered around her. Mother's voice is high-pitched and trembling. After every few words she stops, sniffles, and wipes her eyes, which makes her sound as if she is speaking in a strange staccato.

"I left the night before, and … she seemed to be almost … okay. Told me to bring her some *tvorog* (Russian cottage cheese) next time I came ... She liked *tvorog*, you know ..."

Father appears from behind me. A black yarmulke covers his head and a striped shawl, which I've never seen before, decorates his shoulders.

"I thought, I'd go back … in a couple of days," Mother continues, not noticing our arrival. "But I kept waking up at night … must have been a premonition or something … After work I bought *tvorog* and went to the hospital … Her room was at the end of this hallway ... so I'm walking along and … just next to Mother's room I see a stretcher with a body on it ... The body is covered with a blanket but the feet peek out … I look at those feet and … it just hits me … they are my mother's feet!" And she bursts into loud sobs.

Father makes his way through the crowd of relatives and puts his arms around her, "Fira, calm down." But Mother notices me, breaks free from his embrace, and begins telling me the story I have already heard several times. Grandmother died in the morning, but nobody in the hospital called her children or took her to the morgue in the basement, so my grandmother's body sat on a stretcher in the hallway until Mother arrived for her nightly visit.

A new visitor comes in, "Firochka, I'm so sorry …" Mother stops mid-sentence and rushes toward her. "You know, I saw her the night before …"

"Go, take the last look," my aunt tells me, and I obediently turn around and head to the next room.

In the doorway, I pause. This room is smaller and darker. There are several women here, whispering in the corner. In the middle of the room sits an open casket. For a moment I have an overwhelming desire to run away: I do not know the whispering women, I do not want to approach the casket, and I certainly do not want to see what lies *inside* it. And why should I? It *cannot* be my grandmother, for that would mean that I no longer have a grandmother. True, my friend Ulya never knew even her father, but that's different. My Grandma was with me all my life …

"Go, go!" Somebody pushes me from behind, making me step forward. One more step and I can see a small white-faced woman in the casket. The woman is dressed in a vaguely familiar navy-blue dress and brown shoes. I breathe a sigh of relief. Of course, this is not my Grandma. Mother said that she saw Grandma's bare feet, not these brown shoes … Unless they put the shoes on later?

I look again, now registering Grandma's features, which peer through the white mask of death, and tears begin pouring down my cheeks. Yet the woman in the casket does not react. Her eyes are closed, and the expression on her face is cold, distant, and apathetic. Is it really you, Grandma? Please, give me a sign!

No sign comes from inside the coffin. Instead, I feel something tearing inside *me*, like the fabric belt my aunt tore apart to imitate a mourner's torn clothes. Only this sensation is not an imitation. It is real and painful. I feel it in the pit of my stomach, in my chest, and even in my head.

I search my pockets for a handkerchief. Maybe this pain is a sign? Or, more likely, a punishment? Punishment for not visiting Grandma more often and for not consoling her when she said, "What's going to happen to me?" For leaving her there—for *wanting* to leave, since it felt so uncomfortable to stay.

And now … how will we live without her? What's going to happen to *us*? What's going to happen to *me*? I'm already in trouble. I may never go to college or do anything worthwhile.

I press my hands to my eyes, trying to stop my tears. My legs are trembling, and I cannot catch my breath. I gasp desperately, but my breath does not come. I need help ... Somebody, help me!

Suddenly, I hear an almost indiscernible voice, "Inhale deeply. Now exhale. Inhale again. Good girl. Everything is going to be all right. Just breathe."

My tears stop and I quickly look around. The women in the corner are still whispering, not paying attention to me. The body in the casket is lead-still. Where did these words come from? Not from a window, for there isn't one. Then from … my childhood? From the time when Grandma held me, three years old, by the open window of her apartment, comforting me, "Everything is going to be all right, just breathe."

No matter where the words came from, I obey them. I breathe in and out, in and out—as the voice commanded—and the pain eases, my body straightens, and my breathing relaxes. And with rare certainty, I realize that I'll be all right. Grandma would want that. And although this is the end of her life, it is not the end of mine—just the end of my childhood.

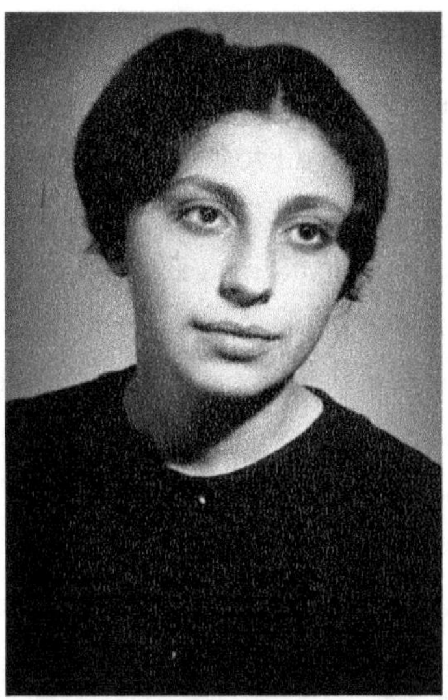

Me at fifteen

The first thing I see when I wake up next Monday is Mother ironing my new school uniform. I grew over the summer and my old uniform became too tight in the shoulders and—finally! —in my budding chest.

"Get up, get up," Mother says. "Get Tanya up, too."

"There's plenty of time," I say, stretching in my bed, still separating dreams from reality in my mind. Then it comes to me—today is the first day of school! My new school is not as close as the old one was, and I have to take a street car to get there. Also, Ulya will be waiting for me at the school entrance, so we can walk into our new lives together.

I jump from my bed, pull the blanket off my loudly protesting sister, and rush to the toilet, silently praying that it will not be occupied. A man's groaning coming from there informs me otherwise, and I head back.

"Hell!" I say. "Naúm Semenovich is in the toilet. Now I'll be late for school!"

"Watch your language," Mother says. "If not for me then out of respect for your grandmother."

I stop short. How could I forget? We are still observing *shiva*, the traditional Jewish period of mourning. Of course, our mourning is not exactly traditional. Instead of staying at home for seven days and grieving over her loss, Mother had to go to work the day after the funeral. She never stopped doing domestic chores either, since who else would do them? Father is already out of town (not that he helps much around the house anyway), and Mother trusts me with simple tasks only.

The mirror in our room is properly covered, though, so my grandmother's soul will not get trapped in it—this is how Mother explained this custom to us. There is another mirror in the bathroom, but since we share the bathroom with our Russian neighbors, that mirror is exempt from the Jewish laws.

"Sorry," I say and quietly proceed with my morning routine. Some forty-five minutes later I leave our apartment and join the crowd of students.

The morning is fresh and clear, and the atmosphere is festive: school-age children wear their dress uniforms, and young kids and their parents brighten the scene with bouquets of flowers and with hope emanating from their eyes.

On my way to the street car, I run into several of my former classmates.

"Hey, where're you going?" one of them says.

"I transferred to another school," I answer.

"You did? Why?"

I shrug and keep walking. I have neither the time nor the desire to explain myself. Besides, my stomach is queasy and my heart is pounding.

A street car approaches and several people get off: a woman with her young daughter carrying a shiny new briefcase, several middle school kids, and a smallish woman in a dark suit. The woman lifts her head and, suddenly, I find myself nose-to-nose with my former principal—her hair is carefully arranged into permanent waves, her lips are pursed into a sharp line, and her eyes are fixed on me like two revolvers.

"Run!" screams something inside my head. "Now!"

I try, but my feet seem stuck to the asphalt, my eyes hypnotized by her hateful stare. I wish I could faint, but I am still upright. "I must say something," goes through my mind. But what? Should I greet her as if nothing has happened, or should I apologize for my behavior?

My head is spinning, and I lower my eyes to the ground to keep my balance. But then, a stubborn voice rises within me, "Why should you apologize? You didn't do anything wrong. Besides, what can she do to you? Just keep going. Ulya is waiting."

I look at the principal, and our eyes spar again. "Good day, Elizaveta Vasilievna," I say. She says nothing. I set one foot onto the streetcar and slowly pull myself up. Then I take a second step, a third, and soon I am inside. Other passengers, annoyed with my sluggishness, push me from behind and shove me to the window. A bell rings, and the streetcar begins to gain speed.

I look out the window at the figure in the black suit—diminishing in size but still ominous, still following me with the cold glare of an assassin—and the old fears wash over me. What if this woman does have the power to ruin me? Should I at least try talking to her? Should I beg for forgiveness? I can get off at the next stop and run back. Yes, yes, I must!

I turn around and begin elbowing my way through the thick crowd, trying to get to the exit. I push and squeeze, and push again, not paying attention to the displeased remarks of other passengers. Finally, I reach the door. It opens, wide and welcoming, and I lean forward, ready to descend.

An old woman in a fallen kerchief looks up to me from the ground. Her hair is thin, her eyes are faded brown, and her pale lips are moving. She reminds me of someone … of … Grandma? What is she saying?

"Be brave, *bubala*. We're all survivors. You have to be brave."

I freeze. Did this woman really say that?!

No, of course not. The old woman is asking about the route. I breathe with relief, "Sorry, I don't know."

"Are you getting off or not?" I hear an annoyed female voice ask behind me. I turn and face the woman. "No," I say firmly. "I changed my mind. I'll ride on."

AFTERWORD

My school principal does not, as I fear, ruin my life. I finish college and, at the age of thirty-nine, leave Moscow and my home country for America. A year after that, my sister and parents immigrate to Israel, where my parents finally separate.

My best friend Ulya will not learn any of this. At twenty-two, just before graduating from Moscow State University and marrying a fellow geology student, she is killed by a drunk driver.

My mother country, the USSR, no longer exists. It crumbled around the edges, revived its old name, Russia, rewrote the words to its anthem—omitting Lenin and other outdated ideas—and blessed itself with a new flag, or rather the long forgotten Andreyevski flag from the Tsarist era.

I left the USSR before its great metamorphoses. My recollections are frozen in time, and as long as I live, things and events from long ago will remain preserved in my memory like fossils.

ACKNOWLEDGMENTS

I am very grateful to my husband for his support and encouragement. Without him this book would never have been written.

TO MY READERS

Word-of-mouth is crucial for any author to succeed. If you enjoyed this book, please consider writing a review online. Even if it is only a few lines, it would be a great help.

You may also drop by my blog: *Writing with an Accent: Diary of a Russian Immigrant* at svetlanagrobman.com, where I publish my stories and essays. If you'd like to send me an email, please do it from my blog, too. Thank you for reading!

www.ingramcontent.com/pod-product-compliance
Lightning Source LLC
LaVergne TN
LVHW051038080426
835508LV00019B/1592